ROUTLEDGE LIBRARY EDITIONS: THE ENGLISHWOMAN'S REVIEW OF SOCIAL AND INDUSTRIAL QUESTIONS

Volume 27

THE ENGLISHWOMAN'S REVIEW OF SOCIAL AND INDUSTRIAL QUESTIONS

THE ENGLISHWOMAN'S REVIEW OF SOCIAL AND INDUSTRIAL QUESTIONS

1894

Advisory Editors
JANET HOROWITZ MURRAY AND
MYRA STARK

LONDON AND NEW YORK

First published in 1984 by Garland Publishing, Inc.

This edition first published in 2017
by Routledge
2 Park Square, Milton Park, Abingdon, Oxon OX14 4RN

and by Routledge
711 Third Avenue, New York, NY 10017

Routledge is an imprint of the Taylor & Francis Group, an informa business

All rights reserved. No part of this book may be reprinted or reproduced or utilised in any form or by any electronic, mechanical, or other means, now known or hereafter invented, including photocopying and recording, or in any information storage or retrieval system, without permission in writing from the publishers.

Trademark notice: Product or corporate names may be trademarks or registered trademarks, and are used only for identification and explanation without intent to infringe.

British Library Cataloguing in Publication Data
A catalogue record for this book is available from the British Library

ISBN: 978-1-138-20875-9 (Set)
ISBN: 978-1-315-39366-7 (Set) (ebk)
ISBN: 978-1-138-22693-7 (Volume 27) (hbk)
ISBN: 978-1-138-22713-2 (Volume 27) (pbk)
ISBN: 978-1-315-39662-0 (Volume 27) (ebk)

Publisher's Note
The publisher has gone to great lengths to ensure the quality of this reprint but points out that some imperfections in the original copies may be apparent.

Disclaimer
The publisher has made every effort to trace copyright holders and would welcome correspondence from those they have been unable to trace.

THE ENGLISHWOMAN'S REVIEW
of Social and Industrial Questions

1894

GARLAND PUBLISHING, INC.
New York & London
1984

Bibliographical Note

This facsimile has been made from
a copy in the collection of
the Bodleian Library.

The volumes in this series are printed on
acid-free, 250-year-life paper.

ISBN 0-8240-3751-0

Printed in the United States of America

THE
ENGLISHWOMAN'S REVIEW

OF

Social and Industrial Questions.

EDITED BY HELEN BLACKBURN.

VOL. XXV.
JANUARY TO OCTOBER, 1894.

LONDON
PUBLISHED AT THE OFFICE OF THE "ENGLISHWOMAN'S REVIEW,"
22, BERNERS STREET, OXFORD STREET, W.
AND FOR THE PROPRIETOR BY
WILLIAMS & NORGATE, 14, Henrietta Street, Covent Garden, London;
and 20, South Frederick Street, Edinburgh.

TABLE OF CONTENTS, 1894.

	PAGE
Alexandra School, Dublin	110
Amateur Art Exhibition	42
Architectural Association, Women and the	39
Aristotelian Society, Miss Jones' Paper	44
ARTICLES, LEADING—	
Austral Salon, Melbourne, The	14
British Workwoman in Danger, The	79
British Workwoman, More Dangers to the	145
Employment of Women, The Report on (Miss J. Boucherett)	1, 73, 149
Exhibition of Women's Work, Proposed Imperial	230
Lead Works and some other Unhealthy Industries (Miss J. Boucherett)	10
Local Government Act, Changes Introduced by	232
Lucy Stone (Miss M. A. Biggs)	84
Maria Deraismes and the Woman's Movement in France (Mme. Schmahl)	90
Technical Training in the Counties	217
Winter is Past, The (Mrs. Warner Snoad)	97
With All my Wordly Goods I Thee Endow (Mrs. Stopes)	157
Arts and Crafts Exhibition	41
Australian Outlook, Miss Shaw on the	63
British Association	262
British Silk Association	190, 279

	PAGE
Characteristics of Women's Pictures	212
Chicago Exhibition, Ladies' Committee of the	189
Chicago Exhibition, New South Wales and the	190
Child Labour	282
China, Empress Dowager of, and the Siamese Question	45
CLUBS—	
Pioneer	125
University	125
Writers'	125
COLONIAL AND FOREIGN NOTES—	
Australia	274
„ New South Wales	100
„ Queensland	100, 139
„ South	60, 100
Africa, South	275
Belgium	60
Denmark	60
Finland	59
France	61, 140, 276
Holland	276
Iceland	62
India	62
New Zealand	100, 101, 108, 275
Switzerland	140, 277
United States, Colorado	65, 140
„ „ Kentucky	141
„ „ Massachusetts	141
„ „ Michigan	277
„ „ New York	239
„ „ Ohio	141
CORRESPONDENCE—	
Deceased Wife's Sister, The	211
Finland, Women's Political and Municipal Reform in	58

Contents.

CORRESPONDENCE—*continued.*
Foreign Homes for Gentlewomen 56
Germany, Progress of Women in 209
L'Avant Courrière 212
Registration of Midwives' Bill 54
Dentists, Women, in Russia .. 144
Domestic Economy Scholarships, London County Council 187
Dufferin Fund, Countess 40, 259

EDUCATION AND UNIVERSITY INTELLIGENCE—
Cambridge 178
Girls' Public Day School Company 114
Glasgow, First Lady Graduates 242
Ireland, Alexandra School 110
„ Royal University 35, 241
London University 34, 241
Oxford 180, 182
„ Lady Margaret Hall 112
Scottish University Scholarships 243
Victoria University 36, 182
Welsh University, The New 116

ELECTIONS AND APPOINTMENTS—
Assistant Anæsthetist ... 107
Assistant Lecturer, History 33, 43
Assistant to Doctor, Lunatic Asylum 33
Co-operative Society, Keighley, Members of 108
Departmental Committee, Scotland, Member of ... 177
Education, Royal Commission on Secondary ... 106
Factory Inspectors 107, 177
Journalists' Institute, Members of 107
Local Government Board, by 240
London County Council, by 178
Master's Clerk 106
Mayor 108
Medical Appointments ... 107, 240, 241
Overseer 107

ELECTIONS AND APPOINTMENTS—*continued.*
Poor Law Guardians 33, 106, 178
Sanitary Inspector... 33, 178
School Boards 33, 107, 178, 241
Employment of Women, Royal Commission on the ... 114
Employment of Women, Royal Irish Association for ... 122
Employment of Women, Society for Promoting the 193
Exhibition of Women's Work 230
Factory Acts, Women Workers and the 183
Foreign Notes, *see* Colonial
Foresters, Women, and Order of 258
Gardening Association, Women's 42
Girls' Public Day School Company 114
Hospital for Women, Chelsea 264
How Colorado was Carried ... 65
Human Prerogative 67
Institute of Journalists — Annual Conference ... 244
Institute of Journalists — Paper by Miss Drew ... 245
IRELAND, *see* Education
Ireland, Royal College of Surgeons, Dublin ... 37
Ireland, Technical Teaching for Girls as it is in ... 202
Irish Schoolmistresses, The Association of 110
Japanese Ladies and the War 263
Jenny Lind, Memorial to ... 193
Journalists, Women as ... 245
Lady Margaret Hall 112
Libraries Association... ... 263
Local Government Act ... 109
Local Government Board, Miss Mason's Report to ... 143
Married Women's Property Act, 1893 37
Medical Students at Geneva... 280
Medicine, Edinburgh School of—Scholarships ... 123
Medicine, London School of —Prizes 38
Medicine, London School of —Students 123

Contents.

	PAGE
Metropolitan Association for Befriending Young Servants	124
Midwives, Registration of	208, 261
Music, and what it is Made of, About	44
National Health Society	125
OBITUARY—	
Collett, Miss Sophia Dobson	139
Cowen, Mrs.	53
Deraismes, Mlle. Marie	90, 135
Evans, Mrs. Wm.	266
King, Miss Anne	266
Lange, Dr. Emmy Kramp	267
Menzies, Mrs.	139
Stone, Mrs. Lucy	53, 84
Webster, Mrs. Augusta	264
Wolverton, Georgiana, Lady	137
Oriental Students	123
Pauper Children, Barrack Life of	251
Physicians and Surgeons, Royal College of Edinburgh and Glasgow	98
Pioneer Lecturers, Association of Women	44, 126
Portugal, The Queen of	126
Post Office Telegraphists	254
Press Reform, Women and	142
Protective and Provident League, Scotland, Conference of Women's	116
Reference Reading Room	45
REVIEWS AND NOTICES—	
Adventures in Mashonaland	128
Autobiography of Mary Smith	49
British Freewoman	194
German View of English Education	270
Harriet, Countess of Granville, Letters of	196
History of English Dress, A	46
Ladies at Work	132
Le Grand Catechisme de la Femme	200
Nursing Record, The	51
Our Exchanges	267
Plea for Appointment of Police Matrons, A	199
Relation of Women to Municipal Reform, The	199
Rights of Women, The	127

	PAGE
REVIEWS & NOTICES—continued.	
Romance of a Country, A	48
Six Weeks in Egypt	51
Two Noble Lives, The Story of	130
Woman and Her Place in a Free Society	201
Women's Herald, The	52
Women Writers, their Works and Ways	48
Work and Leisure	52
Working Woman's Day, A	51
Silk Association, British	190, 279
Stenographers, Women as	277
Swanley Horticultural College	42, 192
Swedish Institute, Clifton Doctors at	257
Telegraphists, Post Office	254
Trades' Union League, Women's	125
Truck Act	261
University Intelligence, see Education	
Welsh University, The New	116
Wesleyan Methodist Conference, Women Delegates	255
Women Dentists in Russia	144
Women and Order of Foresters	258
WOMEN'S SUFFRAGE—	
Appeal Committee Work	19
„ Committee for Scotland	25
„ Meetings in Favour of	22, 104
„ Report	107
„ Signatures	99
„ Supporters of the	19
Colonial Intelligence—	
Australia, Melbourne	173
„ New South Wales	100, 230
„ Queensland	100
„ South	27, 100, 237
„ Victoria	238
New Zealand	18, 26, 100, 101, 171, 238
Foreign Intelligence—	
Colorado	18
New York	173, 239
Leicester Election	239
Local Government Bill, Clauses Affecting Women	27

Contents.

WOMEN'S SUFFRAGE—continued.	PAGE
Meetings at Clifton, Bristol	99
Meeting at Glasgow, Liberal Federation	100
„ „ Manchester	99, 166
„ „ National Liberal Club	100
„ „ Rhyl Liberal Association	100
„ in Queen's Hall	166
„ „ St. James' Hall	166
„ of Central Committee, Annual	166

WOMEN'S SUFFRAGE—continued.	PAGE
Notes of the Quarter	18, 98, 165, 236
Registration Bill	98, 165
Women's Co-operative Guild, Conference	166
Women's Liberal Association, Circular to	100
Women's Suffrage News	98
Women Workers' Conference, The	39
Women's Undertakings and Ventures, Literary and other	43

ERRATUM.—At page 227 of the last issue, in the table of Local Government Franchises, women were, by a clerical error, made to appear as eligible for Poor Law Guardians in Ireland. They can elect in Ireland, but are not eligible for election.

PRICE ONE SHILLING.

New Series—Vol. XXV. No. I.   Jan. 17th, 1894.

THE
ENGLISHWOMAN'S REVIEW

OF

Social and Industrial Questions.

EDITED BY HELEN BLACKBURN.

CONTENTS FOR JANUARY, 1894.

ARTICLES,—The Report on the Employment of Women, by the Lady Assistant Commissioners. Lead Works and some other Unhealthy Industries. The Austral Salon, Melbourne.
WOMEN'S SUFFRAGE.—Notes of the Quarter. Women's Suffrage Appeal. List of Supporters and of Meetings. New Zealand Electoral Act. South Australia. Local Government Bill.
ELECTIONS AND APPOINTMENTS.
UNIVERSITY INTELLIGENCE.
RECORD OF EVENTS.—Married Women's Property Act, 1893. Royal College of Surgeons, Dublin. Women and the Association of Architects. Women Workers' Conference. Countess Dufferin Fund. Arts and Crafts Exhibition. Swanley College. Women's Gardening Association. Ventures and Undertakings. Empress Dowager of China and the Siamese Question.
REVIEWS AND NOTICES.—History of English Dress. Romance of a Country. Autobiography of Mary Smith. Six weeks in Egypt, &c.
OBITUARY.—Mrs. Lucy Stone. Mrs. Cowen.
CORRESPONDENCE.—Midwives Bill. Foreign Homes for Women. Women's Political and Municipal Rights in Finland.
FOREIGN NOTES.
PARAGRAPHS. HUMAN PREROGATIVE.

LONDON

PUBLISHED AT THE OFFICE OF THE "ENGLISHWOMAN'S REVIEW,"
22, BERNERS STREET, OXFORD STREET, W.
AND FOR THE PROPRIETOR BY
WILLIAMS & NORGATE, 14, Henrietta Street, Covent Garden, London
and 20, South Frederick Street, Edinburgh.

PUBLISHED QUARTERLY on the 15th January, April, July, and October.

A Women's Suffrage Calendar for 1894.
Edited by HELEN BLACKBURN.

CONTENTS.—Citizen's and Student's Calendar—Events of the Year—Obituary—Calendar of Events, with Diary—Women's Suffrage: Appeal from Women; Record of Progress in Australasia—Women on School Boards,1893—Public Appointments,1893—Local Government Franchises—Women Poor Law Guardians, 1893—Women Graduates, 1893—Registered Medical Women—School of Medecine for Women—Societies for Promoting the Welfare of Women: England; Scotland; Ireland—Enterprises by Women—Technical Training in Domestic Arts—Figures from the Census—Rates of Postage—Advertisements.

To be obtained of the Publishers, J. W. ARROWSMITH, Quay Street, Bristol; SIMPKIN, MARSHALL, HAMILTON, KENT, & CO., LIMITED, London; And of the EDITOR, 10, Great College Street, Westminster.

PRICE THREEPENCE.

Central Committee of the National Society for Women's Suffrage.

Hon. Sec.: Mrs. FAWCETT.   *Secretary*: Miss HELEN BLACKBURN.

Office: 10, GREAT COLLEGE STREET, WESTMINSTER.

MARRIAGE LAW DEFENCE UNION.

An Appeal from the Women of England … … …	1d.
The Woman's View of the Question … … …	1d.
A Letter to English Wives. By Edith Mary Shaw …	6d.
A Lady's Letter to a Friend, on behalf of those who do not wish to Marry their Brothers … …	½d.
What Miss Lydia Becker says … … … …	½d.
A Sister-in-Law's Plea for Mercy … … …	½d.
A Woman's Opinion on the Wife's Sister Bill … …	½d.

MAY BE HAD AT
1, KING STREET, WESTMINSTER, S.W.

PERIODICAL PUBLICATIONS received during the Quarter:—
AMERICA—*Woman's Journal*; *Woman's Exponent*; *The Woman's Tribune*; *Demorest's Monthly Magazine*; *The Cycle*.
AUSTRALIA—*Dawn*; *The Melbourne Sun*.
AUSTRIA—*Mitheilungen*; *Volkstimme*.
BELGIUM—*Revendication du Droit des Femmes*.
FRANCE—*Le Journal des Femmes*.
SWEDEN—*Dagny*.
DENMARK—*Kvinden og Samfundet*.
SWITZERLAND (Zurich)—*Frauenrecht*.
The Indian Magazine; *Woman*; *Concord*; *The Lady of the House*; *Work and Leisure*; *Women's Union Journal*; *Review of Reviews*; *Threefold Cord*; *Young Gentlewoman*; *The Spinning Wheel*; *Nursing Notes*.

A FAIR FIELD AND NO FAVOUR!

*Office for the Employment of Women as Compositors.
Girls trained and employed for the past twenty years.*

Ladies and Gentlemen are invited to place their orders for

PRINTING

WHERE THEY WILL BE EXECUTED BY

Women

IN A STYLE

EQUAL TO THE BEST.

NO SLIPSHOD WORK!
NO EXORBITANT PRICES!!

Estimates for Book and Magazine Work with Specimens.

JOHN BALE & SONS,

Steam Printers,

87-89, GREAT TITCHFIELD STREET,

OXFORD STREET, LONDON W.

Englishwoman's Review.

CONTENTS FOR OCTOBER 16th, 1893.

ARTICLES:
    Notes on Census. Laundries and Legislation. Women and Local Government. The Intellectual Inferiority of Women (Madame Henri Schmahl). Ladies' Health Society of Manchester and Salford. Poem, Leasing Corn (Mrs. Snoad).

WOMEN'S SUFFRAGE:
    Notes on the Appeal. Women's Suffrage carried in New Zealand. S. Australia. Australasian Women's Suffrage Record.

ELECTIONS AND APPOINTMENTS:
    Poor Law. Workhouse Visiting Committees. School Board.

UNIVERSITY INTELLIGENCE.

RECORD OF EVENTS:
    Irish Women and Home Rule. The New Dominican College for Girls in Dublin. British Association. Women and Overtime. Awards to British Artists at Chicago. The Queen of Rarotonga. Women on Juries for the Protection of Animals in New Zealand. Women and the Foresters. The Coal Strike and the Colliers' Wives. Technical Training. Notes of Progress. Women's Enterprises.

OBITUARY:
    Miss Pratt. Lady Eastlake.

CORRESPONDENCE:
    Proposed Exhibition of Women's Work. Registration of Midwives Bill.

NOTICES. FOREIGN NOTES.

ART AS A PROFESSION. A LADY'S ADVENTURES IN TIBET. WOMEN IN GERMANY.

THE
ENGLISHWOMAN'S REVIEW

(NEW SERIES.)

No. CCXX.—JANUARY 17TH, 1894.

ART. I.—THE REPORT ON THE EMPLOYMENT OF WOMEN, BY THE LADY ASSISTANT COMMISSIONERS.

THIS formidable volume is about fourteen inches long by seven wide, and contains 352 pages of small print in double column. It is written concisely, and is simply packed with information. A glance suffices to show that an account of its contents cannot be compressed into one article of reasonable length. The commissioners who write the Reports are Miss. E. Orme, Miss C. E. Collet, Miss M. Abraham, and Miss M. Irwin. Miss Orme, as the senior commissioner, writes the preface and edits the work.

The Reports were drawn up in pursuance of instructions received at a meeting of the Commission on Labour, in March, 1892, when the lady assistant commissioners were present, and the following points were mentioned as those to be specially kept in view in the investigation of women's work. (*a*) Difference in the rate of wages of men and women; (*b*) Alleged grievances of women; (*c*) Effects of women's industrial employment on their health, morality, and the home.

The assistant commissioners were also instructed to enquire into the existence and causes of the exclusion of women from trades in which women's work is not unsuitable.

The first Report printed in the volume is by Miss Collet, and refers to investigations made among shop-assistants, milliners, dressmakers, laundresses and match-workers. Miss Collet says that she experienced difficulty in getting evidence from the female shop-assistants. A widely circulated invitation to shop-assistants working above seventy-four hours in a week to meet her on a Sunday afternoon met with no response at all, notwithstanding the efforts of the Early Closing Association and the Secretary of the United Shop Assistants' Union. In consequence of this advertisement, however, a former shop-assistant then employed in Ireland wrote and offered to give particulars about sixteen shops in London in which she had been employed during the last five years. This offer was accepted, and the Report is founded in great measure on the account she gives, together with the evidence of eleven assistants, who, after some time, were induced to give evidence. The evidence of the assistant who was in sixteen different shops in five years is certain not to be too favourable to the employers, so we may be sure we know the worst that can be said. Miss Collet also interviewed many employers, and thinks that she has arrived at the truth. Anyone who reads the Report will come to the conclusion that Miss Collet has, at least, done all she can to ascertain the facts, and to put them down fairly.

The Report shows that the wages earned by shop women are very good, and that the hours of work are very long. Board and lodging are almost invariably given, and wages in South London seem to run from £20 a year to £50 and £60 and even more, one assistant receiving above £100. In North London the wages are less, and Miss Collet averages them at £42, with board and lodging. The men assistants earn more. In South London their wages range from £20 to £150, the usual thing appearing to be about £70 or £80. In North London the men's wages average about £65. The hours of work range from fifty hours in the week to seventy-seven hours, including meals. The usual hour of opening is 8.30, the usual hour of closing, 9. On Thursday there is generally a half holiday, when the shop closes at 2, and on Saturday there is a long overtime, when the shop remains open till 11 o'clock. Generally speaking, shops close at 11, but in some cases they remain open till 12, or even till 1 a.m. on Sunday morning. The time allowed for meals is usually half-an-hour for dinner and half-an-hour for tea.

I give an account furnished by an assistant in each of two shops, one being an exceptionally good one, the other exceptionally bad. Oxford Street.—Opens 8.30 ; closes 7.30; Saturday 2 ; time for dinner 25 minutes, for tea 15 minutes; salary nearly £60. Good library and tennis club ; supper 7.45. Perfectly free till 11 p.m. Been there five years. Woolwich.—Opens 8.45 ; closes 10.15 ; Thursday, 2 ; Saturday 12 ; time for dinner, half-an-hour, tea, half-an-hour ; salary £25. Stayed ten weeks. "Thought she would be ill if she remained longer."

One evil which formerly existed seems to be dying out, i.e., the practice of compelling shop assistants to go out for the whole of Sunday after they have breakfasted. The poor girls have nowhere to go, and declare their position to be miserable in the extreme, for " even if a girl has friends, they don't want her every Sunday," said one assistant.

Miss Collet gives no opinion on the subject of the possibility of legislative interference to prevent women from working long hours, but the information she furnishes forms a strong argument against it. The great difficulty in getting female assistants to make any complaints shows that they are not anxious for legislation. They are probably well aware that any attempt to shorten the hours of women's work, while leaving men free, would lead to the substitution of men for women assistants.

It is sometimes said that the difference between the wages of men and women would suffice to prevent this substitution, but a little consideration will show this is not the case. Suppose that a shopman's average pay is £65 a year, and a woman's is £42—as given by Miss Collet—the difference amounts to £23 a year, or about 9s. a week, or 1s. 6d. a day. Now, what amount of goods would a shop assistant sell in an hour? In the very poorest shops where the cheapest materials were sold could a man fail to sell less than 4s. worth of goods in a busy hour? In two hours this would be 8s., and the profit to the employer at 25 per cent. (the usual thing) would be 2s. on the two hours. If, therefore, the choice lay between closing his shop two hours earlier, or employing men instead of women, it would clearly be to his advantage to employ men. When more valuable goods were sold it would be still more to his advantage to do so. Now I ask my readers to ponder on this calculation, because it is a complete answer to the argument that women's wages being lower than men's would prevent them from being dismissed, and that argument is a very dangerous one. The only way, it seems to me, in which legislation is possible is that all shops, whether employing men or women, should be closed at 11 o'clock. Neither on Saturday nor on any other day should drapery or clothing shops be allowed to be open after 11 o'clock at night.

Milliners and Dressmakers. — These are already under the Factory Act. There can be no objection to enforcing the Act in this case, because there is no danger of men being extensively employed as dressmakers. Neither is there any danger of foreign ready-made dresses being imported. The chief grievance of dressmakers, and a very real one, is that when women are kept beyond the usual hours of work they are not paid for overtime. This is very hard, but could scarcely be removed by legislation. Miss Collet suggests that girls under 18 ought to be more protected against overwork than they are now—a very reasonable suggestion. The wages are sadly low in the dressmaking trade, but are better in millinery.

A theory is held by some people that if any trade was brought under the Factory Act, and the working hours were thus shortened, it would have the effect of raising the wages in that trade. The dressmaking industry is, unfortunately, an example to the contrary —eight shillings a week, without board or lodging, is quite usual.

Laundresses. — Miss Collet's report on the laundresses is very important, because at the present moment a movement is being made for the purpose of placing the trade under the Factory Acts.

The hours of work in London and neighbourhood are, generally speaking, for washers in steam laundries, from 8 to 8, with an hour and a-half allowed for meals on five days of the week, with shorter hours on Saturdays. Ironers' hours are rather shorter. Sometimes they do not come at all on Monday; sometimes they come later.

It appears that the machinery in many of these laundries is insufficiently fenced, and is dangerous to the workers. The sanitary arrangements are not always good, but the law as it exists at present is capable of removing this last evil if put in motion. The wages are good, as the following table, taken from a wage-book, shows:—

Workers.
1 earned 25s.
5 ,, 20s. to 25s.
2 ,, 18s. ,, 20s.
12 ,, 15s. ,, 18s.
13 ,, 12s. ,, 15s.
6 ,, 10s. ,, 12s.
11 ,, 8s. ,, 10s.
7 ,, 6s. ,, 8s.
6 ,, under 6s.

Of these six, three were learners, one was the messroom girl, and two were absent the greater part of the week.

The usual wages for washers seem to be 2s. 6d. a day, with 3d. an hour if kept overtime; ironers rather more. The greater number of the employers in steam laundries were of opinion that the extension of the Factory Acts to them would do them no harm, and they seemed to be generally in favour of such extension. One employer objected on the generous ground that a limitation by law of the hours of women workers would be unjust towards the hand laundries. In hand laundries there is very often no work done on Mondays, and sometimes none on Saturdays, but rather longer hours are worked on the other days, and overtime is frequent.

The hand laundries are preferred by women with children, as the arrangements leave them free on one or two days in the week to attend to their household affairs. These laundries afford a useful means of livelihood to widows, and married women whose husbands are ill or out of work.

The same conditions are found in all laundries in which steam is not used. The wages earned are about the same—perhaps a little higher, certainly not less. The sanitary arrangements are often bad, but the existing law is sufficient to cope with that evil.

Young girls are less frequently employed in hand than in steam laundries. The easy work of putting articles under the steam-rollers to be mangled suits them very well, but the hours are too long, and the heat in the ironing rooms too great for them.

Any limitation of the hours of work of women would be disadvantageous to the hand laundries and to all small laundries. If there was a press of work they would be unable to get through it if overtime were illegal. It would be advantageous to the steam laundries, as it would send them the custom which would be withdrawn from the small laundries. The chief promoters of the agitation in favour of putting laundries under the Factory and Workshops Acts are, in our opinion, (1) the owners of steam laundries, (2) the manufacturers of the machines therein used, and (3) the men who are employed in the steam laundries to manage the machinery, and who are often employed during their spare time to do the washing.

The persons who are chiefly opposed to the extension of the Acts are the owners of small laundries and of cottage laundries. It seems rather cruel to pass an Act against these poor women, who themselves work in their own laundries, in favour of the great capitalists who set up the steam laundries.

It is our opinion that legal limitation of the hours of young persons, boys as well as girls, is required, for boys are sometimes employed in the mangling department, and also that machinery ought to be safely fenced, and that the existing law with regard to sanitary arrangements should be enforced. Beyond this the law should not go.

Match Workers. — Inquiries were made by Miss Collet with regard to necrosis of the jaw, which is prevalent among match workers. It appears that the safety matches made by Messrs. Bryant and May, and also those made by the Salvation Army, are innocuous. But the ordinary matches made by Messrs. Bryant and May, and other firms, are dangerous. The proportion of persons attacked compared to those employed is small. Messrs. Bryant and May employ 1,150 women and 250 men in their ordinary match factory. Of these there were, at the time of Miss Collet's visit, on the sick list from necrosis one boy, four men, and seven women. It seems to be possible, by taking more care of the teeth, and by proper ventilation, to diminish the proportion still further. Necrosis causes disfigurement, and is sometimes, though very rarely, fatal.

The second Report is also by Miss Collet, and refers to industries carried on in Luton and in Bristol.

Straw-Plaiting.—This is a declining trade. One cause of the decline is that straw-plaiting is no longer taught in the schools, as it was in the days of the old dames' schools. In 1870 the teaching of straw-plait in schools was prohibited. In 1873 Chinese straw-plaiting was first introduced, which has almost supplanted the native industry. Still, in Luton and neighbourhood straw-plaiting continues to be done, though the pay is very poor owing to the Chinese competition. One witness said she only received 6d. now, where formerly she earned 1s. 2d. Another said she earned ½d. an hour. A third said she earned now 4d. instead of 10d. A plait collector told Miss Collet that 1½d. an hour was the maximum that could be earned. The homes* visited by Miss Collet did not appear to her to be uncomfortable as a general rule.

Straw Hat Making.—The machinists in factories earn pretty good wages, and are generally unmarried. In the slack time of the year the earnings of machinists are only about 3s. or 4s. a week, but in the busy season they range from 16s. to 25s. A manager of a factory said that the very best machinists could earn in the busiest season from 40s. to 50s. a week; the best hand sewer of hats only 15s.

Sometimes whole families work at the trade in their own houses, the man blocking the hats, his wife or daughter machining. Sometimes a workshop is attached to the house. The father and sons block, wife and daughters machine and finish. Sometimes women are hired to machine if there are no daughters, or a niece comes in to help. The hired women are paid by piece work, and earn from 12s. to 15s. a week. Hours from 8 to 8, or 8 to 4, with an hour for dinner and half-an-hour for tea.

This is, in our opinion, one of the best of women's trades, especially for single women, the absence of all injurious smells, and the position while employed—sitting instead of standing—rendering it suitable for the delicate as well as for the strong.

Bristol.—Miss Collet give a table of the earnings in the various trades for women.

PERCENTAGE OF WOMEN AND GIRLS EARNING :

	Under 8s.	8s. to 12s.	12s. to 15s.	15s. to 18s.	Over 18s.
Boots and Shoes	28.6	21.4	16.0	16.0	18.0
Corsets	20.3	31.8	24.6	16.7	6.6
Clothing	38.2	30.4	14.3	8.9	8.2
Laundry	16.6	47.6	20.2	13.1	2.5
Paper bags	30.3	40.9	21.3	.9	6.6
Cocoa	21.8	37.3	36.9	3.6	.4
Confectionery	95.8	4.2	—	—	—

It will be seen that the best paid trades are boots and shoes, corsets, laundry work, and cocoa-making. The worst is confectionery. Clothing work, which is probably the largest trade, holds a medium position. Miss Collet visited the houses of many home-workers.

---

* The straw-plaiters are generally married.

She says: "The London work girl generally dislikes working at home, but the Bristol girl prefers it. One reason for this will be seen when the home accommodation in the two cases is compared. The London and Bristol factories may be equally uncomfortable, but in London the home is very frequently worse than the factory, while in Bristol it is better. In not one single instance did I find the home workers in Bristol working in a bedroom." The reason is apparently that the rents are so much less than in London. Witness 231 paid 6s. a week for a cottage of five rooms, but let off two rooms for 3s. a week. The family living in these three rooms consisted of husband, wife, and two daughters. Witness 289 paid 3s. 9d. a week for a four-roomed cottage with garden. She considered herself better off than her sister in Paddington, who had to pay 5s. a week for a single room. In the Winterbourne district, Witness 270, working with her mother, said they paid 2s. 6d. a week for their four-roomed cottage, with a garden, in which they grew their own vegetables. This seemed about the usual rent, Miss Collet says.

Perhaps this Report may indicate a means of relieving in some degree the national distress under which we are now suffering. The empty cottages of the agricultural labourers in Essex and other parts where the land has gone out of cultivation might be made useful by affording cheap and comfortable habitations to workers in the clothing and other trades, where they could grow their own vegetables, cultivate fruit for their own eating, keep poultry, and perhaps pigs, and lead much happier and healthier lives than they now do in London.

It has been suggested that home workers in the clothing trade are paid less than the workers in factories, but Miss Collet thinks that the work done at home and in factories is not generally of exactly the same description, and that whenever it is exactly the same the pay is similar.

JESSIE BOUCHERETT.

(To be continued.)

ART. II.—LEAD WORKS AND SOME OTHER UNHEALTHY INDUSTRIES.

A DEPARTMENTAL Committee appointed by the Home Secretary has lately been enquiring into the health of persons employed in lead works, and has made a Report. Unfortunately the evidence on which the report is founded has not yet been printed. To some degree, however, this defect is diminished by the circumstance that the lady sub-commissioners have also been investigating the subject. Miss Abraham visited a large factory near Newcastle, and Miss Orme and Miss Irwin conjointly visited a factory near Glasgow.

Lead work is very unwholesome, because the dust is inhaled into the lungs, is absorbed by the skin, and if food be eaten with dirty hands, is actually swallowed. The employment is more or less unwholesome according as certain precautions are observed or disregarded. The precautions are: (1) A short day's work; (2) Not to work on an empty stomach; (3) To wash the hands and face before eating, and to eat in a room free from lead dust; (4) To take a warm bath once a week; (5) To wear respirators on occasion; (6) To wear a dust cloak over the dress.

In the factory near Newcastle visited by Miss Abraham, these precautions were very imperfectly observed, and the consequences were indeed terrible. She visited sixteen women who were suffering from illnesses caused by the lead, and four of these were blind, one of whom is mentioned as being permanently so and in the workhouse. Several others were suffering from "wrist drop," colic, and various forms of illness which, though severe, one may hope were not incurable.

Miss Abraham is of opinion that women suffer more than men from lead poisoning. She tells us that 135 cases of this sort were admitted into the Newcastle Infirmary in five years, 94 women and 41 men, of whom eight in all died—five women and three men. If the numbers employed were equal, the disproportion is very large, but if twice as many women as men were employed the disproportion would be small, and Miss Abraham omits to give the numbers employed. Dr. Oliver, of the Infirmary, however, says that women suffer more frequently and severely than men, and that young women are specially susceptible, which is the exact contrary of the case with men, who, he alleged, rarely suffer at all before the age of 23.*

At the factory in Scotland visited by Miss Orme and Miss Irwin, a better state of things exists owing to the necessary precautions being observed more closely, though not perfectly. The day's work is short, and owing to fluctuations in the trade, the work is seldom continued the whole year round. Witness 411 —a fine healthy working girl—said she had worked for nine months and felt no ill effects. 412 had worked seven months and had not suffered, but knew a girl who had been seriously ill with convulsions in consequence. No. 413 feels her head trouble her occasionally, but not seriously. 414 has no complaints to make. 415 has headache occasionally and internal pains. None of these have been employed more than a year. No. 416 has been employed sixteen or seventeen years and has not found her health impaired, but the manager said she had been often employed in "orra jobs" about the place, so was not a fair specimen. 417 has slight headaches. Most of the women interviewed made light of the danger to health. Their complaint is that the work is not regular and the wages too low. They earn from 10s. to 14s. a week. The authorities at the Western Infirmary, where workers are sent when suffering from lead poisoning, said they had had very few cases. The medical officer of the lead works said that during the fifteen years the factory had been in existence " There has been no death from lead poisoning. We have

---

* Part of the reason of this extra sensibility of women is owing to their dress, which, if too long, stirs up the dust, and which affords no protection to the legs.

occasionally a case of colic, causing inability to work for a few days. This mostly occurs where the general surroundings are bad, causing impairment of the general health, and thereby predisposing to illness, but as a rule we have a healthy lot of girls and women to deal with, who are rarely ill, although many of them have been employed in the factory a great number of years; but my belief is that by proper attention to the appliances provided by the firm for the safety and comfort of their workers, we ought to have almost complete immunity from any bad effects which lead may tend to have. The state of matters which I see reported from Newcastle has no existence here."

Probably the most important precaution is that of not working on an empty stomach. This Scotch firm provides a dining-room and soup and porridge free of charge, so that no worker need ever be hungry. This is probably the secret of the good health of the persons employed. In a very sad case occurring at Bilston, mentioned in the Report of the Departmental Committee, of a girl of 17 employed as a lead enameller, who died from lead poisoning, it appears that when she began work the firm provided each worker with a cup of milk and a biscuit when she arrived at the factory. Subsequently this rule was altered, and acid drink provided instead. Soon afterwards the poor girl fell ill and died. A case occurred in December last of a woman who died in London from working in a lead factory. It appeared at the inquest that warm baths and acid drinks were provided by the firm, but no mention was made of food. When we consider how poorly fed working women generally are, and that want of nourishing food is the cause of consumption and many other fatal diseases, it is evident that a good meal is the most effectual preventive measure that can be taken to protect them against lead poisoning or any other complaint.

It is said that the Government contemplate bringing in a Bill to prohibit the employment of women in lead works. Would it not be better to require all firms to follow the example of the Scotch firm, and so, while permitting the women to earn their livelihood, to secure them from suffering from the effects of the lead? A further precaution might be taken by requiring the women to wear knickerbockers under their dresses, and forbidding them to have dresses so long as to trail on the ground and so stir up dust.

Miss Abraham reports that babies sometimes die in convulsions if their mothers have suffered from lead poisoning before their birth. This is very sad, but by due precautions we may hope that the mothers will no longer be seriously affected by the lead. Also we must remember that every employment has its accompanying disease. Probably the women employed by the Scotch firm are healthier, happier, and stronger than ordinary dressmakers. If we consider the welfare of the next generation, there is no occupation so injurious to it as that of the tailor. Dr. Arlidge, in his book, "Diseases of Occupations," thus speaks of tailors: "Confinement indoors, the cramped and unhealthy mode of sitting at work, the want of physical exercise, the frequent use of artificial light, and the emission of heat in the operation of pressing—in these conditions we find an array of disease-producing factors not often surpassed." Dr. Smith, who wrote "The Sanitary Circumstances of Tailors in London" in 1863, was of opinion that two-thirds of the mortality of tailors are due to phthisis and chest diseases. Dr. Ogle, who has written since, believes this statement to be beyond the truth, but statistics show that their mortality from phthisis greatly exceeds the average.

When we consider that consumption is hereditary from the father even more than from the mother, it is evident that we have here one of the chief causes of consumption in children. It is bad that babies should die of convulsions, but far worse that children should be consumptive. Women suffer less than men from sedentary employment, so that needlework is a trade not unsuitable to them. To prohibit women from engaging in lead work, while permitting boys of 14 to engage in the tailoring trade, is to strain at a gnat and swallow a camel. To turn men or women out of their employment, to take from them their means of living without giving them compensation, is an act of cruelty, while to prohibit boys or girls from engaging in trades unhealthy to them is no cruelty but a kindness. If a lad of 18 has a turn for needlework, or finds no other opening, let him, being then old enough to judge for himself, become a tailor, and if a girl of 18 can earn an honest livelihood in the lead works, and sees no other good opening, let her go also. She will not contribute so much to the deterioration of the national health as the tailor will.

Pottery work is also unwholesome from clay dust, flint dust, and in some departments from lead. Both boys and girls suffer in the Potteries.* Neither ought to be in future employed till old enough to choose for themselves, but to turn out of work those already engaged, many of whom are quite healthy and suffer no inconvenience, would be an act of injustice which will, we hope, never be committed.

JESSIE BOUCHERETT.

ART. III.—THE AUSTRAL SALON, MELBOURNE.

BY ONE OF ITS FOUNDERS.

EARLY in January of 1890, a few of the women journalists of Melbourne held an impromptu sort of meeting at a private house with the view of forming a Woman's Club. Rumours of the Somerville Club of London, and still more of the new Somerville which sprang from its ashes, had come across the ocean frequently, neither was the Sorosis of New York altogether unknown, and it was felt that the time

---

* The Potteries Committee of Inquiry states that lads suffer from lead poisoning, and classes "lads and young women" together, stating that of these many break down, while others do not suffer at all. There is a curious contradiction between Miss Abraham's report and the Inquiry report on this point.

had come for Melbourne to make a beginning. It was found on inquiry that none of those concerned possessed even one copy of the constitution of either of those organisations, so that there was much groping in the dark as it were, but Mrs. Zadel Gustavson, of New York, joint author with her husband of a peculiar work, " The Foundations of Death," was in Melbourne at the time, and was able to give some information concerning the Sorosis, but as, although a member, she had never attended any of the meetings, knew little of the procedure prevailing, and had been some time absent from America, her information was so vague as to be of no practical benefit. Attention had been awakened, however, and from five at the first meeting early in the month, the attendance rose to considerably over twenty at the third, before the month's end; as we have said, the idea had been initiated by some of the women journalists, but as Melbourne, though a good sized city, is still considerably smaller than several of the bigger towns of Great Britain, it was felt from the beginning that it would be impossible to make a club out of the scanty ranks of press-women or writers, either amateur or professional. This difficulty was disposed of at the very first meeting, when it was resolved that the proposed club should be composed of women actively engaged in all professions. These early meetings were of the most intense interest, so various, and in many cases curious were the views put forth. Even those who first mooted the project were in anything but agreement as to its constitution, and had all the ideas put forward been adopted, the organisation would have been a trades' union, a luncheon and dining-room, a boarding house, a young women's mutual improvement society, a gymnasium, a mechanics' institute, an amateur musical and dramatic club, and a mutual admiration society rolled into one. As it is, it is none of these things, though it partakes of the nature of some of them. A most animated discussion was that which decided the name. A large number of cognomens were proposed, only to be rejected as indescriptive or too general; even the picturesque and descriptive title of "The Ink and Art Club" was decided to be not comprehensive enough, and on the proposition of a member who knew something of the London *Salon*, the style and title became with geographical fitness that of "The Austral *Salon*."

All decisions were, and still are, made by the rough-and-ready method of taking the vote of the majority, but after the baptism of the yet inchoate scheme, the way seemed to grow plainer. A committee was appointed to draw up a constitution in the form of rules and regulations, and as this committee was composed of women with a praiseworthy belief in their own sex, and a laudable wish to see it progress, it is to be feared that the four years of history now behind the Salon have scarcely been lived up to the high level indicated in that constitution, of which the first article is that "The object of the Austral Salon shall be the intellectual advancement of women." Be that as it may; the first launching of the Austral Salon excited attention, and even some degree of enthusiasm. The Salon, as it is universally called—the word "club" having long been dropped—began to work out its destiny by holding fortnightly women's meetings in a small hall, and it was formally inaugurated in June, 1890, with a grand invitation entertainment, at which the Governor of Victoria and his wife were present. All the professional talent of the Salon was utilised for this performance—a sort of dramatic reading of "Lalla Rookh," with the action given in dumb show, interspersed with songs, which was an immense success, and the rush of people anxious to join was so great that the committee imposed an entrance fee, and proposed a subscription ball. This took place in August, at the Melbourne Town House, and was attended by about 1,000 people.

The Salon has had other invitation entertainments and other subscription balls since, successful, but not either so successful or so brilliant as those that marked its first year of existence. It has given of its substance towards charity by a grand dramatic performance at one of the theatres two years ago. It raised enough money to enable a blind girl to proceed with her studies for the B.A. degree at the Melbourne University. It is frequently called upon to give its patronage to a benefit concert or entertainment, not necessarily, and indeed not often, for a member. Many very clever and very instructive papers have been read and followed by discussion at the monthly evening meetings. A series of flower festivals, both novel and tasteful, have been held during the past eighteen months, and the Monday " afternoon teas," when programmes of music, recitations, and comedies are submitted, and young talent has a chance of a hearing, are invariably very largely attended. But withal the Austral Salon cannot be said to have fulfilled the hopes and intentions of its founders. Perhaps the hopes were too exalted, the intentions too vague.

The Salon was first constituted with a president, two vice-presidents, and an executive vice-president or perpetual chairwoman. This latter arrangement was not found to work well, and at the end of the first year the office was abolished. The Salon is now administered by a committee of seven, with honorary treasurer and secretary. A distinction is made, in the articles, between members and associates—to quote : " Membership is limited to women actively engaged in literature, science, and the fine arts," but " Associates may be either men or women who are in sympathy with, and willing, by personal effort and influence, to promote the objects of the Salon." Associates have the right to vote upon any paper or subject of general discussion at the regular meetings, but they have no voice in the government of the Salon, with the exceptions recently made that women associates are eligible for the offices of treasurer or secretary, and that one is elected annually to represent the associates on the committee. All elections, whether of officers and, committee, or new members and associates, are on the votes of members only.

After several removals, the Salon now occupies very handsome rooms, open all day, in the centre of the city. Light luncheon and afternoon tea can be had, but the day seems to be yet remote when the members shall have a club house of their own, with all its attendant privileges and conveniences.

WOMEN'S SUFFRAGE.

NOTES OF THE QUARTER.

The event of the past quarter has been the admission of women to the Parliamentary Franchise in New Zealand, when the act conferring the rights of citizenship on women for the first time in any British Parliament, received the Governor's assent on September 19th.

The text of those passages of the act which describe the qualifications of electors, will be found on another page.

As a general election was close at hand, no time was lost by the women of New Zealand in enrolling their names on the register, and when the day of election came they were ready to vote in thousands. Speaking of Auckland, the *New Zealand Herald* says: "About 5,000 women have been added to the roll. It may be supposed that about 4,500 of these voted, recording (allowing for plumpers) about 12,000 votes."

From Colorado, good news has come. That State, which in 1877 rejected Woman's Suffrage by a majority of 9,000, has in November, 1893, adopted Woman's Suffrage by a majority of over 7,500.

These good things have not come of themselves. In New Zealand, as recorded in our former issue, measures for Women's Suffrage had been carried through many of the necessary Parliamentary stages in 1878, in 1887 and in 1892. The petitions presented by Sir John Hall in 1893 contained the signatures of 29,548 women, while other members had presented petitions, bringing the total to 31,872.

In Colorado a very widely ramified campaign of work had been carried on quietly, but continuously, for many months.

A summary of the debates in the House of Commons on the clauses affecting women in the Local Government Bill is given at page 28.

Women's Suffrage.

The Women's Suffrage Appeal has been making steady progress, and has called forth a large amount of energy amongst the supporters of Suffrage in all parts of the Kingdom—as may be seen by the subjoined record of meetings held, and list of ladies who have rendered valuable service.

The present position of Parliamentary business indicates that a longer time may be allowed for the collection of signatures than could have been at first anticipated; accordingly the special Committee have decided to continue the work of collecting signatures to the 31st of March.

The Central Committee, 10, Great College Street, have issued a circular to their members and friends, in which the Committee earnestly beg those friends who have not yet returned their books of signatures to kindly send in all that are already filled at once, either to the office of the Central Committee, to their local centre, or to the Special Appeal Office, as the case may be, and to continue working for additional signatures till March 31st, when all books must be sent in.

SUPPORTERS OF THE APPEAL.

Valuable support has been given to the work of the Appeal, either by their sympathy or their active work, by many ladies of influence throughout the kingdom.

The Editor is fully aware that the following list of ladies who have rendered good help to the Appeal is very incomplete, seeing it has been prepared in haste, in view of the extension of time for collecting signatures. She trusts it will nevertheless serve to indicate the widely diffused character of the work which is going forward.

† Denotes members of the Special Appeal Committee.
* Denotes hon. secs. of Local Appeal Committees.

A'Court, the Hon. Mrs. Holmes (Clifton)
*Adair, Mrs. H. (Oxford)
Adamson, Mrs. and Miss (Tynemouth)
Alexander Miss (The Palace, Londonderry)
Allen, Miss Gray (Londonderry)

Anderson, Mrs. Garrett, M.D.
Ashford, Mrs. (Birmingham) President Birmingham W.S. Committee
Atkinson, Miss, Hon. Sec. Manchester W. S. Committee
Austen, Mrs. Roberts

†Balfour, The Lady Frances
†Balfour, Miss
Bateson, Miss M., Hon. Sec. Cambs. W. S. Committee
Barber, Miss, Hon. Sec. Leeds W. S. Committee
Barratt, Mrs. Francis (Prideaux)
*Baynes, Mrs. (Rochester)
Beddoe, Mrs. (Bradford-on-Avon)
Beddoe, Miss (Clifton)
Benson, Mrs. (Lambeth Palace)
Bevan, Mrs. Wm.
Bewicke, Mrs. Calverley
Bigg, Miss Louisa, Hon. Sec. Luton W. S. Committee
Blackett, Miss Ida (Chertsey)
Booth, Mrs. Alfred (Liverpool)
Boucherett, Miss Jessie
Bright, Mrs. Alan H. (Liverpool)
Brocklebank, Mrs. (Liverpool)
Brodie-Hall, Miss (Eastbourne)
Brook, Mrs. C. J. (Huddersfield)
Browne, Mrs. Morgan
Brown, Mrs. Dixon (Haltwhistle)
Brown, Mrs. E. Stewart, Hon. Sec. Liverpool W. S. Committee
*Butterfield, Mrs. (Northampton)

Clark, Mrs. W. S. (Somerset, East)
Clayton, Mrs. (Hexham)
Cowen, Mrs., Hon. Sec. Notts W. S. Committee
†Courtney, Mrs. Leonard
Courtney, Miss (Penzance)
Culme-Seymour, Mrs.
Currey, Miss F. W. (Lismore)

Davenport-Hill, Miss F.
Davies, Miss Llewelyn, Hon. Sec. W. Co-operative Guild

*Eaton, Mrs. Lauder (Falmouth)
Eccles, Miss (Westminster)
Egerton, Hon. Lady Grey
Elder, Miss C.
*Eunson, Mrs. (Northampton)

†Fawcett, Mrs.
Fawcett, Miss Philippa
Fenwick, Mrs. Bedford
Fitzgerald, Mrs. Penrose
Ford, Miss I. O.
Ford, Mrs. Rawlinson (Leeds)
Fordham, Mrs. (Royston)
Fuller, Mrs. G. P. (Corsham, Wilts)

Gardiner, Miss (Manchester)
Garrett, Miss Ruby (Aldeburgh)
Gaskell, Miss (Weymouth)
Gilliland, Miss (Londonderry)
Gittens, Miss, Hon. Sec. Leicester W. S. Committee
Green, Miss (Gorton)
Groser, Miss (Plymouth)
Gurney, Miss Mary

Hale, Mrs. H. M. (Stoke Bishop)
Hallett, Mrs. Ashworth, Hon. Sec. Bristol W. S. Committee
Harle, Mrs. (Thornbury, div. Gloucester)
Haslam, Mrs., Hon. Sec. Dublin W. S. Committee
Hodgson, Mrs. C. H.
Hogg, Mrs. (Leeds)
Hollond, Mrs. John
Holman, Mrs. Arthur (Torpoint)
Hughes, Miss E. P. (Cambridge)
Hume, Lady (Clifton)

Irton-Smith, Mrs. (Ilkley)

James, Mrs. E. (Aberystwith)
Jebb, Mrs. (Cambridge)
Jeune, Lady
*Johnson, Mrs. Arthur (Oxford)
Johnstone, Mrs. (Tavistock)
Jones, Mrs. Viriamu (Cardiff)
Joy, Mrs. Algernon

†Knightley, The Lady; of Fawsley
Kerr, Miss Malcolm (Ventnor)
Kingsley, Miss

Latchmore, Mrs. (Leeds)

Latimer, Miss Frances (Plymouth)
Lawrence, the Misses (Brighton)
Leeds, Mrs. (Croydon)
Luttrell, Mrs. A. (Bridgwater)
Lyttelton, Hon. Mrs. Arthur (Eccles)
Lyttelton, Hon. Mrs. E. (Hertford)

McCullagh, Mrs. (Londonderry)
McLaren, Mrs. Charles
†McLaren, Mrs. Eva
Mallock, Mrs. (Torquay)
Manners, Mrs., Hon. Sec. Mansfield W. S. Committee
*Martindale, Mrs. (Brighton)
Martin, Miss (Cork)
Martin, Miss (Handsworth)
†Massingberd, Mrs.
Mellor, Miss (Birkenhead)
Mitchell, Mrs. (Caerleon)
†Mordan, Miss (Reigate)
*Morgan, Miss Gwenlian (Brecon)
Moroney, Mrs. (Miltown Malbay)
†Morrison, Mrs. Frank
Munro, Mrs. (Chelsea)
Mylne, Mrs. (Paddington)

Osler, Mrs. Alfred, Hon. Sec. Birmingham W. S. Committee

*Patteson, Miss (Ipswich)
Paull, Miss Lillie (Truro)
Payne, Mrs. (Cuckfield)
Peard, Mrs. (Croydon)
Pender, Mrs. (Rugby)
*Perrott, Mrs. (Brighton)
†Phillips, Mrs. Wynford
Polglase, Misses (Falmouth)
Powell, Mrs. (Reigate)
Priestman, Misses (Bristol)

Reid, Mrs. (Birmingham)
Reid, Miss A. M. (Hammersmith)
Reid, Miss Emily (Eastbourne)
†Reid, Mrs. Broadley

Rennick, Mrs. G. (Newcastle-on-Tyne)
Reynolds, Mrs. (Bridport)
Roberts, Miss Dorothea, President Mansfield W. S. Committee
Roper, Miss, B.A., Sec. Manchester W. S. Committee
Rylands, Mrs. (Birmingham)

Salmon, Mrs. (Bury St. Edmunds)
Sawyer, Lady
Schaw-Protheroe, Miss (Carmarthen)
Scholefield, Mrs. A. (Newcastle-on-Tyne)
Shore, Miss Arabella
Sidgwick, Mrs. Henry
Sidney, Miss (Bath).
Singleton, Mrs. (Melbourne)
Simpson, Mrs. H. T. (Gloucester)
Snoad, Mrs. Warner
†Somerset, Lady Henry
Spring Rice, Mrs. S.
Stacpoole, Miss Florence
*Stapleton, Miss (Tunbridge Wells)
Stewart, Miss Gertrude, Sec. W. S. Committee, Parliament Street
Stopes, Mrs. Carmichael
Storey, Miss (Newcastle-on-Tyne)
Swanwick, Miss Anna

Tanner, Mrs. Arthur (Wells Division of Somerset)
†Taylor, Mrs. (Chipchase Castle)
Taylour, Miss (Saffron Walden)
Thew, Mrs. Arthur (Southport), Hon. Sec. Guild of the Unrepresented:
Tod, Miss Isabella M. S., Hon. Sec. N. of Ireland W. S. Committee
Twining, Miss Louisa

Vernon, Hon. Mrs. (Kettering)
†Vernon, Miss

(Continued at p. 25)

RECORD OF MEETINGS AT WHICH THE APPEAL HAS BEEN ADVOCATED.

*Those marked * have been expressly held in support of the Appeal.*

Date.	Place.	Description.	Chairman.	Speakers.
Aug.	*Reigate	Drawing Room Meeting, by invitation of Mrs. Powell	Mrs. Sambrook	Miss Mordan
,, 29	*Ventnor (Albert Hall)	Lecture (organized by Miss Malcolm Kerr)	Mr. Albert Bull, C.C.	Miss Mordan
	*Luton	Conference at Lyndhurst House (in connection with Luton W.S. Committee)	Alderman Blundell	
Sept. 18	*Nottingham (Central Hall)	"At Home" of Notts. W. S. Committee	Mrs. Cowen	Miss D. Roberts, Prof. Viriamu Jones, Miss Wright, Miss Blackburn
,, 25	Epsom	Lecture (Epsom and Ewell W. L. A.)	Mr. Lewis Fry	Mrs. G. P. Fuller, Lord Edmond Fitzmaurice, Mrs. Emma Marshall
Oct. 7	*Bradford-on-Avon (The Chantry)	Drawing Room Meeting, given by Mrs. Beddoe		Mrs. Fawcett
,, 10	*Mansfield (Albert Street Hall)	Public Meeting, organised by Mansfield W. S. Committee	Mr. H. E. Hollins	
,, 12	*Manchester (Congregational Hall, Eldon Street)	Public Meeting	Mr. Councillor Southern	Mrs. Fawcett
,, 13	*Edgbaston (Birmingham Committee)	Drawing Room Meeting (Mrs. H. N. Rylands)		Mrs. Rylands, Mrs. Ashford, Mrs. Fellowes, Mrs. Hallwright, Mrs. Sonnenschein
,,	Westminster	In connection with W. L. A.	Mrs. Lidstone	Miss Holah
,, 19	*Bristol (69, Park Street)	Conference of Workers	Mrs. Beddoe	
,, 23	*Handsworth (Birmingham Committee)	Drawing Room Meeting (Mrs. Wilkinson)	Mrs. Ashford	Lady Sawyer, Mrs. Phillp, Miss Martin
,, 24	*Tunbridge Wells (Sussex Assembly Rooms)	Meeting, by invitation of Miss Stapleton	Mrs. Fawcett	W. H. Browell, Esq., Rev. T. R. Stebbing, Miss Blackburn
,,	*Falmouth (Penmance House)	Drawing Room Meeting, by invitation of Mrs. Lauder Eaton	Mrs. Genn	Miss Mordan
,, 26	*Chatham	Lecture		Miss Friend
,, 27	*Weymouth (Cookes' Room)	Lecture	Mrs. Samson	Mrs. Morgan Browne
,, 30	*Bridport	Lecture	Mrs. Bryant Reynolds	Mrs. Morgan Browne
,,	*Truro (Bosvigo House)	Drawing Room Meeting, by invitation of Miss L. Powell	Rev. R. E. S. Buck	Miss Mordan
,, 31	*Oxford (105, Banbury Road)	Drawing Room Meeting, by invitation of Mrs. Adair	Mrs. A. Johnson	Miss Blackburn
,, 31	*Dorchester	Drawing Room Meeting, by invitation of Mrs. Arthur Lock	Rev. J. McClure Uffen	Mrs. Morgan Browne
,,	*Somerville Club	Lecture		Mrs. Stopes
,,	*Islington	Lecture		Mrs. Holah
Nov. 2	*Harborne (Birmingham W. S. Committee)	Drawing Room Meeting (Mrs. Godlea)		Mrs. Fellowes, Mrs. Ashford
,, 4	*Northampton (Old Reading Room, Town Hall)	Public Meeting	Lady Knightley	Mrs. Pender, Mrs. Hickson, Lord Knightley, Mrs. Manfield, Mr. Manfield, M.P., Miss Blackburn, Mayor and Mayor Elect
,, 6	*Newcastle-on-Tyne (Y.W.C.A., Saville Place)	Conference of Workers, organised by Mrs. T. Taylor		
,, 7	*Leeds (Brayshers' Rooms, Bond Street)	"At Home," by invitation of Leeds W. S. Committee	Mrs. Edward Walker	Mrs. Beddoe, Lady Frances Balfour, Hon. Mrs. Arthur Lyttelton, Miss I. O. Ford, Miss Blackburn, Miss Connon

Date	Location	Meeting	Chair	Speakers
Nov. 8	Clapham Reform Club			Mrs. Bamford Slack, Dr. Harris, L.C.C.
,, ,,	*Huddersfield (Mayor's Parlour)			Mrs. Fawcett
,, ,,	*Birmingham (Birmingham Committee)			Mrs. J. K. Reid, Miss Bonrly, Mrs. Farrow
,, 10	St. James's Hall, London			The Rt. Hon. Leonard Courtney, M.P.	Mrs. Fawcett, Sir Wilfrid Lawson, M.P., Mrs. Wynford Phillips, Mrs. Bamford Slack
,, 13	*Melbourne Vicarage (near Derby)	Drawing Room Meeting, by invitation of Mrs. Singleton	Canon Singleton	Miss Mordan, Mr. Briggs, R.C.
,, 14	Burgess Hill (Institute)	In connection with W. L. A.	Hon. Mrs. A. Brand	Mrs. Morgan Browne
,, 15	Hayward's Heath (Assembly Rooms)		Mrs. Payne	Mrs. Morgan Browne
,, ,,	Colchester	Public Meeting		Mrs. Mallet
,, ,,	*Brighton (Mayor's Parlour)	Conference of Workers		
,, ,,	*Handsworth	Drawing Room Meeting, Mrs. Pearson	Mrs. Haycraft	Mrs. Reid, Mrs. Philip
,, 21	*Mosley (Birmingham Committee)	Drawing Room Meeting, Mrs. James Smith	Mrs. Darby Weston	Mrs. E. E. Matthews, Mrs. Philp, Miss Norah Morris
,, ,,	*Barnt Green (Birmingham Committee)	Drawing Room Meeting, Mrs. H. Lee	Mrs. J. Moore Bayley	Mrs. Osler, Mrs. Eric Carter, Mrs. Ashford
,, 21	Pembroke Dock			Mrs. McLaren, Mrs. Wynford Phillips
,, 22	Tenby			Mrs. McLaren
,, 24	Narberth	In connection with W. L. A.		Mrs. McLaren
,, 27	Pembroke			Mrs. McLaren, Miss Jenkins
,, 28	Cardiff			Mrs. McLaren
,, 27	Southport	Annual Meeting of the Guild of the Unrepresented	Mr. J. J. Cockshott	Mrs. Mallet
,, 28	*Withington (Town Hall)	Public Meeting	Mr. J. Southam	Mrs. Fawcett [chester, &c.
,, 29	Manchester (Memorial Hall)	Annual Meeting	Rev. S. A. Steinthal	Mrs. Fawcett, the Archdeacon of Manchester
,, ,,	Wakefield	Lecture (W. L. A.)	Mr. George Webster	Mrs. Mallet
,, ,,	Pateley Bridge	Pateley Bridge Lecture		Mrs. Mallet
,, 29	{Eccles (Hon. Mrs. A. Lyttelton)	Drawing Room Meeting and Lecture; Two Drawing Room Meetings (in connection with Women's Liberal Association)		Miss Whitehead
,, 30	Bristol	Drawing Room Meeting		Mrs. Fawcett
,, ,,	Islington	In connection with W. L. A.		Mrs. Holah
Dec. 1	*Clifton (Clifton Down Hotel)	Lecture	Mrs. Ashworth Hallett	Miss Balfour, Mrs Beddoe
,, ,,	Stowmarket	Meeting of Ladies	Mr. H. Robinson	Miss Friend
,, ,,	*Liverpool (Temperance Hall)	Public Meeting	Mrs. A. H. Bright	Miss E. Hornby, Mrs. Stewart Brown, Mrs. Fawcett, Hon. Mrs. A. Lyttelton, Mrs. Alfred Booth
,, 2	Ripon (Temperance Hall)	Women's Liberal Association	Miss H. Hargrave	Mrs. Mallet
,, 4	*Brighton (Prestonville)	Drawing Room Meeting given by Mrs. Martindale	Mrs. Longton	Mrs. Morgan Browne
,, 5	Hoxton	Drawing Room Meeting by invitation of Mrs. Buss		Mrs. Holah
,, 6	*Brighton (Sussex Square)		Miss M. Lawrence	Mrs. Fawcett, Mrs. Morgan Browne
,, ,,	West Kensington	Lecture to Pupil Teachers' Society		Mrs. Holah
,, 7	Walworth (St. John's Schools)	Lecture		Miss Mordan
,, ,,	*South Kensington (Bramham Gardens)	Drawing Room Meeting, Misses Jacomb Hood		Miss Mordan, Miss Stackpoole, Miss Blackburn
,, 7	Wellingborough	Social gathering of Hatton Habitation of P.L.	Mr. Herbert Dulley	Mrs. Pender, Miss Friend
,, 11	Plymouth	Women's Liberal Association, Social Gathering		Mrs. Swann
,, 12	*Tynemouth (St. Oswin's Hall)	Public Meeting	Mrs. Taylor, of Chipchase	Mrs. Fawcett
,, ,,	*Shields (Congregational Hall)	Public Meeting	Mrs. Taylor, of Chipchase	Mrs. Fawcett

DATE.	PLACE.	DESCRIPTION.	CHAIRMAN.	SPEAKERS.
Dec. 11	*Newcastle-on-Tyne (Art Gallery)	Public Meeting	Alderman W. D. Stephens	Mrs. Fawcett, Mr. Geo. Renwick, Mrs. Spence Watson
,, 13	*Jarrow (Mechanics' Institute)	Public Meeting	Mr. W. S. Dalgliesh	Mrs. Fawcett, Mrs. John Wimbolt
,, 13	Bedminster (Bristol)	Lecture in connection with Primrose League		Miss Blackburn
,, 14	Birmingham (Priory Room)	Lecture in connection with Women's Liberal Association		Miss C. M. Collett, of Leicester
,, 15	*Kensington (46, Queen's Gate Terrace)	Drawing Room Meeting by invitation of Mrs. Bevan	Sir Wm. Wedderburn, M.P.	Mrs. Fawcett, Mrs. Bamford Slack
,, ,,	Maidenhead			Mrs. McLaren
,, 19	Barry Dock (Baptist Chapel)	Lecture (Young Wales Society)	Dr. Edwards	Miss E. P. Hughes

THE FOLLOWING MEETINGS HAVE BEEN HELD IN SCOTLAND IN CONNECTION WITH THE SCOTCH APPEAL COMMITTEE.

DATE.	PLACE.	DESCRIPTION.	CHAIRMAN.	SPEAKERS.
Oct. 17	North Berwick (Odd Fellows Hall)	Lecture	Rev. J. Davidson	Miss Taylour
Nov. 8	Dalkeith (Glencairn House)	Drawing Room Meeting		Miss Louisa Stevenson, Miss Kirkland
,, 13-16	Aberdeen	A series of Drawing Room Meetings by invitation of Mrs. Adamson, Mrs. Ker, Mrs. Rodger, Mrs. Duthie, Mrs. Ramsay; also Meeting at Y.W.C.A. and Girls' Club		Mrs. Stopes
,, 21	Chirnside (Erskine U. P. Manse)	Conference of Workers		Mrs. Gillies
,, 21, 22	Inverness	Drawing Room Meetings by invitation of Mrs. James Innes and Mrs. Mackinnon		
,, 23, 24	Inverness	Public Meetings in Station Hotel and in Council Chamber, Town Hall		Mrs. Stopes
,, 27	Tain	Drawing Room Meeting, Mrs. Matheson		
Dec.	Edinburgh	A series of Drawing Room Meetings by invitation of Mrs. Muir Dowie, Mrs. Balgarnie, Mrs. Lang Todd, Mrs. Kitchins, Mrs. Lewis		Various Speakers
	Edinburgh (Newington House)	Conference of Workers	Mrs. Shaw	
	Edinburgh (West Edinburgh W. L. A.)	Social Gathering given by Miss Methuen		
	Edinburgh (West End Café)	Social Gathering given by Executive of Special Appeal Committee		
,, 5	Paxton (Berwick)	Drawing Room Meeting by invitation of Mrs. Prentice		Mrs. Gillies
,, 11	Aberdeen (Y.M.C.I.)	Public Meeting	Sir W. Henderson	Prof. Adamson, Mrs. Ramsay, Mrs. Stopes
,, ,,	Dundee (Friends' Institute)	Lecture		Mrs. Stopes
,, ,,	Perth (Station Hotel)	Drawing Room Meeting by invitation of Mrs. Whitelaw	Mr. Leonard Plaigner	Sir John Leng, M.P., Dr. White, Mr. Blair, Mrs. Stopes
,, 13	Broughty Ferry	Drawing Room Meetings by invitation of Mrs. Crowdas and Mrs. Steele		
,, 14	Stirling	Drawing Room Meeting by invitation of Miss Maclagan		
,, 15	Dundee (Town Hall)	Public Meeting	Lord Provost Low	Mrs. Stopes

(Continued from p. 21.)

Walker, Mrs. Cotton (Dublin)
Walker, Mrs. Edward (Leeds)
*Wallis, Mrs. Percy (Kettering)
Watson, Mrs. Spence (Gateshead)
White, Miss C. E. (Roscrea)
White, Miss (Dublin)
Winbolt, Mrs. John (Stockport)
Wright, Miss (Mansfield)

THE SPECIAL APPEAL COMMITTEE FOR SCOTLAND.

Honorary President—The Right Hon. the Countess of Aberdeen.
President—Mrs. McLaren (Newington House, Edinburgh).
Vice-President—Miss Louisa Stevenson (13, Randolph Crescent, Edinburgh).
Honorary Treasurers—Miss Balfour (Whittinghame, Prestonkirk). Miss Methven (25, Great King Street, Edinburgh).
Honorary Secretaries—Miss Wigham (5, South Gray Street, Edinburgh); Miss E. Scott Kirkland (13, Raeburn Place, Edinburgh).
Secretary—Miss H. B. Thompson.
Office—8, York Buildings, Edinburgh.

Lady Frances Balfour (Whittinghame, Prestonkirk)
Miss Burton (Liberton Bank, Edinburgh)
Mrs. Edward Caird (1, The University, Glasgow)
Mrs. Campbell (Tulliechewan, Dumbartonshire)
Miss M. Cunningham (12, Marchhall Road, Edinburgh)
Mrs. Muir Dowie (5, Howard Place, Edinburgh)
Mrs. Lindsay Forbes (Drydenbank, Loanhead)
Mrs. Fremantle (19, Athol Crescent, Edinburgh)
Mrs. Gillies (Chirnside, Berwickshire)
Lady Macpherson Grant (Ballindalloch)
Mrs. Greenlees (Langdale, Dowanhill, Glasgow)
Mrs. Henderson (4, Windsor Terrace, Glasgow)
Miss Lees (8, Wemyss Place, Edinburgh)
Mrs. Lindsay (37, Westbourne Gardens, Glasgow)
Lady Agnes Macleod (Granton House, Edinburgh)
Miss S. E. S. Mair (5, Chester Street, Edinburgh)
Mrs. Carlaw Martin (7, Lauder Road, Edinburgh)
Mrs. Millar (26, York Place, Edinburgh)
Miss Oswald (of Dunnikier, South Bank, Edinburgh)
Miss Grace Paterson (247, Bath Street, Glasgow)
Mrs. Herbert Paul (Edinburgh)
Mrs. Hugh Rose (Kilravock Lodge, Edinburgh)
Mrs. Steel (Boroughfield, Edinburgh)
Miss Flora C. Stevenson (13, Randolph Crescent, Edinburgh)
Mrs. Lang Todd (50, Great King Street, Edinburgh)
Miss Urquhart (5, St. Colme Street, Edinburgh)
Miss Waddel (37, Monteith Row, Glasgow)
Mrs. Watson (118, Findhorn Place, Edinburgh)
Lady Maud Wolmer (Edinburgh)

NEW ZEALAND.

Subjoined is the full text of the enfranchising clauses of the Electoral Act of New Zealand, 57 Vict., 1893, No. 18, entitled "An Act to amend and consolidate the Law relating to the Qualification and Registration of Electors, and the Conduct of Election of Members of the House of Representatives," September 19th, 1893.

Clause 3 (*interpretation*) provides that "person includes woman."

Clause 6 (*qualification male and female*).

The Members of the House of Representatives shall be chosen in every electoral district appointed for that purpose by the votes of the inhabitants of New Zealand, who shall possess within the district the qualifications defined by this Act, that is to say—

(*Freehold.*) (1) Every person of the age of 21 years or upwards having of his own right, and not as a trustee, a freehold estate in possession situated within any electoral district of the value of twenty-five pounds, whether subject to incumbrances or not, and of or to which he has been seised or entitled either at law or in equity for at least six months next before the registration of his vote, and is not registered in respect of a freehold or residential qualification in the same or any other district, is entitled (subject to the provision of this Act) to be registered as an elector, and to vote at an election of members for such district for the House of Representatives; or

(*Residential.*) (2) Every person of the age of 21 years or upwards, who has resided for one year in the colony and in the electoral district for which he claims to vote during the three months immediately preceding the registration of his vote, and is not registered in respect of a freehold or residential qualification for the same or any other district, is entitled (subject to the provisions of this Act) to be registered as an elector and to vote at the election of members for each district for the House of Representatives.

(*No person to be registered in more than one district*). (3) No person shall be entitled to be registered on more than one electoral roll within the colony, whatever the number or nature of the qualifications he may possess, or wherever they may be.

(*Women not qualified for election.*) Clause 9.—No woman, although duly registered as an elector, shall be capable of being nominated as a candidate, or of being elected a member of the House of Representatives, or of being appointed to the Legislative Council, and every nomination paper of a woman as a candidate shall be absolutely void and of no effect, and shall be rejected by the returning officer without question.

Separate provision is made for the Maori vote in Part V. of the Act.

SOUTH AUSTRALIA.

On November 13th, a deputation from the Women's Franchise League of South Australia waited on the Premier to ask that the Government would reintroduce the Women's Suffrage Bill during the present session. The deputation was introduced by the Hon. Dr. Magary, M.L.C.

Mr. C. Proud said they had come to respectfully ask the Premier to restore the Adult Suffrage Bill to the notice paper of the Assembly, by whom it had been laid aside because the third reading had passed by only a bare majority, and not by the absolute majority required by the Constitution Act. They understood this could be done on the Government giving seven days' notice.

Miss George, Mrs. Zadow, Mrs. Lee and the Rev. J. Day Thompson also supported the request.

The Premier said on the question of Women's Suffrage the Government were in the position of just persons who needed no conversion, as they were thoroughly at one on the matter, and were willing to do all they could to place Women's Suffrage on the statute book. They might rely on the Government doing what they could to help them.

LOCAL GOVERNMENT BILL.

The debates in the House of Commons, to which the various clauses affecting women in the Local Government Bill have given rise, testify to a marked advance in parliamentary opinion in regard to the relations of women to public duties. The Bill has not yet reached the House of Lords; meantime the clauses affecting women have passed the House of Commons in the following terms :—

Clause 6 (2).—No person shall be disqualified *by sex or marriage* for being elected or being a member of a parish council.

Clause 21.—The chairman of a district council, *unless a woman* or personally disqualified by any Act, shall be by virtue of his office justice of the peace for the county in which the district is situate.

Clause 22 (2).—A person shall not be qualified to be

elected or to be a councillor unless he is a parochial elector of some parish within the district, or has during the whole of the twelve months preceding the election resided in the district, and no person shall be *disqualified by sex or marriage* for being elected or being a councillor.

New Clause added after Clause 29.—For the purposes of this Act *a woman shall not be disqualified by marriage* for being on any local government register of electors, or for being an elector of any local authority, provided that a husband and wife shall not both be qualified in respect of the same property.

The following is a summary of the series of debates which have taken place on the above clauses.

November 16th. - Instruction to Committee.

Mr. McLaren moved :—" That it be an instruction to the committee that they have power to insert provisions [to prevent the disfranchisement of those married women who as ratepayers are now entitled to vote at elections of guardians, and] to enfranchise, for the purposes of this Act, all those women, whether married or single, who would be entitled to be on the local government register of electors, or on the parliamentary register of electors if they were men." The first portion of the instruction he was glad to find was unnecessary; and he therefore moved the instruction with the omission of the words in brackets. The instruction, as all such instructions were, was permissive; and he only asked that the committee should be empowered to deal with the matter at the proper time. He simply desired to extend local franchises for the purposes of this Act to women on the same terms as to men. Married women who were ratepayers were now entitled to vote for Poor Law guardians, because the rate-book was the register. With regard to the local government register, which the Bill would introduce, the opposite was the case. If the Bill passed in its present form, and the local government register were made the register upon which votes were to be given for parish and district councils, married women would be effectually excluded. The second portion of his instruction aimed at placing upon the register women freeholders, women entitled to vote under the service franchise and women lodgers.

Mr. H. Fowler said that in the debate on the previous instruction, the Government were blamed for having made the Bill a measure of very great extent and complicity, and his hon. friend now asked him to put a very heavy piece of cargo on what he had already been told was an over-laden ship. He was afraid he must ask the House, if the Bill was to pass, not to encumber it with that grave question.

Sir C. Dilke said the President of the Local Government Board had spoken of this matter as a very heavy piece of cargo, but the heavy cargo was the change in the electorate which the right hon. gentleman himself proposed. This Bill for the first time introduced the lodger voter, the service voter, and the Parliamentary voter into local elections, and while thus adding largely to the electorate in its present form, it would disfranchise all married women who had voted in elections of the kind. He thought the matter should be discussed in committee.

Mr. STANSFELD and Sir MICHAEL HICKS BEACH also supported the instruction.

The House divided, when the numbers were—

For the instruction 147
Against... 126

Majority 21

November 21st.

The House again went into Committee on the Local Government (England and Wales) Bill.

Mr. W. M'LAREN rose to move an amendment to Clause 2, providing for the inclusion, among those entitled to vote at elections for parish councils, " of all married women who would be entitled to be on the local government register of electors if they were single." The object of the amendment was, he remarked, to prevent the disfranchisement of those married women who were ratepayers, and were entitled to vote at present for vestries and boards of guardians. The position of those married women was one of considerable doubt in regard to all other elections, but with regard to the old parochial franchises relating to the election of vestrymen and guardians, there was great simplicity in the matter, as the register in these cases was the rate-book, and every woman whose name was on it was entitled to vote for both. Since the Married Women's Property Act a considerable number of married women who were actually ratepayers paying rates in their own names had been put on the register. A very great change would be made by the Bill in its present form. The rate-book was no longer to be the register, but the Government proposed that the local government register and the Parliamentary register were to be the register on which, in future, parochial elections should be conducted. His amendment would prevent the only injustice that would arise owing to the change of register. The position of married women on the local government register was wholly different. No doubt the local government and burgess lists were made up from the rate-book, but they had to pass through the hands of the assistant overseer, whose duty it was to make up a preliminary register and submit it to the revising barrister. In case after case the revising barrister had had struck off the name of a married woman if he knew she was married and was a widow. There were cases here and there in which married women had been allowed to remain on the register by accident, or oversight, because the revising barrister believed they were widows.

Mr. H. FOWLER said in the case of boards of guardians the

franchise had always been that of the ratepayer; women registered as ratepayers, and as such always claimed the right to vote in the election of guardians, although the Local Government Board had invariably declined to pass an opinion on the legality of that vote, or on the election of married women as guardians. They were advised that the disqualification which, according to the decision of the Court of Queen's Bench, was imposed by the common law applied in all cases, whether to the election of School Boards or boards of guardians, inasmuch as being married women they were disqualified from exercising the franchise. Of course, that was not a decision, but an opinion, but it was an opinion the Government could not disregard. Now, if he understood the decision of the House correctly on this subject it was this—that the disqualification of married women should cease; that was to say, where a woman was otherwise qualified, and was on an existing register, and as such entitled to vote, she should not be disqualified by reason of being a married woman. That was, as he understood, the intention of the House, and it was a decision which the Government would endeavour to carry out. There was, however, another question raised. His hon. friend said, create a new register altogether, which was not in existence at the present time, a register of women who, if they were men, would be entitled to vote. That, of course, would involve a new register, a new revision, and a variety of other procedure. He would ask his hon. friend to withdraw his amendment, and he, on his part, should propose to insert a new clause removing the disqualification of married women altogether — in other words, to rescind or repeal the decision in the case of " The Queen v. Harrald."

Sir H. JAMES said that, although he had no cause to regret the opposition which he offered in former years to women exercising the Parliamentary franchise, he did not wish to exaggerate the extent of the proposition now before the Committee for conferring the vote upon women for local purposes, and he would not offer any opposition if the amendment were not carried to a greater extent.

Mr. STANSFELD advised that the offer of the amendment by the President of the Local Government Board be accepted.

Mr. G. T. BOWLES opposed, arguing that it was a tremendous change. Sir Charles Dilke regarded it as a conservative rather than a radical change.

Mr. BALFOUR said they must face this fact—that if this amendment be accepted the whole controversy with regard to the women franchise in political matters will enter upon a new phase, and, do what they will, they would not be able to exclude married women possessing certain qualifications for a vote for this House whenever this House attempted to extend the women franchise in the smallest degree. His impression was that personally he should be prepared to assent to the proposals of the Government. He could only draw two conclusions from what had been done. In the first place, they had made it absolutely impossible in the future to keep off those women they were putting on this register from the Parliamentary register; and, in the second place, he believed it was impossible in the compass of this Bill to exclude from the existing register these women owners of property who did not happen to be rated as occupiers.

After some further discussion, Mr. McLaren's amendment was by leave withdrawn.

November 25th.

Mr. FOWLER moved an amendment on Clause 3, that no person should be disqualified by sex or marriage from being elected or being a member of a parish council. Sir Henry James protested; Sir Julian Goldsmid, Sir Albert Rollit supported. Mr. Tomlinson and Mr. Bowles were opposed.

Mr. PLUNKETT said in his ten years' experience in Wyoming he had noticed that the fears that were expressed as to women unduly pushing themselves into public and official life had not been realised.

Sir R. PAGET was opposed.

Mr. E. STANHOPE looked with some fear on the suggestion that women might be elected chairmen, but on the whole was inclined to leave the matter to the good sense of the parishes themselves.

The amendment was agreed to.

November 25th.

In Clause 21 (making the chairman of a district council *ex-officio* a J.P.),

Mr. H. FOWLER proposed "after the word council to insert 'unless a woman, or personally disqualified by any act.'"

Mr. CARVELL WILLIAMS thought this perpetuated a principle the Bill professed to abandon.

Mr. CONYBEARE protested against it as the introduction of a disqualification.

Sir HENRY JAMES thought if women were to be justices it should be by a general law to that effect, and not that the only women eligible should be chairmen of district councils.

Mr. H. FOWLER held that the Government were introducing no disqualification, and they had no intention of altering the general law on the subject.

Mr. MORTON did not see why women should not be on the bench.

Sir JOHN GORST thought this was an entirely new departure, and the Committee should resist any fresh disability on women.

Sir ALBERT ROLLIT held that it was upon the office the privileged position was conferred, and the distinction that the amendment would draw was both illogical and improper.

Mr. BOWLES thought the amendment unnecessary.

The SOLICITOR-GENERAL said that the Government did not intend to remove the disqualifications which at present existed, and they thought it more frank and advisable to put their object in precise language.

On a division being taken there were

For the amendment	144
Against	38
Majority	106

An amendment moved by Mr. LODER "that the chairman be a male" was negatived.

January 1st.

Mr. H. FOWLER introduced a new clause, to follow clause 29, dealing with the qualification of married women. In consequence of Mr. Fowler having undertaken to do so, an amendment on clause 31 providing for the registration of married women, of which Mr. M'Laren had given notice, was not pursued; and after clause 31 had been passed, the new clause was introduced. Some discussion arose as to the limitation of the clause by the words "for the purposes of this Act."

The CHAIRMAN feared without these words it would not be in order.

Mr. COURTNEY suggested they should come at the beginning of the clause, which was then moved by Mr. FOWLER in these terms:—"For the purposes of this Act, a woman shall not be disqualified by marriage from being on any local government register of electors, or from being an elector of any local government authority, provided that a husband and wife shall not both be qualified in respect of the same property."

In this form the amendment was carried.

January 9th.

A motion by Mr. Atherley Jones, to add a new clause allowing women as lodgers or possessing the service franchise, to be placed on the parochial register, was after some discussion withdrawn.

January 12th.

On the Bill being reported to the House, a motion, of which Mr. Storey had given notice, was moved by Mr. Dodd, to provide that a woman should not be qualified in respect of the occupation of any house in which she and her husband resided, was negatived.

Mr. FOWLER, who had given notice of his intention to have the Bill recommitted in order to omit from the new clause passed on January 1st the limiting words "for the purposes of this Act," explained that he ought to have moved that the Bill be recommitted for the purpose of inserting the amendment of which he had given notice; but as the Deputy-Speaker had informed him that the instruction would be out of order, he had omitted to make the motion. Perhaps the Deputy-Speaker would publicly state that from the chair for the information of hon. gentlemen to whom he pledged himself to move the instruction.

The DEPUTY-SPEAKER said he told the right hon. gentleman that, in his opinion, the instruction referred to was clearly out of order and that to introduce such a proposal into the Bill was beyond the province of the House.

The Bill passed third reading.

ELECTIONS AND APPOINTMENTS.

POOR LAW GUARDIANS.—Three ladies have been elected guardians since the last issue, on the occasion of bye-elections, viz.—
Barton-Regis Union (Clifton).—Mrs. Trebilco.
Southport.—Mrs. Helen B. Taylor.
Gateshead.—Miss Alice Featherstonhaugh.

SCHOOL BOARD ELECTIONS.

Bardfield (Essex).—Miss E. A. Smith, junr.
Barking (Suffolk).—Miss R. P. Jeff (bye election).
Bradford (Yorks).—Mrs. Armitage (bye election).
Braintree (Essex).—Mrs. S. L. Courtauld.
Brighton.—Mrs. Roth.

SANITARY INSPECTORS.

The Vestry of St. Mary Abbott's, Kensington, has appointed two ladies, Miss Lucy Dean and Miss Rose Squire, Sanitary Inspectors under the Administration of the Factory and Public Health Acts, in places where women are employed. The appointments are made, in the first instance, for a period of six months. The salary is at the rate of £60 per annum. Both ladies were trained by the National Health Society, and hold its diploma for teaching.

Miss Elenora Fleury has been appointed assistant to Dr. Connolly Norman, in the female department of the Richmond Lunatic Asylum, Dublin.

Miss Alice M. Cooke, B.A., late Jones Fellow of Owens College, has been appointed an assistant lecturer in History at Owens College.

UNIVERSITY INTELLIGENCE.

LONDON UNIVERSITY.

B.A.

Coombs, Agnes Fanny, Royal Holloway College (honours in German).
Brake, Elise Florence M., Royal Holloway College (honours in English).
Barrows, Maude Marion, University College, Aberystwith, and Masons College (honours in English).
Smith, Annie Florence, Bedford College (honours in English).
Garbutt, Eleanor, Bedford College (honours in English).
Lorimer, Elizabeth Hilda L., University College, Dundee.
White, Anne, Royal Holloway College.
Bennie, Maria Elizabeth, private study.
Blanch, Mary Elizabeth, University College, Aberystwith.
Coryn, Ida May, private study.
Doulton, Maud May, Royal Holloway College and private study.
Duke, Lucretia Smith, Westfield College.
Dunman, Agnes Caroline, University College, Cardiff.
Hellings, Rosetta, Bedford College, London.
Howard, Elizabeth, Ladies' College, Cheltenham.
Howard, Kate Maria, Royal Holloway College.
Ironside, Edith Mary, Ladies' College, Cheltenham.
Jones, Annie Jane, University College, Bangor.
Lloyd, Kate May, Milton Mount College.
Marshall, Grace Elizabeth, University College, Aberystwith.
Moulton, Emily Margaret, University College, Aberystwith.
Nott, Ellen Louisa, University College, Cardiff.
Pickford, Mary Ann, Milton Mount College.
Price, Emily, Mason College and private study.
Salt, Lizzie Godwin, University College, Aberystwith.
Stevens, Louisa Jane, private study.
Stiff, Kate Mary, University College, Bangor.
Thompson, Kate Elizabeth, private study.
White, Edith Lillian, Ladies' College, Cheltenham.
Whitley, Mary Winifred, private tuition.

B.A. AND B.Sc. CONJOINTLY.

Madison, Ada Isabel, University College, Cardiff, Girton and Bryn-Mawr, U.S.A. (honours in Mathematics).
Hewart, A. Beatrice, B.Sc., University College, Aberystwith (honours in Mental and Moral Science).

B.Sc.

Black, Gertrude, University and Bedford Colleges, London (honours in Experimental Physics and Botany).
Clarke, Lilian Jane, University College (honours in Botany).
Selby, Eliza Lucy, University College, Bangor (honours in Botany).

Ebden, Isabel Frances E., Ladies' College, Cheltenham, and Bedford College.
Haslewood, May, Ladies' College, Cheltenham.
Hewart, Annie Beatrice, University College, Aberystwith.
Newbigin, Marion Isabel, University and School of Medicine, Edinburgh.
Patch, Winifred S., University College and School of Medicine for Women.
Rennison, Edith, Royal Holloway College.
Silcox, Lilian Alice, Newnham College.
Taylor, Millicent, Ladies' College, Cheltenham.
Wardell, Phœbe, Royal Holloway College.

M.A.

Heath, Bertha Mary (Gold Medal), private study (Classics).
Brebner, Mary, University College, Aberystwith (Classics).
Evans, Florence Anne, University College, Cardiff (Classics).
Lee, Florence Kate, University College (Mathematics and Natural Philosophy).
Robertson, Mary Alice, University College (Mental and Moral Science, &c.).
James, Mary M. Price, University College, Cardiff (Mental and Moral Science, &c.).

D.Sc.

Ogilvie, Maria Matilda, University, Munich, and private study.

B.S.

First Division.—Blake, Louisa B. Aldrich, London School of Medicine for Women and Royal Free Hospital.

M.B.

Jones, Lillie Mabel A., London School of Medicine for Women and Royal Free Hospital.
Piercy, Anne Frances, London School of Medicine for Women and Royal Free Hospital.

M.D.

Bateson, Annette M., B.Sc., London School of Medicine for Women and Royal Free Hospital.
McLaren, Alice Janet, B.S., London School of Medicine for Women and Royal Free Hospital.

ROYAL UNIVERSITY, IRELAND.

B.A.

First Class Honours, Modern Literature. — Chapman, Agnes Sloane ; Joynt, Mabel Sarah.
Second Class Honours, Classics.—Sayers, Wilhelmina Jane.
Second Class Honours, Modern Literature.—Fogarty, Mary Jane ; Woods, Annie Ray ; Stone, Anna Maria.
Second Class Honours, History.—Craig, Mary C. F. ; Buchannan, Josephine ; Koehler, Martha Maud.

Bolger, Angela,
Boyland, Helen E.
Bradshaw, Charlotte Mary.
Corby, Alice M.
Costello, Harriet.
Deacon, Edith Frances.
Fitzgerald, Annie Mary.
Green, Sarah Finlay.
Hewetson, Mary Elizabeth.
Hogben, Maud Mary.
Kingston, Eileen Lucie.

Murray, Annie Maud.
O'Reilly, Susanna.
Orr, Mary E. S.
Palton, Annie Stockbridge.
Ross, Elizabeth.
Scott, Katherine Ann.
Temple, Annie Elizabeth.
Thorpe, Jane.
White, Edith Mary.
Woods, Sarah Frances.

M.A.

Cantillon, Emmeline Gertrude (2nd Class Honours).

LL.B.

Egan, Letitia Elizabeth.

VICTORIA UNIVERSITY.

B.A.

Fallowfield, Annie G.; Hall, Marion; Halstead, Nancy W.

M.A.

Cooke, Alice Margaret; Crompton, Alice; Trevor, Adelaide.

RECORD OF EVENTS.

MARRIED WOMEN'S PROPERTY ACT, 1893.

The following is the text of the Married Women's Property Act of 1893, which received the Royal assent on December 5:—

56 and 57 *Vict.*, *Chap.* 63.
An Act to amend the Married Women's Property Act, 1882.

Be it enacted by the Queen's most excellent Majesty, by and with the advice and consent of the Lords Spiritual and Temporal, and Commons, in this present Parliament assembled, and by the authority of the same, as follows:

(1) Every contract hereafter entered into by a married woman, otherwise than as agent,

(*a*) shall be deemed to be a contract entered into by her with respect to and to bind her separate property whether she is or is not in fact possessed of or entitled to any separate property at the time when she enters into such contract;

(*b*) shall bind all separate property which she may at that time or thereafter be possessed of or entitled to; and

(*c*) shall also be enforceable by process of law against all property which she may thereafter while discovert be possessed of or entitled to;

Provided that nothing in this section contained shall render available to satisfy any liability or obligation arising out of such contract any separate property which at that time or thereafter she is restrained from anticipating.

(2) In any action or proceeding now or hereafter instituted by a woman or by a next friend on her behalf, the court before which such action or proceeding is pending shall have jurisdiction by judgment or order from time to time to order payment of the costs of the opposite party out of property which is subject to a restraint on anticipation, and may enforce such payment by the appointment of a receiver and the sale of the property or otherwise as may be just.

(3) Section twenty-four of the Wills Act, 1837, shall apply to the will of a married woman made during coverture whether she is or is not possessed of or entitled to any separate property at the time of making it, and such will shall not require to be re-executed or republished after the death of her husband.

(4) Sub-sections (3) and (4) of section one of the Married Women's Property Act, 1882, are hereby repealed.

(5) This Act may be cited as the Married Women's Property Act, 1893.

(6) This Act shall not apply to Scotland.

ROYAL COLLEGE OF SURGEONS, DUBLIN.

DISTRIBUTION OF PRIZES.—At the annual distribution of prizes awarded at the examinations held during

the winter session, 1892, and the summer session,
1893, which took place on November 1st, in the
board room of the Royal College of Surgeons,
Stephen's Green, the following prizes were awarded
to women students. *Practical Pharmacy.*—Miss S.
L. Glynn, first prize, cheque and medal. *Forensic
Medicine.*—Miss J. B. Ferguson and Mr. A. Leverton,
equal, first prize, cheques and medals. Miss E. L.
Micheson and Miss A. M. Thornett, equal, second
prize, cheques and certificates.

The President of the Council, Mr. Edward Hamilton,
who occupied the chair, concluded his address to the
pupils as follows :—I cannot conclude without alluding
to our sisters in science. Whatever opinion we may
hold respecting their presence here, they are now
amongst us, and we must give them all welcome.
They have competed and won our prizes, and we
gladly give the honour to which they are entitled.
We can learn much from them—their indefatigable
zeal, the way in which they have triumphed over
obstacles which have come in their way. Their
devotion and self-denial have shown that woman's
intellect is in no way inferior to ours. They have
more endurance, because they are not weaned by such
trivial allurements as we men are beset with, but
continue steadfast until the end."

FELLOWSHIP EXAMINATION. — After passing the
necessary examination, Miss Emily Winifred Dickson,
L.B., C.P.I., L.R.C.S.I., M.B., B.Ch., Royal University, Ireland, has been admitted a Fellow of the Royal
College of Surgeons, Dublin.

At the London School of Medicine for Women the
Mackay Prizes of twenty-five pounds and fifteen
pounds respectively have been awarded to Miss Stoney
and Miss Vaughan.

Miss Rose Govindarajulu (of Madras) has passed
the first Examination of the Royal College of Physicians and Surgeons, Edinburgh and Glasgow.

WOMEN AND THE ARCHITECTURAL ASSOCIATION.

The Architectural Association has followed the example of the Geographical Society in rejecting women associates. Two ladies, whose names are not given, but who have been, says the *Builder*, "working for some time in the office of an eminent London architect" were proposed at the meeting on November 10th. The proposal called forth "indignant epistles from two members of the Association (not very much known to fame)," and hearing that an opposition to their election was being organised the ladies withdrew their names. A special general meeting to consider the point was called on December 15th, when it was proposed, "That in the opinion of this meeting it is expedient that ladies engaged in the study or practice of Architecture shall be eligible for election on the same terms, and under the same conditions, as men." In spite, however, of the advocacy of the President, Mr. Mountford, who "had spoken to a great many of the leading members, and thought all agreed with him that the election of ladies was desirable, and of the fact that neither laws nor bye-laws forbade their admission," the motion was lost by forty-one votes, thirty-seven voting in favour of it (we presume the leading members), and seventy-eight (among them some not very well known to fame) against. Well, women can wait! It is better to build a house than to be a member of an Architectural Association, and the day may come when even that honour may be accorded them.

THE WOMEN WORKERS' CONFERENCE.

The Women Workers' Conference held their now annual gathering at Leeds from November 6th to 12th, and brought together about 230 delegates from all parts of the country, as well as large audiences of resident ladies. The Albert Hall, where the meetings were held, was well filled day after day, and the arrangements for reception and writing rooms, luncheon and postal arrangements, &c., in the crypt below, were admirable. The local Committee spared no thought or pains to make all pleasant and easy for their guests.

Comparing the gathering with that of Bristol, there

was less animation in the discussions, due perhaps in part to the relaxation of the rule that obtained last year, that every paper must be read by its writer. On this occasion, several of the most valuable papers were read for their writers. Such an exception might indeed well be made in the case of Miss Florence Nightingale, who contributed a valuable paper on Health Teaching in Villages, but to permit it in the case of so many of the most important papers was undoubtedly detrimental to the liveliness of the discussions.

Pressure on space this quarter permits only of a very brief record of this gathering, and we must—for the present at any rate—pass over many facts of interest, especially in such papers as those on "Anglican Sisterhoods," by Miss Maria Trench, and on " Bible and Domestic Missions," by Mrs. Leonard Selfe, and on "Training Teachers for Technical Classes," by Mrs. Walter Ward. One point, however, was noticeable—throughout the whole of the Conference indeed, but in these papers perhaps more particularly—viz., the insistance on the necessity of training for the workers. This is surely a part of the general recognition that responsibility attaches to all good work, which is one of the most hopeful features of the whole woman movement.

THE COUNTESS DUFFERIN FUND.

The United Kingdom Branch of the "National Association for Supplying Female Medical Aid to the Women of India," generally known as the "Countess Dufferin Fund," has just issued its fifth annual report, from which we learn that there are now twelve lady doctors of the first grade working in connection with the fund in hospitals in India.

One of the most important features of the United Kingdom Branch is the maintenance always of a lady doctor "in waiting," a post "intended only for ladies new to India, who are unacquainted with the language and manners of the people, and not for those who have resided some time in the country." The doctor "in waiting" has opportunity, by being attached to some hospital, to become acquainted with the peculiarities of climate and treatment of Indian diseases, also she has time to learn the language, and further, there is thus always a supernumerary lady doctor in India ready for any post that may become vacant.

The four scholarships offered to ladies in England in connection with the fund are now opened also to Indian ladies studying in England. We regret to see that while the Branch requires an income of £1,000 to carry out all its projects fully, it last year received only £215. We cannot but think this must be due, not to want of interest so much as to want of knowledge, on the part of the many persons interested in India, of the needs of the Society.

The post of Hon. Sec. has been undertaken ·by Susan, Countess of Malmesbury, but we fail to notice any address in the report to which persons desiring information may apply. We believe, however, that any enquiries may be addressed to Miss Helen Grant, Secretary to the Countess, 9, Beaufort Gardens, S.W.

ARTS AND CRAFTS EXHIBITION.

The fourth Exhibition of the Arts and Crafts Society was held in the New Gallery in October and November, 1893. It will be remembered that the Society did not exhibit in 1892, but this omission was fully made up for by the high standard reached in the last exhibition. The Arts and Crafts is not an exhibition of amateurs, and it is encouraging to note the place taken by women among professionals of so high a class. The names of 92 appear in the list of exhibitors, some as artists, some as craftswomen, some combining the characters of designer and executant. Of the exhibits, 104, about one-fifth of the whole number are wholly or in part the work of women. The essentially feminine handicraft of needlework accounts for nearly one-half of these, but the remainder give tokens of skill in many varying directions, among them book-binding and illustrating, copper-etching, designing, decoration, work in plaster and gesso, pottery and glass, enamel, metal work, carving, &c. It is an augury of good things to come when so many avenues are opened to women by the cultivation of their artistic capacity.

THE AMATEURS had it all their own way in the Annual Amateur Art Exhibition, which was held in November in some rooms in the Imperial Institute. But here, too, considerable cleverness was shown, especially in carving, modelling, iron work, and photography. The drawings and paintings are always amateurish, and this time was no exception to the general rule, but in some of the other classes there was a distinct improvement on previous exhibitions.

WOMEN AT THE HORTICULTURAL COLLEGE, SWANLEY.

The Kent County Council, which has already been so generous to the Horticultural College in the matter of founding scholarships for men, has now extended its liberality to the women's branch. Out of the thirty scholarships it has established for residents in the county, five of the value of £60 a year each, as well as some of those at £30, are now thrown open to competition among girls of between 15 and 20 years of age. Some of these may be held by members of the industrial classes, but considering the success already achieved by women gardeners of higher education, and the many and varied appointments for which they are eligible, it is to be hoped that mistresses of high schools and others interested in the employment of ladies will encourage competition among students of wider culture. Forms for application may be had from the hon. sec., Miss Goodrich Freer, Women's Branch Horticultural College, Swanley. It is much to be desired that other County Councils should also offer scholarships to be held at the College. Influence in this direction might be most usefully brought to bear on individual members of County Councils.

WOMEN'S GARDENING ASSOCIATION.

The Women's London Gardening Association, which contracts for the stocking and care of conservatories, window-boxes, balconies and gardens, and for the care of graves in cemeteries, is increasing its work so much that it has found it necessary also to extend its premises, and on the 31st of October Mrs. Chamberlain gave an "at home" in celebration of the event in the new shop, No. 64, Lower Sloane Street, which has been added to No. 62. The new premises consist of a large room, which was gracefully decorated for the occasion, a secretary's office adjoining, and a basement running under both shops, which is used as a storehouse for gardening tools, flower-pots, &c., and as a kitchen for making the jams and pickles sold by the Association. This branch of their work is growing fast, and a new department has been opened (at No. 64) for the sale of choice fruits. The charge of plants during the owner's absence from town is undertaken, and every kind of floral decoration. All the orders are executed by ladies except very heavy work, for which men are employed.

WOMEN'S UNDERTAKINGS AND VENTURES.

More than fifty pages of the October number of the *English Historical Review* are occupied by a very careful, learned, and elaborate article on "The Settlement of the Cistercian Monks in England," by Miss Alice M. Cooke, whose appointment as assistant lecturer is recorded at page 33. This piece of work is the firstfruits of the valuable Fellowship established three years ago by the late Mr. T. E. Jones, of Manchester, for the encouragement of historical research among the graduates of the Owens College in the Victoria University. Miss Cooke, who took her degree with first-class honours in the School of History in the Victoria University in 1890, was soon afterwards elected as the first Jones Fellow of the Owens College, and the essay on the Cistercians represents the results of the work which she was thus enabled to undertake.

Nature says: "The volume of selections from the philosophical and poetical works of Miss Constance C. W. Naden, compiled by the Misses E. and E. Hughes, and published by Messrs. Bicker & Son, is one of the daintiest we have seen for some time. The selections from the essay on induction and deduction contain some remarkably fine expressions, and many other parts of the book are of great interest."

At a meeting of the Aristotelian Society on December 4th, Miss Constance E. E. Jones read a paper on the "Import of Categorical Propositions." Miss C. E. E. Jones, our readers will remember, is lecturer at Girton College, and author of the "Introduction to General Logic" already reviewed in these pages in October, 1892.

Miss Wilkinson, as landscape gardener to the Metropolitan Public Gardens Association, is now engaged in laying out St. Mary's Park, Woolwich, and Victoria Park Cemetery. Myatt's Fields, Camberwell, and Vauxhall Park are other open spaces recently laid out by Miss Wilkinson.

Mrs. Calverly Bewicke will give one of her Shakesperian Dramatic Recitals in aid of the Samaritan Fund of the Westminster Hospital, on February 20th, in Queen Anne's Mansions Theatre. H.R.H. the Duchess of Albany has graciously promised to be present. Canon Farrar will take the chair. This is the sixth Recital Mrs. Bewicke has given for the Samaritan Fund, resulting each time in a substantial sum, never less, and last year very much more, than £50.

ABOUT MUSIC AND WHAT IT IS MADE OF.—Under this conversational title Miss Oliveria Prescott gave a series of lectures at the Church of England High School in Baker Street. She pointed out the structure of old popular and scholastic music, and how modern music has gradually "built in" the old material upon a new foundation, that foundation having, at the same time, its first stones laid in old popular tunes.

THE ASSOCIATION OF WOMEN PIONEER LECTURERS has now removed to 4, Caroline Place, Mecklenburg Square. Its object is to form centres and deliver courses of lectures on various subjects by thoroughly competent University and non-University women, in places not ready to receive University Extension teaching. Particulars can be obtained from the Secretary, Miss Edith Bradley.

REFERENCE READING-ROOM. — Miss Hubbard is arranging a Reference Reading and Resting Room at 7c, Lower Belgrave Street, S.W., for the use of workers on women's questions. Suggestions would be welcomed, of books, articles, reports, &c., bearing on subjects of interest to women, which would render the Reading Room a useful place of study for those engaged n women's questions.

THE EMPRESS DOWAGER OF CHINA AND THE SIAMESE QUESTION.

The following paragraph, from the *Times* of November 3rd, shows that the Empress Dowager of China still impresses the force of her character on the Empire she ruled so firmly during her Regency :—

"According to the latest information from Pekin, the inactivity of China during the recent crisis in the relations between France and Siam was due to the counsels of the Empress Dowager. It appears that the Chinese Consul-General at Singapore kept the Government fully informed of the state of affairs at Bangkok, and that the Emperor and his Ministers were much concerned at the situation of Siam, which is regarded in China as 'a vassal State.' Before convening a meeting of the Grand Council to come to a conclusion on the course China should pursue in the matter, the Emperor, as the story goes, went to consult his aunt. Having laid the facts before her, she inquired how long it was since Siam had last recognized the suzerainty of China by sending tribute. On being told that it was very many years and that no reason had been assigned for this neglect, the Empress Dowager is represented to have spoken as follows:—'In what Siam thought were her days of power and wealth she pretended to despise China by casting her off and confiding in the protection of a foreign Power in case we should resent it. She has chosen her part, let her abide by it. We have everything to lose and nothing to gain by interfering, and at most it would be a thankless task. Your first duty is to look after the security, wealth, and happiness of your own Empire. We have enough to do as it is without interfering with outside. If China were strong for aggression it would be quite another matter, for a word would then be enough to secure the integrity of Siam. As things are at present, and until you have strengthened the Empire internally, it would be folly to meddle with other countries.' How far this interview and speech are apocryphal it would be difficult to say, but in Pekin the neutrality of China in the Franco-Chinese dispute is attributed to the influence of the Empress Dowager."

REVIEWS AND NOTICES.

A History of English Dress, from the Saxon Period to the Present Day, by Georgiana Hill. London : Bentley & Son.

This book is a rich storehouse of entertaining information, collected with much industry and research. But it is more than this. Miss Georgiana Hill has so marshalled the vagaries of fashion that dress, which might seem as a mere accidental appendage, takes its place as a component element of history.

Many curious side lights appear as the Saxon, Norman, Plantagenet, Lancastrian, Tudor, and Stuart periods are passed in review, the fashions of each period reflecting the social characteristics of the time. Curious, for instance, is the contradiction history affords of the notion that women are more given than men to mutability in fashion.

"There was a time when they showed far less disposition than men to adopt new fashions. Because in the present day men have chosen to affect a certain rigour in dress which does not admit of much variation, they are pleased to forget the quality of their toilet in the past, the number and mutability of their fashions, the elaboration and costliness of their attire, which equalled—nay, exceeded— that of women. During the earlier portion of the Plantagenet Period, while Lords and Knights were launching out into all kinds of extravagancies, their wives and daughters clung to the simple Græco-Roman dress which was worn under the Normans, and indeed earlier. The long gowns falling to the feet in ample folds, the wide mantles, the simple kerchief, which were seen up to the reign of the second Edward, were almost the same as those worn by ladies in the Saxon era." (Page 67.)

"With the influx of foreign goods and foreign fashions, and the growing taste in Western Europe for novelties and display, the classic simplicity of female costume was corrupted. Women began to dress to match the men." (Page 68.)

The long gowns and graceful loose dresses which for four hundred years had held their own amongst women began to give way towards the middle of the 15th century; garments became shorter, "there was a tendency to cut the figure into sections." Following the fashion of the gentlemen in shortening their garments, women in the fifteenth century began to shorten their trains, and to abandon the loose flowing dresses they had retained from Saxon times, gradually taking up fashions with the tendency to cut the figure into sections which became so marked in the Tudor period when simplicity and grace gave away to stiffness and artificiality.

It is curious also to find how slow women were to adopt gloves, which were worn by men in the higher ranks, while women still used the long sleeves of their gowns to cover their hands. A couple of centuries later muffs were first worn by men.

The student of social conditions would find material here wherewith to trace the gradual change in the effect of dress: how from being eminently a means to distinguish class rigidly from class, and stamp the rank of the wearer, it has now become rather a means to obliterate class distinctions, and conceal the social standing of the wearer.

The tendency to "adaptation," which Miss Hill calls the keynote of our modern dress, is still carrying on this destruction of social stratification, but may it not be aiding greater freedom for individuality, notwithstanding the "neutrality" which is "coming more and more to be the basis of costume." "We cease to desire to be distinguished by our clothes; we study to make them harmonious parts of ourselves." The struggle between individuality and collectivism may be reflected for the future historian in our dress!

The Romance of a Country: a Masque, by M. A. Curtois. Fisher Unwin.

It is refreshing to meet a purely imaginative work like this in days when fiction has become so realistic. The Fair Country of this Masque belongs to no land known to any geographer, its people have no chapter in any history, yet it fascinates by its truthfulness, by its vivid picture of human nature in full and free play. Miss Curtois gives us none of that morbid introspection, that minute dissection of the baser qualities of life which vitiates the fiction of the present day. Her characters belong to lands as much *terra incognita* as those wherein the romances of chivalry had their heroes, mid "antres vast and deserts idle," and yet we individualise them all, and their strange names and quaint titles soon become familiar. Alvo "the young Leader," Ivlon, Escar, the treacherous Ursan, the cruel tribes of the Rema, stand out as only the touch of genius can make them. The plans of the exiles to win back the Fair Country, the dangers and difficulties that assail them, the treachery that dogs them, draw out scenes of heroism and aspiration which those who look to fiction to take their thoughts away from carking cares and lift them to a bracing mental atmosphere will read with rejoicing that even in this material generation a book has been produced so full of true and fair imaginings.

Women Writers, their Works and Ways; Second Series, by Catherine J. Hamilton. Ward Locke & Co.

Miss Hamilton, in the second series of Women Writers, fully sustains the promise of her first volume. In one sense the first series may seem to have an advantage, inasmuch as it dealt with writers of an earlier period, whose histories might have more novelty for the ordinary reader than those of the writers belonging to the beginning and middle of our own century. But on the other hand the second series has the advantage in the fact that while many readers may be unfamiliar with the literature of the past century, all will have friends amongst the creations of this company of noble writers which includes

Mrs. Jameson, Mrs. Gaskell, Miss Bremer, Mrs. Browning, Adelaide Ann Procter, George Eliot, &c. If the most important fact of any man's (or woman's) performance be, as Carlyle says, the life he has accomplished, we should welcome glimpses into the lives of the workers who, amid difficulties oft, discouragement oft and toil always, raised enduring monuments for the inspiration of unborn generations. Such glimpses Miss Hamilton's carefully-written pages give. She had a noble subject, and she has dealt with it in a manner pleasant to read, and reliable for its care. The portraits in this series are superior in execution to those in the first, and enhance the value of the volume.

The Autobiography of Mary Smith, Schoolmistress and Nonconformist. Miscellaneous Poems, by Mary Smith (M.S.), Schoolmistress and Nonconformist. London : Bemrose & Sons ; Carlisle : The Wordsworth Press, 75, Scotch Street.

It gave a certain added interest to these volumes to find that they were the works of the Miss Smith whose name was familiar to early workers in the Women's Suffrage cause as an active coadjutor in Carlisle, and to find that that lady had a history ; for these volumes show that hers was a self-made, self-educated career.

Under such circumstances the temptations to write a biography is easily understood. When the tempted person is the one being with literary aspirations in an unlettered class of society, the centre of an admiring and uncritical audience ; when, in addition, she is almost wholly self-educated, and has no opportunity of measuring herself with cultivated people, the temptation to write an Autobiography is most natural.

Perhaps the chief inducement to bring the posthumous volumes to light has been the letters from Mrs. Carlyle, which are given as an appendix to the first volume. In one of these Miss Smith seems to have sought Mrs. Carlyle's aid to find her some situation which would bring her more in contact with literary society. Mrs. Carlyle's characteristic reply concludes :

" Meanwhile, believe a woman older than yourself, who has seen, and *seen thro'*, all you are now longing after. There is as little *nourishing* for an aspiring soul in literary society as in any civilised society one could name! and for 'clear ideas' and 'broad knowledge,' they are not secreted in any corner of life, but lie in all life, for whoever has faculty to appreciate them."

The next letter, written three years later, opens thus:—

"*This* time you come to me as an old acquaintance whom I am glad to shake hands with again. The mere fact of your being still in the same position after so long an interval, and with such passionate inward protest as that first letter indicated, is a more authentic testimony to your worth, than if you had sent me a *certificate of character* signed by all the clergy and householders of Carlisle!"

These letters are in truth the most attractive part of the book, which, nevertheless, is not devoid of interest. It is not well written, and is disfigured here and there by narrow prejudices and a bitter partisan spirit in religion and politics, yet it leaves some pleasing pictures on the mind. The writer's father, the kindly, gentle old shoemaker, so conscientious in his Dissent, yet so devoid of sectarian spirit, is one. Another is the kindly Quaker family with whom Mary Smith lived as nursery governess, with their precise ways and gentle, considerate, courteous manners. And we obtain a glimpse—not, perhaps, a very interesting one—of what has not often been portrayed, the everyday life among Dissenters of the small tradesman class forty years ago. And the writer was better than her works. She was not, as she thought herself, an "incomprehensible being," a poet, or a learned literary lady. She was no bright particular star, but an ordinary candle, which yet did its work in lighting up dark corners. Narrow and self-conceited, she was yet religious, conscientious, hardworking, and her character was redeemed from the common-place by an honourable independence of spirit and a loyalty to her friends which might be called Quixotic if it did not deserve a higher name. Her leisure hours, of which she had but few, she devoted to good works, and she aided with her pen, to the best of her powers, every movement which seemed to her likely to benefit her fellow-creatures, whether Women's Suffrage, the employment of women, or local, political and social matters. She was born at Cropredy, in Oxfordshire,

February 7, 1822, and died in Carlisle, where she had spent the greater part of her life, on January 9, 1889.

Six Weeks in Egypt. Fugitive Sketches of Eastern Travel, by Mrs. C. J. Brook. London: Marshall, Simpkin & Co.; Huddersfield: E. W. Coates.

Out of these sketches, " fugitive " though they be, the stay-at-home traveller may gain a reflex of the enjoyments of travel. They have just enough of the personal element to give cohesion to the narrative, and never so much as to weary the reader. For those who have not time or opportunity to consult the great writers on Egypt ancient or modern, this little volume will be welcome, for it gives information of the latest aspect of the things of to-day, and of the latest results of the explorations into things of the past history of that wonderful land. Mrs. Brook refers specially to the favourable position of women in ancient Egypt, forming so marked a contrast with their position there to-day, and in some respects even with their position amongst ourselves. After reading these bright pages we feel a wish to thank the " old friends " at whose desire Mrs. Brook was induced to give them to the public.

A Working Woman's Day, 1d. *Cookery for Sick People*, 1d. *A Homely Talk on Health*, 2d. By Florence Stacpoole, and published for the National Health Society, 53, Berners Street, London, W.

Miss Stackpoole has enriched the literature of the National Health Society with three capital little books full of clear, practical suggestion and information on matters useful in every household. *A Working Woman's Day* gives a very good glimpse into the many ingenious contrivances to which a thrifty working man's wife needs to resort in order to maintain order and comfort on the limited income and in the still more limited space which forms her kingdom.

The NURSING RECORD, published at 376, Strand, has passed to the able editorship of Mrs. Bedford Fenwick. H.R.H. Princess Christian contributed an article to the number for October 7th, on the Royal British

Nurses' Association, which concludes with the following passage:—" Not every one can be an artist, a musician, a sculptor, or put great thoughts into becoming words. How few can even prepare a meal to satisfy a discriminating palate? Neither, then, can all women nurse, and here falls a heavy responsibility on Matrons and Sisters. They, and they alone, have power and the opportunity of doing the needful sifting, and by kindly disillusioning the Probationer who is labouring to misapply her gifts, to save her from the bitterness of a wasted life. It is from the standpoint of such considerations as these that I have always regarded the Presidency of the Royal British Nurses' Association as one of the highest honours which it is my happiness to bear.

"I am deeply penetrated with the conviction that it will create for women a recognised profession which will give scope to all that most adorns their nature; that it is destined to take an honoured place amongst the many great institutions of our country, and that it will be ladened with blessings to future generations. With all my heart I devote to it such loving thought, labour, and strength, as I have to give."

The number for January 6th includes papers by Dr. Annesley Kenealy—who was judge of awards in the Hygienic Section of the World's Fair—on "Women Judges at Chicago," and by Rachel Foster Avery, on "The National and International Councils of Women."

The WOMEN'S HERALD is no more. It has been absorbed by the *Women's Signal*, the first number of which appeared on January 4th, edited by Lady Henry Somerset and Miss Annie H. Holdsworth.

WORK AND LEISURE.—With the close of 1893 our excellent contemporary, *Work and Leisure*, bids farewell to its readers. Under the title "Vale," in the December number, Miss Hubbard reviews the many advances and new enterprises which have been treated of, year by year, in its pages during the eighteen years of its useful career.

The editor intimates that she has arranged with

Miss Janes, editor of *The Threefold Cord*, to give brief insertion of information bearing on the topics hitherto treated of in *Work and Leisure*.

OBITUARY.

LUCY STONE.—Our American co-workers have had a heavy loss in the death of Mrs. Lucy Stone, who passed away on October 18, at her home near Boston, at the age of 75. Mrs. Stone will be most widely known as editor, in conjunction with her daughters, H. B. Blackwell and Alice Blackwell, of the *Woman's Journal*. That journal was started in 1870, but long before that Mrs. Stone had been labouring in the cause to which she gave the best energies of her life. If she did not live to see the full result of her labours, at least she had seen sufficient to leave the world with serene hopefulness, which found frequent expression in her last days. "I am so glad to have lived," she said one day shortly before the end, "and to have lived when I could work." To a friend who expressed grief that she should not see women obtain the vote, she answered, "Perhaps I shall know it where I am, and if not I shall be doing something better. I have not a fear, nor a dread, nor a doubt." "I have not the smallest apprehension," she said to her daughter when it began to be feared her illness would terminate fatally; "I know the eternal order and I believe in it."

Fuller notice of Mrs. Stone's life and work will, we hope, appear in a future issue.

MRS. COWEN.—It is with deep regret that we have to announce the death of Mrs. Cowen, who died at her residence in Nottingham, after a brief illness, on January 8th, aged 62. As hon. sec. to the Notts

Women's Suffrage Committee, as President of the Women's Liberal Association, Mrs. Cowen had long taken a leading part in the various phases of women's interest. In the Suffrage work, more especially, her quick, steady effort will be seriously missed. Mrs. Cowen had also served on the Nottingham School Board from 1884 to 1893.

CORRESPONDENCE.

REGISTRATION OF MIDWIVES BILL

TO THE EDITOR OF THE "ENGLISHWOMAN'S REVIEW."

MADAM,—I have read with much interest the letter signed "Country Lady" in your last number. Your correspondent truly says "the bill requires much consideration" and "may fail, and do actual harm." As a midwife with experience in work among the very poor, where the services of a doctor are often quite beyond their means, I have seen much injury and suffering inflicted on the mothers by untrained and unskilled attendants; who claim the title of midwife, and thus easily impose on the poor women.

Such untrained attendants are only allowed to practise in the United Kingdom; in all other European countries midwifery laws are enforced; and no woman may practise as a midwife without passing an examination in practice and in theory. "Country Lady," in speaking of her own village, which is evidently well provided, mentions two women who act as midwives, but the services of a doctor are apparently easily available; but in many poor and populous districts seven out of ten births take place without a medical man, and in such districts, statistics show that 3,000 mothers die annually over and above the general statistics of puerperal mortality. That is, women having skilled attendance die one in 600 births; women in the hands of unskilled attendants die one in 200.

I am sure "Country Lady" will be glad to know that she is misinformed as to the intention of allowing women to obtain certificates and practise as midwives, under the proposed new Bill, without practical as well as theoretical training. The London Obstetrical Society demands, as a primary condition for going up for its examination, due evidence that the candidate has conducted twenty-five births under authorised supervision.

In the suggestions for the terms of the new Bill, this requirement will probably be extended.

Theoretical knowledge alone would indeed be dangerous, not only in conducting a case, but in nursing mother and child afterwards, so that I cannot agree with the opinion given: "Their knowledge will be useful after the birth in attending properly to the patient."

As to the statement, "It will be impressed upon them that they are to do nothing themselves, but in all cases to send for a doctor," I do not understand what is meant. Every educated midwife knows that she is certified to attend *natural labour*, and that it is her duty to send for medical aid when the *labour is abnormal;* the power of recognising danger depending greatly on the education of the midwife; and the fact of being unable to diagnose it at an early stage being one of the gravest dangers of untrained midwifery. The points requiring attention which your correspondent mentions, are all dealt with in the report of the select committee of the House of Commons, August, 1893; and would occupy too much space to be answered in detail.

As many are in the same position as "Country Lady," anxious to know more on this subject, they may be interested to hear that an Association of Ladies has been formed for the purpose of interesting and informing women on this subject, and of endeavouring to help the mothers among the poor to good attendance.

Any further information about the Association will be most gladly given.

Letters can be sent to me, as I am acting as Honorary Secretary.

LUCY M. ROBINSON.

95, *Philbeach Gardens, London, S.W.*
December 27th, 1893.

Owing to the kindness of the Editor I have seen the letter of Mrs. Robinson.

Whether the Bill about midwives proves to be a blessing or the contrary, depends on what the form of the Bill is when brought before Parliament. As I saw it last autumn it might have been called " A Bill for the Abolition of Midwives."

A clause ought certainly to be inserted to the effect that no one should be certificated as midwife who had not attended twenty-five births, and when the certificate is given to the midwife it should bear upon it a licence to practise in all cases of natural birth.

The medical man who explained the matter to me was of opinion that a midwife ought in all cases to call in a doctor, and ought never to act at all, because, as he said, only a qualified surgeon could tell whether the birth was going to be natural or otherwise, and he thought the Bill before Parliament was intended to have, and would have, that most desirable effect. He said no midwife should ever act herself, but should always send for the doctor, because nothing was so dangerous as " a little knowledge."

Let the Association of Ladies look carefully to the framing of the Bill, or they will find their poor women deprived of all assistance, except that of surgeons, whose charges are too high for the poor to pay.

A COUNTRY LADY.

FOREIGN HOMES FOR GENTLEWOMEN—AN ENQUIRY.

TO THE EDITOR OF THE "ENGLISHWOMAN'S REVIEW."

MADAM—Can any of your correspondents, foreign or otherwise, furnish any information concerning those foundations or institutions dating from mediæval times for the purpose of supplying a home and a living to decayed gentlewomen? I am under the impression that such institutions, not partaking of the nature of convents, but resembling them in so far as to promote a species of communal life for purposes of living and perhaps association in work, are still to be found in Germany under the name of Stiften (the participants in their benefits being styled *Stiften-damen*), and it is also my impression that similar institutions exist in Denmark.

The idea of these Stiften, so far as I can ascertain, is directly derived in these Protestant countries from the Catholic notion of convents, or rather from a modification of the same, as a means of providing for the surplus or indigent daughters of the higher classes for whom marriage seemed an unlikely contingency, and whose dispositions were unsuited to the cloister. For these, we are told, in an account of France before the Revolution, a middle course existed, by which, on the payment of a somewhat smaller dowry than that exacted by most convents, they were able to become *chanoinesses*, vowed indeed to celibacy, but otherwise occupying a position midway between the religious and the worldly life, and far more allied in its liberty and interests to the latter than to the former. Except that after making their final vow they were not able to marry, the chanoinesses had no other obligation than that of residing for four months in the year in the communal establishment or settlement provided for them; the rest of their time might be spent in their own families, sharing in all the pursuits and amusements of a French lady's existence. In their own establishment (consisting of small dwellings, like those of the Benguines at Ghent, which two or more ladies occupied in common) they were subject to little or no restraint, and might receive visitors as often as they chose, even male ones, so that love-affairs and marriages—perhaps almost the only marriages of inclination possible to the daughters of the French nobility—sometimes resulted to the younger canonesses, who had not yet completely given up all thought of changing their state.

It would, therefore, appear as if the women of earlier times were not so absolutely compelled to choose between the life of a wife by necessity, or of a nun, as we have been led to believe; moreover, that in the rudest times society recognised the duty of providing effectually for those who could not stand alone. In our own century, when the state of society no longer renders it unsafe for an unencumbered woman to live in the world, if she has enough, and when opportunities of training and self-support are so multiplied as to put them within the reach of all who have health and capacity, it may seem at first sight as if nothing of the kind could be needed. But we must not forget that we have unhappily among us numbers of poor ladies, nearly or quite destitute, who are neither young enough nor strong enough to become really capable of self-support; such, therefore, are, notwithstanding the advantages of our time, in very much the same position as the helpless ones, namely, all women and all men also of weak physique, were in the middle ages, and it seems but reasonable that some similar provision in accordance with the spirit of our own age were made for them. If, therefore, this can be done in other countries, and foundations for this purpose exist, I should be grateful for information as to conditions and methods of working.

I am, &c.,
INQUIRER.

WOMEN'S POLITICAL AND MUNICIPAL RIGHTS IN FINLAND.

TO THE EDITOR OF THE "ENGLISHWOMAN'S REVIEW."

DEAR EDITOR,— I have read with considerable interest the paper on "Women's Political and Municipal Rights in Different Countries," in the last issue of the ENGLISHWOMAN'S REVIEW; but as I found that there were some omissions as to women's municipal and parochial rights in Finland, I enclose an extract I have copied from a report given this summer at Chicago by the Union, a Society for the promotion of women's interests in Finland. The report was read at the Women's Congress at the World's Fair, and was entitled "Women and Women's Work in Finland." Hoplng that this extract will be of some interest to the English public,

Believe me, yours truly,
ANNIE FURNHJELM.

Urdiala, November 13.

"Unmarried women who are of age, widows and divorced wives, provided they fulfil other necessary conditions, possess the right of municipal vote (Laws of January 6th, 1865, and December 8th, 1873). This right, however, proves very different in the communes managed directly by municipal assemblies, from what it is in those communes (for instance, most cities) where the government and management are entrusted to a municipal board.

"The general rule is that women are entitled to take part and vote in the municipal assemblies according to this rule; they may in communes of the first kind take part in decisions on the management of the communes, as well as vote on the election of its functionaries, &c.

"In communes of the latter kind, women are entitled to take part in the election of the municipal board as well as in that of some functionaries (in cities they may accordingly vote on the election of mayors, councillors, and physicians), but they may not be elected members of the board, and consequently they cannot take part in decisions on the government and management of these communes.

"In connection with the municipal rights of women, some few words may be said about their *parochial rights*. Unmarried women of age, widows, and divorced wives, are entitled to take part in parish meetings, and vote in the election of the clergy, as well as in that of churchwardens; but a woman may not be elected churchwarden. (Ecclesiastical Law of December 6th, 1869).

"Women are, according to lately issued regulations, eligible as members of the communal Poor Board. Women may sit on school committees in high schools for girls. The members of these committees are proposed by the local board, and chosen by the supreme school council in Helsingfors. The duties of these school committees are limited to an unimportant supervision of the school.

"Public elementary school boards, chosen by the communal assembly or board, are of much greater importance, and direct the affairs of public elementary schools in town and country.

"The eligibility of women to sit in the school board of public elementary schools in towns depended, until quite lately, on the different regulations of the different towns; and in many places women have also been elected to fill it, though the general school law did not pronounce them eligible. Lately, however, the matter has been settled in a satisfactory way; a statute issued March 7th, 1893, decrees women to be *eligible members of the school boards* in town and country. In this, as well as in many other respects, the general opinion and custom have preceded and prepared the way for legislation, and the law, such as it existed, had come to be interpreted in a much more liberal way than was formerly the custom. In consequence of a similar liberal interpretation of the laws existing, women have been considered competent to fill offices which formerly belonged exclusively to men, such as those of *trustees* in cases of bankruptcy.

"Widows are, of course, the lawful guardians of their own children. The law is, however, generally understood not to allow women to act in the same capacity for the children of other people. There have been cases, however, when women, without being widows, have been elected to fulfil the position of guardians."

FOREIGN NOTES.

BELGIUM.

At the University of Brussels, Mesdemoiselles Herswingels and Derscheid have passed as doctors in medicine, surgery, and midwifery.

The *Liège Express* has appointed Mdlle. Delchevalerie on its staff as a reporter—the first lady to fill the position of reporter in Belgium.

DENMARK.

LOCAL GOVERNMENT FRANCHISE FOR WOMEN—DEBATE IN THE FOLKETING.—The first reading of the Bill for Communal Suffrage and Eligibility for Women aroused extremely little interest in the Folketing. A few more ladies in the reserved seats than usual, and that was all. The house was empty, and the members who were present paid no particular attention to the motion. After the minister had explained his attitude in a few words, no one felt inclined to take up the debate. Perhaps this was a sign that the demands of the Bill seemed so reasonable that it was not worth while arguing over them.

Trier, who introduced the Bill, declared that it was unnecessary to speak at length on a question which had been discussed again and again in the Folketing. It was one of those measures which would always keep cropping up until it became law. In 1888, a petition from about 20,000 women from the whole country was sent into the Rigsdag, expressing their view of the "pressing necessity" of this measure.

The present Bill differed from that which was introduced in the Landstag, in the spring of 1888, in two points. First, it assumed eligibility as a natural sequel to women's suffrage. In Iceland, where communal suffrage was carried first, they were now approaching the question of adding eligibility to the measure. The same consideration which had allowed men, from 25 to 30 years of age, to be eligible without possessing the franchise, should influence many who objected to women's suffrage, and lead them to see the practical use of making women eligible, and thus enabling them to exercise their powers in those branches of communal work for which they are peculiarly fitted, such as School Boards, Poor Law Guardians, the Relief of the Sick, Protection of Children, &c. The second point regarded the position of married women. In the first Bill they had been absolutely excluded; the case of widows and unmarried women had alone been dealt with. Meanwhile, however, the supporters of the cause had come to the conclusion that there could be no reason for excluding married women if they fulfilled the same conditions as unmarried women and as men, namely, if they paid taxes independently to the commune. There were two classes of married women whose claims stood foremost—those who, by the law of 1880, had secured the disposal of their own earnings, and those who, by marriage contract, had an independent power over their property and income. A census of 1890 showed that in Copenhagen alone there were 5,287 women who paid taxes. It was not stated how many of these were married, but it might be presumed that some of them were. The question had been so often discussed on both sides that he hoped the measure would soon make further progress, and that in its present form it would be accepted not by a party only, but by the whole Rigsdag.

The Minister of the Interior (Ingerslev), after pointing out that the supporters of the Bill evidently did not expect it to pass in the near future, referred them, for his opinion on the subject, to a speech made by him in the debate on the Law of 1882, for Iceland, when he had declared that he could see no objection to the same regulations applying in Denmark as in Iceland. Further than that he would not go.

Here the debate ended; the Bill was sent to its second reading without a division. The house did not go into committee on it, but it was read a second time a week afterwards, and went on to the third reading without a word. At the third reading, Scharling made a few remarks against the measure, which went thus to the Landsting, where it was rejected Thursday, Nov. 28.—*Abridged from Qvinden og Samfundet.*

FRANCE.

Mademoiselle Klumpke, who has for several years worked at the Paris Observatory, has just taken her degree as Doctor of Mathematical Science. She presented a brilliant thesis at the Sorbonne, " A Contribution to the Study of Saturn's Rings."

In granting the degree Mr. Darbours addressed the gifted authoress as follows :—

" You have occupied yourself with one of the most interesting questions in astronomy. The great names of Galileo, Huyghen, Cassini, Laplace, without speaking of those of my illustrious colleagues and friends, are connected with the history of each of the great advances in the attractive but difficult theory of the Rings of Saturn. Your work is not a slight contribution to the subject, and it places you in an honourable position among the ladies who have devoted themselves to the study of mathematics.

"During last century Mdlle. Maria Agnesi gave us a work on the differential and integral calculus. Since then, Sophia Germain, as remarkable for her literary and philosophical talent as for her mathematical faculties, was held in esteem by the great geometers who honoured our country at the beginning of this century. And but a few years ago the Academy of Science, on the report of a commission on which I had the honour to take part, awarded one of its best prizes to Madame Kowalewsky, placing her name by the side of those of Euler and Laplace in the history of discovery relating to the theory of the movement of a solid body round a fixed point.

"In your turn you have entered upon your career. We know that for some years you devoted yourself with great zeal and success to investigations connected with the star chart. Your thesis, which you have prepared according to our course of higher mathematics with an assiduity that we could not ignore, is the first that a lady has presented and successfully sustained before our Faculty, to obtain the Degree of Doctor of Mathematical Science. You have worked in a deserving manner, and the Faculty has unanimously decided to declare you worthy of the grade of Doctor."

ICELAND.

In Iceland women who, since 1882, have been entitled to vote in local elections, have this autumn been rendered eligible also for election.

INDIA.

It is with the greatest regret that we learn from the *Indian Magazine*, that the school for Hindu widows, founded by the Pundita Ramabai, is doomed, so far as its original design is concerned.

Only in the last issue of this Review the report of the Ramabai Association was quoted, showing steady increase of numbers in the school. But all is now changed. The strictly unsectarian character of the school alone enabled it to face the storms of opposition, but latterly the Pundita Ramabai has determined to introduce instruction in the Christian religion.

"The upshot of this is that the Sharada Sadan is ruined as an institution for educating the high caste Hindu widows, though it may continue to remain as a mission school for a score of daughters of native Christians of Poona.

"Meantime, a new movement is set on foot in Poona which, if it succeeds, will do great credit to its promoters. A new Sharada Sadan, entirely under Hindu management, is, it seems, to be started. Preliminary to starting a regular school, provision has been made for the education of such of the widows as had to leave Ramabai's school at this crisis. Some of the leading men have each undertaken to bear the annual cost of maintenance, lodging and education of two widows."

H.H. the Maharaja of Mysore has issued a draft regulation to be considered by his Government, the object of which is to prevent infant marriage in Mysore. He proposes to fix the minimum age at which the ceremony can be performed at eight for a girl, fourteen for a boy. It is expected that the regulation will be adopted, and though the improvement is limited, it will help decidedly to diminish the very large number of child widows in Mysore.

Two instances of the re-marriage of widows are recorded from Ahmedabad, at one of which more than a hundred leading native gentlemen were of the company.

Babu Benod Lal Ghose, vice-chairman of the Baranagar Municipality, has given 1,400 rupees for the erection of a Women's Hospital at Baranagar in connection with the Dufferin Fund.

At Madras the Social Reform Association are arranging lectures for Hindu ladies. The third lecture was given on October 21st by Miss A. Shunmugum, on "Scenes in Europe," illustrated by a magic lantern.

PARAGRAPHS.

MISS SHAW ON THE AUSTRALIAN OUTLOOK.

MISS FLORA L. SHAW read an interesting paper on January 9, at a meeting of the Royal Colonial Institute, held in the Whitehall Rooms of the Hôtel Métropole. The writer insisted on the distinction, too little realised at home, between the temperate Australia of the south and the tropical Australia of the north, and pointed out the different political conditions which this distinction made necessary or desirable. The conflict of races, the undeveloped wealth of the continent, particularly in its vineyards, the need of female immigration, the subjects of finance and land settlement, and the question of separation or closer union were also fully discussed. The chair was taken by Sir Frederick Young.

The CHAIRMAN observed that this was a red-letter day in the history of the institute, inasmuch as it was the first occasion on which they had had the pleasure of hearing a paper read by a lady. Miss Shaw was well known for the searching and profound analysis which she had applied to colonial questions, and the paper which they were about to hear would be found fully to justify the writer's reputation. Miss Shaw's contribution might almost be said to be the most striking which had ever been added to the records of the institute.

In the course of her paper, speaking of the need for female emigration, Miss Shaw remarked : " One of the needs of the society appeared to me to be young unmarried women, and in visiting the homesteads and finding young men engaged, as they easily may be, in washing dishes, scrubbing kitchen tables, feeding the fowls, or attending to the flower garden, one cannot but think that for such colonisation as this there would be a good deal to say in favour of allowing the girls of big families to accompany their brothers. Many and many an English girl, who, unless she marries, has no other prospect at home than to be a governess or a telegraph clerk, would, I believe, be glad to go out under the safe guardianship of her brother, sharing his hardships, mitigating the first loneliness of the great wrench, which is the cause perhaps of more of the recklessness of young Englishmen abroad than has ever been admitted, and taking her part in that most entertaining of natural interests, the creation of a home. No healthy, sensible girl fears work. It is the dulness of the left-behind which makes so many of those whose circumstances are not altogether prosperous discontented."

A discussion followed this paper, opened by Sir JAMES GARRICK, who, in expressing his high appreciation of Miss Shaw's address, concurred with the chairman in holding this to be a red-letter day in the history of the institute. The paper was only one more link in the powerful chain which Miss Shaw had been forging, not only between Australia and this country, but between all parts of the Empire. Miss

Shaw had had all the best sources of information at
her command, and was well qualified to represent
the colonies. She had resolved to see for herself, to
verify or correct the information with which she had
equipped herself. Her papers from Australia were
so accurate, so profound, and in difficult questions so
abstruse, that men friends of his expressed incredulity
that they had been written by a woman. With regard
to Queensland in particular, Miss Shaw's letters were
so very valuable that he had on his own initiative distributed those letters broadcast. He could only hope
that the hostile critics of the Australian colonies
would adopt the views of their recuperative powers
which were expressed in the paper, and all would
recognise that Miss Shaw had pointed out the way
to retrieve the errors of the past. The colonists were
learning to be self-denying and self-relying, and to
depend upon their own efforts instead of English
money. No man could predict the future of those
great communities, but the highest ambition might
well be satisfied in maintaining the great inheritance
which had come down to us. (*Abridged from "Times"
of Jan.* 10.)

HOW COLORADO WAS CARRIED.

The *Boston Woman's Journal* contains a long account of the Suffrage Campaign in Colorado, whence
the following extracts are taken:—

" The first thing we did was to address a circular
letter to each political county convention in Colorado,
accompanied in every case by a set of suffrage resolutions. There are fifty-five counties. Each county
held two and most of them three conventions. Three
or four counties held more. As far as possible, the
resolutions sent out were placed in the hands of known
friends, and, where this was done, they never failed to
get before the convention. Out of 180 sets of resolutions, over two-thirds were endorsed, the convention
in most cases putting a woman suffrage plank into its
platform. This action on the part of the convention
of course bound no one to vote for us, but it gave us

wide advertisement over the State as in the field and
at work. . . .

"One great feature of the campaign has been the
support received from prominent politicians, lawyers
and ministers throughout the State. Nearly every
minister of any prominence in Denver, Pueblo, Leadville, and many other towns has preached in our favour
from one to three times, and many of them have spoken
from our platforms. From the leaders of the Populist
and Republican parties we have received financial aid,
as well as help in the way of advice, that can never be
estimated nor forgotten by the women of Colorado.

"Another strong point of the campaign was the absolutely non-partisan stand which we have been able
to maintain throughout. We have never committed
ourselves in any direction, not even by sending
speakers to political platforms. This did not prevent
the Populists and Republicans, however, from advocating our cause everywhere, and we have made many
friends by sticking closely to a non-partisan basis of
action."

And now a word to allay the apprehensions of
Eastern suffragists as to another constitutional fight.
When the constitution of Colorado was prepared in
1877, Judge Bromwell, who still lives in Denver,
caused to be inserted in it a provision that whenever
the legislature saw fit to submit the question of equal
rights to the people it could do so by a simple majority
vote, and that the law should then be referred to the
voters, a majority of whose votes should ratify it,
whereupon the right to vote would be bestowed upon
women. It is simply a case of "Referendum."

The following editorial, taken from the Denver *Republican* of November 10, explains the matter more
fully:—

THE EQUAL SUFFRAGE LAW.

"Many inquiries have been made regarding the
rights acquired by women as voters in Colorado under
the law approved by a large majority of the popular
vote on Tuesday, and some persons seem to think

that women will not be permitted to vote for elective federal officers, on account of some clause in the constitution or laws of the United States. This is a mistaken view. The new law gives women exactly the same rights as men in exercising the elective franchise in Colorado, as will be clearly seen by reference to Section 1 of the Act passed by the Ninth General Assembly, which reads:

"'That every female person shall be entitled to vote at all elections, in the same manner in all respects as male persons are or shall be entitled to vote by the constitution and laws of this State, and the same qualifications as to age, citizenship and time of residence in the State, county, city, ward and precinct, and all other qualifications required by law to entitle male persons to vote shall be required to entitle female persons to vote.'

"Male persons who possess the necessary qualifications are permitted to vote for presidential electors and members of the House of Representatives, and it follows as a matter of course that women possessing the same qualifications will hereafter be permitted to vote on exactly the same terms as men."

HUMAN PREROGATIVE.

IT would be interesting to hear the opinions of various thinkers on the subject of human prerogative, for, judging of humanity by their acts, the idea seems to obtain that human prerogative has no limits. It has been made a reproach to the generations of the past that under their sway might was right, and we are wont to congratulate ourselves upon the fact that in these days justice reigns, and that the bad old rule of our ancestors is ended. Is might indeed no longer held to constitute right, and does justice reign? We can hardly affirm that it does when we dispassionately consider the things that are.

In this realm those who are able to uphold their rights, or to clamour for them, obtain a certain something which for lack of a better name we call justice. "Legal sanction and support" is popularly confounded with justice; to the unreflecting the terms are synonymous, and it is piteous indeed that such should be the case, that the meaning of justice should be so desecrated. Justice is all-embracing, and when we say that those who can uphold their rights obtain justice we express ourselves very foolishly. Justice cannot be agitated for—justice is free. Legal countenance and support may be warred for and gained by coercive measures, but, in a land acknowledging the sway of the great sovereign justice, legal countenance and support would be given as a matter of course to all the feeble millions who are unable to raise any cry in their own defence. In England they are not so given; and the mercy of legislators for the non-speaking creatures in their power may be defined as an unknown quantity. Mercy, however, might be dispensed with if justice were given, but, roughly speaking, it may be asserted that humanity in general in their dealings with the lower animals have absolutely no understanding of equitable treatment; it does not, so to say, occur to them that justice may be involved in such dealings.

A certain amount of legal protection—of a poor and limited kind—is given to so-called domestic animals, but wild creatures are held to be outside the pale of anything of the kind, and the ordinary individual is quite within his rights—is held to be merely exerting his human prerogative—when he chooses to torture to death some hapless non-domestic animal that fate has put in his power. By might he has possessed himself of his mute fellow-mortal; the law gives him the right to do what he likes with it.

Might must be right no longer! The cultured peoples of the 19th century must defer to some diviner rule. Let us see if we can find out what should be the leading feature of the ethics that may fitly govern us in these times.

In considering ethics we remember that we are

occupied with the science of duty, and going straight to the root of the matter we discover that the incentive treated of is defined as "that which a person is bound by any obligation to do or to refrain from doing." The words, *by any obligation* we mentally put in italics, and having thus given them prominence we inquire, What obligation do we acknowledge? The searcher who desires to yield homage to the highest obligation only will determine that he is bound, in the way of doing, to give help and service to every fellow sentient, and in the way of not doing to refrain from causing hurt of whatever description to the same. Whether a being is soulless or not, whether it suffers a greater or lesser degree of pain, are circumstances quite beyond the question, because duty affects the *one who acts*, not the one acted on, and when we disregard any heart's anguish, any body's agony, we show ourselves wanting in thoroughness, and fail miserably in our pursuit of right.

Those who are properly imbued with the sacredness of the obligation that controls them, will see in the helplessness or inferior worth of any creature impressive reasons for especially remembering the rights of that insignificant individual.

There has been a good deal of talk lately on the subject of cruelty to birds because the Moloch fashion casts envious eyes upon their plumage, and woeful accounts are given of the unpardonable wrong done to the helpless in the name of those who prostrate themselves before the false fetich spoken of. We could give heartrending details of the savagery perpetrated; of wings torn from little glad, bright, living bodies; of innocent, useful lives mercilessly cut short for no good purpose; but it is better to dwell upon the moral aspect of cruelty, as it affects the soul of right, than on the material aspect.

The physical suffering we cause, keen and unendurable though it may be, has an ending, but there is no end to the evil moral force we send forth into the world when we outrage the laws of justice and humanity; there is no end to the wrong we do when we are false to the divine principle within. Many, however, who are anxious to be true to that principle, *unconsciously* give countenance to cruelty. Some critics have a somewhat hysteric way of inveighing against certain fashions whilst quietly accepting others equally objectionable, and of taking it for granted that the votaries of the mode worshipped savagely cry out for victims, well knowing what the victims endure. The assumption is altogether gratuitous ; probably not one woman in fifty is aware that the wing she wears is the result of cruelty. The ordinary human unit is not reflective, but does as others do, and wears what they wear without any thought whatever. If the average subject were to be inspired with a ray of reflection she could only feel—looking at the customs in the midst of which she lives—that animals exist merely for the use of man, and that as they are slaughtered in hordes every day the anguish of one dumb heart more can be of little consequence.

The *circumstances* in the midst of which the unthinking are brought up are responsible, not the unthinking individuals, for existing abuses, and those circumstances are the result of the wrong-thinking of the past. The cruelty that exists to-day does not proceed from the selfishness of fashionable women, but is simply the outcome of erroneous ideas on the subject of human prerogative established by man in the past.

For the guidance of many who have involuntarily countenanced barbarity, we would say in conclusion that as nearly all animal material is produced by means of suffering, it would be well for those who desire to wear skins, feathers, &c., to acquaint themselves with the methods by which those beautiful things are prepared for the market. A few quotations are appended, giving a faint idea of all that we tacitly encourage when we choose the plumage of dead birds instead of the other lovely things offered for adornment.

"It was estimated nine years ago that twenty to thirty millions of birds were annually imported by this country. . . . Birds had been so persecuted to get their plumes for the northern market that they were practically exterminated." Macleod Island :

"found a huge pile of half decayed birds lying on the ground; all of them had the plumes taken with a patch of skin from the back, and some had the wings cut off. . . . Within the last few days it [the rookery] had been almost destroyed, hundreds of old birds having been killed, and thousands of eggs broken. I do not know of a more horrible and brutal exhibition than that which I witnessed here." . . . Sarasota : "all birds killed off by plume hunters (similar sickening details follow.)" Extracts from papers by Mr. W. E. Scott, the well-known American ornithologist : "The small snow-white heron, which has, during the nesting time, a plume of lovely feathers growing out of its back, is ruthlessly killed when it has its young ones, as the feathers are then in the greatest perfection. Dozens, nay hundreds, of men are employed in slaughtering the parent birds as they hover over their nests. . . . Not only are they killed by hundreds, but they are also tortured by having their wings torn off whilst still alive. Many are only wounded by the shots, and fly away to die slowly, hearing the cry of their offspring perishing miserably of hunger." From "A Talk about Birds," by Mrs. Brightwen : "If to the starved young we add all the birds that fly away with pellets of lead in their bodies to languish and die of their wounds . . . it would be no exaggeration to say that for every bird worn in a lady's hat, at least ten birds have suffered the death pang."—W. R. Hudson, C.M.Q.S.

The commissioner of Sind says: "I have known that in a few days' time no less than 30,000 black partridges have been killed in certain provinces to supply the European demand for their skins. One dealer in London is said to have received, as a single consignment, 32,000 dead humming birds, 80,000 aquatic birds and 800,000 pairs of wings. A Parisian dealer had a contract for 40,000 birds, and an army of murderers were turned out to supply the order. . . . The slaughter is simply beyond calculation." From "As in a Mirror," by the Rev. H. Greene, M.A. : We cannot even honestly believe that birds have no depth of feeling. "The dying cries of the fledglings left to

starve to death in their nests by hundreds, is described as heart-rending," and the following touching episode shows us something of the faithfulness and heroism and depth of affection of the little pretty things that we pursue and torture for such pitiful ends. . . .
" One day George Stephenson went into a room to close a window which had been open for some time. A day or two afterwards he noticed a bird dash itself repeatedly against the window panes. He went to see why he did this, and opened the window. Immediately the bird flew past him with a worm in its mouth, and went straight to a corner of the room. Stephenson followed it with his eyes, and saw that a nest had been built there. The bird took one long look into the nest, then fluttered down to the ground gasping and almost lifeless. He crossed the room to learn the cause, and saw in the nest a mother bird and three or four young ones, all dead. He was filled with pity and picked up the poor bird; he tried to nurse it into life, but it was of no avail, it died broken hearted."

O. ESLIE-NELHAM.

London School of Medicine for Women.
IN ASSOCIATION WITH
THE ROYAL FREE HOSPITAL.

THE Course of Study includes a complete preparation for the Medical Examinations of the University of London, the Royal University of Ireland, the Conjoint Examinations of the King and Queen's College of Physicians and the Royal College of Surgeons, Ireland, and the Conjoint Examinations for the Scottish Triple Qualification of the College of Physicians and College of Surgeons, Edinburgh, and the Faculty of Physicians and Surgeons, Glasgow. Also for the Diploma of the Society of Apothecaries, London, in Medicine, Surgery and Midwifery. For information respecting Scholarships, &c., apply to the Dean, Mrs. GARRETT ANDERSON, M.D., or to Mrs. THORNE, *Honorary Secretary*, 30, Handel Street, Brunswick Square, W.C.

EDINBURGH SCHOOL OF MEDICINE FOR WOMEN,
SPECIALLY RECOGNISED AS
Qualifying for the University of St. Andrews.
President:
H.R.H. The Duchess of Fife.
Vice-Presidents:
The Marchioness of Tweeddale. The Lady Helen Munro Ferguson. The Lady Reay.

This School forms an integral part of the Extra Mural School of Edinburgh. Its five years' curriculum is specially adapted to the requirements of the University of St. Andrews and of the Conjoint Scottish Colleges, but qualifies for all other examining Boards. Winter Courses, 100 Lectures each; Summer Courses, 50 to 60 Lectures each. Clinical instruction in the Royal Infirmary, with special cliniques in the Eye, Throat, and Ear, Skin, Gynæcological, and Lock Wards, with Clinical Lectures in Medicine and Surgery. School Fees, £75 in four instalments; or total Fees for qualifying course in School and Hospital, £95 in one payment. For information as to Scholarships, &c., apply to Dr. JEX BLAKE, *Dean;* or Miss BLACK, *Secretary*, Surgeon Square, Edinburgh.

THE UNITED SISTERS' FRIENDLY SOCIETY
(SUFFOLK UNITY).

"Work and Leisure" Court, No. 15.

The object of the Society is threefold; to afford
1. A weekly allowance in sickness.
2. An annuity commencing at the age of 65.
3. A sum of money (£6 or upwards) payable at death to the duly nominated representative of a Member.

All single women and widows of good health and character, between the ages of 16 and 45, are eligible for Membership in the "Work and Leisure" Court, subject to election by the Committee, and to a satisfactory Medical Certificate from a duly qualified Medical Practitioner. A further examination by one of the Physicians of the Court may be required by the Committee.

President: Miss L. M. HUBBARD, Editor of "Work and Leisure."
Secretary: Miss EDITH M. MASKELL, 7c, Lower Belgrave Street London, S.W.
(To whom all communications should be addressed.)

THE NEW HOSPITAL FOR WOMEN,
144, EUSTON ROAD, N.W.

THE PHYSICIANS ARE WOMEN.

Treasurer:—Mrs. WESTLAKE, The River House, 3, Chelsea Embankment, S.W.
Hon. *Secretary:*—Miss VINCENT, 6c, Hyde Park Mansions, N.W.
Physicians and Surgeons to the Patients:—Mrs. MARSHALL, M.D.;
Mrs. DE LA CHEROIS, M.D.; Miss COCK, M.D.;
Mrs. SCHARLIEB, M.D., B.S.Lond.
Physicians and Surgeons to Out Patients:—Miss WALKER, M.D.;
Miss WEBB, M.B.; Mrs. STANLEY BOYD, M.D.
Ophthalmic Surgeon:—Miss ELLABY, M.D.
Assisted by a Consulting Staff of Physicians and Surgeons.

This Hospital is established to enable poor women to be attended by FULLY QUALIFIED WOMEN DOCTORS.

A Report and further information may be had on application to MISS MARGARET M. BAGSTER, *Secretary.*

Bankers:—BANK OF ENGLAND (Western Branch), Burlington Gardens, W.

JUST PUBLISHED, in 2 vols., Crown 8vo., Cloth Neat, Price 3s. 6d. each.

THE AUTOBIOGRAPHY and MISCELLANEOUS POEMS of MARY SMITH (M.S.), Schoolmistress and Nonconformist. With Letters from JANE WELSH CARLYLE and THOMAS CARLYLE. London: BEMROSE & SONS, LD.; Carlyle: G. & T. COWARD.

COMFORTABLE HOME FOR LADIES in 8-roomed Cottage adjoining Girls' Training Home. Large healthy village, 2 miles from sea. Terms moderate, including cooking and attendance. LADY C. BARNE, Wrentham, Suffolk.

Society for Promoting the Employment of Women.
22, BERNERS STREET, OXFORD STREET, W.

Established 1859. *Incorporated* 1879.

This Society was established for the purpose of finding openings for girls to learn different kinds of trade and business. Also for aiding those already trained to procure employment. A register is kept for experienced and certificated Bookkeepers, Saleswomen, Matrons, Sick-nurses, Engravers, Law Writers, Printers, Gilders, and other assistants. Orders for copying MSS., circulars, &c., and for directing envelopes, are promptly executed.

Bookkeeping.

A class for training young women as Clerks and Bookkeepers is held on the evenings of Monday and Thursday.

PRICE ONE SHILLING.

New Series—Vol. XXV. No. II.   April 16th, 1894.

THE
ENGLISHWOMAN'S REVIEW
OF
Social and Industrial Questions.

EDITED BY HELEN BLACKBURN.

CONTENTS FOR APRIL, 1894.

ARTICLES.—The Report on the Employment of Women by the Lady Assistant Commissioners, by Miss J. BOUCHERETT (continued). The British Workwoman in Danger. Lucy Stone, by Miss M. A. BIGGS. Maria Deraismes and the Woman's Movement in France, by Madame SCHMAHL. The Winter is Past (Poem) Mrs. WARNER SNOAD.

WOMEN'S SUFFRAGE. — Notes of the Quarter. Resolutions of Liberal Associations. South Australia. New Zealand. Second Record of Meetings.

ELECTIONS AND APPOINTMENTS.

RECORD OF EVENTS.—The Local Government Act. The Association of Irish Schoolmistresses. The Alexandra School. Lady Margaret Hall. Girls' Public Day School Company. The New Welsh University. Conference of Women's Protective and Provident League (Scotland). The Royal Commission on Employment of Women. Irish Association for Employment of Women. Edinburgh School of Medicine. London School of Medicine. Oriental Students. M.A.B.Y.S. Clubs, &c., &c.

REVIEWS.—The Rights of Women. Adventures in Mashonaland. Two Noble Lives. Ladies at Work.

OBITUARY.—Mdlle. Maria Deraismes. Georgiana Lady Wolverton. Miss Dobson Collet. Mrs. Menzies.

FOREIGN AND COLONIAL NOTES.

PASSING NOTES.—Women and Press Reform. Miss Mason's Report. Women Dentists in Russia.

LONDON

PUBLISHED AT THE OFFICE OF THE "ENGLISHWOMAN'S REVIEW,"
22, BERNERS STREET, OXFORD STREET, W.

AND FOR THE PROPRIETOR BY

WILLIAMS & NORGATE, 14, Henrietta Street, Covent Garden, London
and 20, South Frederick Street, Edinburgh.

PUBLISHED QUARTERLY on the 15th January, April, July, and October.

A Women's Suffrage Calendar for 1894.

Edited by HELEN BLACKBURN.

CONTENTS.—Citizen's and Student's Calendar—Events of the Year—Obituary—Calendar of Events, with Diary—Women's Suffrage: Appeal from Women; Record of Progress in Australasia—Women on School Boards, 1893—Public Appointments, 1893—Local Government Franchises—Women Poor Law Guardians, 1893—Women Graduates, 1893—Registered Medical Women—School of Medicine for Women—Societies for Promoting the Welfare of Women: England; Scotland; Ireland—Enterprises by Women—Technical Training in Domestic Arts—Figures from the Census—Rates of Postage—Advertisements.

To be obtained of the Publishers, J. W. ARROWSMITH, Quay Street, Bristol;
SIMPKIN, MARSHALL, HAMILTON, KENT, & CO., LIMITED, London;
And of the EDITOR, 10, Great College Street, Westminster.

PRICE THREEPENCE.

Central Committee of the National Society for Women's Suffrage.

Hon. Sec.: Mrs. FAWCETT.   *Secretary:* Miss HELEN BLACKBURN.
Office: 10, GREAT COLLEGE STREET, WESTMINSTER.

MARRIAGE LAW DEFENCE UNION.

An Appeal from the Women of England	1d.
The Woman's View of the Question	1d.
A Letter to English Wives. By Edith Mary Shaw ...	6d.
A Lady's Letter to a Friend, on behalf of those who do not wish to Marry their Brothers	½d.
What Miss Lydia Becker says	½d.
A Sister-in-Law's Plea for Mercy	½d.
A Woman's Opinion on the Wife's Sister Bill	½d.

MAY BE HAD AT
1, KING STREET, WESTMINSTER, S.W.

PERIODICAL PUBLICATIONS received during the Quarter:—
AMERICA—*Woman's Journal; Woman's Exponent; The Woman's Tribune; Demorest's Monthly Magazine; The Cycle.*
AUSTRALIA—*Dawn.*
AUSTRIA—*Mitheilungen; Volksstimme.*
BELGIUM—*Revendication du Droit des Femmes.*
FRANCE—*Le Journal des Femmes.*
NORWAY—*Nylaende.*
SWEDEN—*Dagny.*
DENMARK—*Kvinden og Samfundet.*
SWITZERLAND (Zurich)—*Frauenrecht.*
The Indian Magazine; Woman; Concord; The Lady of the House; Women's Union Journal; Review of Reviews; Threefold Cord; The Spinning Wheel.

A FAIR FIELD AND NO FAVOUR!

*Office for the Employment of Women as Compositors.
Girls trained and employed for the past twenty years.*

Ladies and Gentlemen are invited to place their orders for

PRINTING

WHERE THEY WILL BE EXECUTED BY

Women

IN A STYLE

EQUAL TO THE BEST.

NO SLIPSHOD WORK!
NO EXORBITANT PRICES!!

Estimates for Book and Magazine Work with Specimens.

JOHN BALE & SONS,

Steam Printers,

87-89, GREAT TITCHFIELD STREET,

OXFORD STREET, LONDON W.

Englishwoman's Review.

CONTENTS FOR JANUARY 16th, 1893.

ARTICLES:
    The Report on the Employment of Women, by the Lady Assistant Commissioners. Lead Works and some other Unhealthy Industries. The Austral Salon, Melbourne.

WOMEN'S SUFFRAGE:
    Notes of the Quarter. Women's Suffrage Appeal. List of Supporters and of Meetings. New Zealand Electoral Act. South Australia. Local Government Bill.

ELECTIONS AND APPOINTMENTS:

UNIVERSITY INTELLIGENCE.

RECORD OF EVENTS:
    Married Women's Property Act, 1893. Royal College of Surgeons, Dublin. Women and the Association of Architects. Women Worker's Conference. Countess Dufferin Fund. Arts and Crafts Exhibition. Swanley College. Women's Gardening Association. Ventures and Undertakings. Empress Dowager of China and the Siamese Question.

REVIEWS AND NOTICES:
    History of English Dress. Romance of a Country. Autobiography of Mary Smith. Six weeks in Egypt, &c.

OBITUARY:
    Mrs. Lucy Stone. Mrs. Cowen.

CORRESPONDENCE:
    Midwives Bill. Foreign Homes for Women. Women's Political and Municipal Rights in Finland.

FOREIGN NOTES.

PARAGRAPHS.

HUMAN PREROGATIVE.

THE
ENGLISHWOMAN'S REVIEW

(NEW SERIES.)

No. CCXXI.—APRIL 16TH, 1894.

ART. I.—THE REPORT ON THE EMPLOYMENT OF WOMEN, BY THE LADY ASSISTANT COMMISSIONERS.
(*Continued.*)

MISS COLLET obtained the evidence of 125 persons in Birmingham, forty-eight of whom were employers; the rest were workwomen. Those workers who were interviewed in the factories or workshops are not, Miss Collet states, included in this list. The pen manufacturers, generally speaking, objected to allow their premises to be seen. Messrs. Gillott alone permitted their factory to be visited, but it was impossible to obtain a table of wages; as pen making is considered to be the largest manufacture in Birmingham, this was unfortunate. We must, I am afraid, draw very unfavourable deductions from these circumstances.

Button making.—Hours of work, ten a day, with an hour and a quarter for meals, so the actual period of work is eight hours and three-quarters. Wages generally about 10s. a week. *Umbrella makers* are worse paid, 8s. being about the average. *Bedstead lacquerers.* —The pay here is very good, ranging from 8s. to 18s., the average being about 15s. *Jewellery trade.—*

Average wages 10s. a week for fifty-two hours' work. *Cocoa factory.*—This factory is at Bourneville. Wages range from 8s. to 18s., generally from 12s. to 15s. Only single women are employed.

The manufactures at Birmingham are very numerous, and include buttons, picture frames, bedsteads, buckles, boots, furniture, screws, boxes, silver chains, jewel and spectacle cases, umbrellas, pens, saddlery, earthenware, cocoa, clothing, coffins, bolts, &c. Miss Collet could not discover that the women thus employed had any particular diseases.

The physician at the Hospital for Diseases of Women thought that "By far the greater number of women who had suffered from excessive overstrain were domestic servants." Sometimes women engaged in emery works are hurt by the wheel breaking. Sometimes "stampers" lose a finger, if careless. In bedstead lacquering the work is dirty, but not unwholesome. Enamelling iron is decidedly injurious to health on account of the lead dust inhaled, but though some girls suffer, others are not in the least affected. The example of the Scotch firm of lead manufacturers shows that with proper precautions the suffering from this cause may be almost, if not quite, prevented.

Miss Collet thinks the worst feature of the industrial life at Birmingham is the employment of married women in manufactories, whose husbands earn good wages, and are well able to support them. Infant mortality is high in Birmingham, and she thinks that the absence of the mothers from home may be the cause. This is quite possible, but it would clearly be cruel to forbid the employment of married women unless stringent measures were at the same time taken to compel husbands to provide for their wives and families. A single woman can go to the workhouse if in want; a married woman cannot unless her husband will go also. So a married woman is in a dreadful position if her husband spends his wages on himself; her only resource is to work. This is injurious to her infant, but if forbidden to work both she herself and the elder children would suffer from want, and ultimately the infant would too, for, if without food herself, she would be unable to nourish it.

The *pearl button* trade has declined; possibly the cause may be the action of the men's Trades Union, which passed a rule that "no female is allowed in the capacity of either piece-maker, turner, or bottomer. Any member working where a female does either, shall forfeit one pound, or should he continue to do so, be excluded." A rule was also passed against the use of machinery.

Employment of women at Walsall.—Saddlery and harness making is the chief employment, though there are other manufactures. The hardest work done by women in this trade is the "shaft tug." For tugs with seven stitches to the inch they are paid 5d., with eight stitches 6d., and so on up to 10d. A pair of 6d. shaft tugs can be made by a good worker in an hour and a-half. The girls wished more shaft tugs were wanted. The heavy government shaft tugs are not made at Walsall. Women stitch bridles and also saddles. They are paid by time. The usual earnings are from 8s. to 12s. a week, but some earn less and some more, according to the number of hours worked. Their hours are not long, and the girls often come late, and so are paid less. There is a good deal of tailoring done also at Walsall. In one factory 700 women and girls are employed, and there are several factories. They earn according to skill and hours of work, from less than 6s. up to 18s. a week; nearly half earn from 6s. to 10s. a week, and a fourth from 10s. to 15s.

Dudley.—The clothing trade is worse paid than at Walsall. More than half of the women employed earn under 8s. a week, the rest earn from 8s. to 18s.

Staffordshire Potteries.—Here the girls often work as attendants on the men, who do the skilled work; one girl waits on two men, and they each pay her 5s. a week. Girls also make cups with a machine called a "jolly." Girls also make plates by means of a steam "whirler." They rub the edges of the plates with tow, hence they are called "towers." Men are employed to print the patterns, women to transfer them. The women earn about 11s. 3d. a week as transferrers. The paintresses earn from 8s. to 15s. a week. Some of the work done is unwholesome. "Towing" is unwholesome, unless the dust is carried away by machinery. Ware cleaning is the most unhealthy work, as the dust is inhaled. Miss Collet gives the case of a girl of 15 who died in consequence. Glazing is also somewhat unhealthy, but as a general rule Miss Collet thought the women looked more healthy than the men. Three witnesses said the moral conduct of the women was good. There was some immorality in the neighbourhood, but it was amongst the servant girls, not the factory girls. Thirteen factories employ 1,279 women and girls; nearly one-third are married. The hours are from 7 a.m. to 6 p.m., with an hour and a-half for meals. Paintresses work shorter hours.

Liverpool.—There is much poverty at Liverpool, owing to the immigration of large numbers of Irish men and women. An instance is given of the harsh action of the Factory and Workshop Act. Cotton, when drying, must be watched at night, lest it should catch fire, also the fires must be kept up, and (probably) the cotton turned at intervals. It is very easy work; one woman must keep awake, but the others employed can sleep until their services are required. The merchants prefer to employ women, but are fined for doing it, so this light, easy and healthy occupation is lost to women.

Women are employed at *sack making* and *paper sorting*, and are very poorly paid; wages vary from 4s. to 10s. a week, but few get as much as 10s. *Rope making* is a better trade, wages from 6s. to 12s., and the work is healthy and clean.

One of the largest industries is the *tobacco and cigar* trade. The wages vary in a remarkable manner—some earn less than 6s. a week, others more than 21s., according to skill. The hours of work are fifty a week, exclusive of meal times.

Book folding and book sewing employ a large number of women at poor wages, 1s. 8d. a day for working fifty-four hours a week, and a three years' apprenticeship. This is remarkable, because generally where there is an apprenticeship the wages are good. Box making is better paid.

There is an admirable *jam factory* at Aintree. To obviate the necessity of having heavy trays carried by the girls, the floors are interlaced with tram lines, along which small trucks are rolled to and fro.

Tailoring work seems to be better paid at Liverpool than is usual. A coat maker said she earned 4s. 6d. a day, working from 9 till 7, and on Saturdays from 9 till 4. Formerly they had worked two hours a day more, but by the action of the Women's Trade Union, the hours had been shortened. Beginners earned 2s. 6d. a week, and wages went up to 18s. or more. A dull girl would earn 10s. or 12s., a " really smart " girl 18s. or 20s. Another coat maker said she was paid 3s. 6d. a day. This witness said that the hours at her factory had also been shortened, in consequence of the Women's Union.

Extract from Miss Collet's Report :—

" The president and secretary of the Liverpool Tailoresses' and Coatmakers' Union gave the following account of its formation and progress. It was formed in the summer of 1890 ; the Jewish tailors had formed a society and gained a reduction of hours. The woman coat makers thought that ' What a foreigner could do a woman could.' They therefore prepared slips of paper and went round to the workshops and persuaded 260 women coat makers to sign their names and addresses in favour of a Trade Union and a reduction of hours. The Trades' Council assisted them, and they called a meeting at the Oddfellows Hall, and formed themselves into a union and elected a president, secretary and committee. Then they sent a memorial to the Middlemen's Society, asking for a two hours' reduction. No notice was taken of their request. They therefore blocked two shops, and sent a letter to say that the reduction of hours must be given without any reduction of wages and without adopting the piece-work system. They had so far no funds, but they had agreed to support those who were out. The middlemen held a meeting and decided to lock them out, thinking that without funds they would be frightened. The Trades' Council had, however, promised them support, and the girls kept together, and patrolled the streets to show what respectable-looking people they were, as statements to the contrary had been made. The middlemen still held out, but one firm was known to want to make the concession ; the girls went to this employer, and told him that if he would pay the foreman a weekly wage he could employ them. He dismissed his middleman, but could not get a Liverpool man in his place. The Manchester Tailors' and Pressers' Society, however, sent down a foreman, and about thirty women went into this shop. In another fortnight the 'middleman' at another large firm was persuaded to make the concession, and then all the rest gave in. In one case afterwards an outdoor shop wanted to increase the hours ; the Union took out the women and paid them 20s. a week for three weeks, and places were found for them elsewhere."

This account is very pleasant reading, as it shows that the men's Trades Union behaved kindly to the women and assisted them.

A trouser maker said she earned about 2s. 6d. a day. A trouser machinist said she had earned from 20s. to 24s. a week at a factory, but now worked at home, which she preferred. Makers of jackets, vests and shirts are less well paid, and earn from 1½d. an hour to 3d. This gives for ten hours' work from 1s. 3d. to 2s. 6d. a day.

Manchester.—This city appears to be specially unsanitary. It is, however, provided with a "Ladies' Health Society" which is very diligent in visiting the poorer districts, and endeavours to enforce sanitary rules, so perhaps it will improve. The wages are not so good as in Liverpool. In needlework the makers of *aprons and pinafores* are the best paid; 80 per cent. of these earn from 10s. to 18s. a week, the other 20 per cent. earn less. *Mantle makers* are less well paid, the greater proportion of better class mantles being supplied from Germany. *Corset making, ready made tailoring* and *shirtmaking* are badly paid. *Machinists* earn generally from 8s. to 18s. a week, a few earn less. Skilled *umbrella machinists* earn from 10s. to 18s., ordinary umbrella makers are fairly paid. The price paid is about 1s. a dozen. One witness said it would take a quick woman to make two dozen a day;

another witness said she could finish a dozen in three hours, but preferred working at 13s. weekly wages. Miss Collet is of opinion that the shirtmakers are the worst paid class; 94 per cent. earn only from 8s. to 12s. a week in factories, and she thinks that those who work at home are worse off, as they would probably have to hire machines, and certainly to buy cotton. The enquiry of the the Lady Commissioner apparently did not include persons engaged in cotton factories, as Miss Collet makes no mention of them at Manchester.

JESSIE BOUCHERETT.

(*To be continued.*)

ART. II.—THE BRITISH WORKWOMAN IN DANGER.

THE British workwoman of to-day is in serious danger, and the misfortune is that she is most in danger from those who are most anxious to serve her.

When educated women first began to try to qualify themselves to follow professional work, they were continually confronted with the assurance that a woman's place is at home, and she ought not to seek work outside. But now when industrial workers wish to carry on their industries at home, they are ordered off by their supposed friends to the factory, and told that if they do their work at home they beat down wages, encourage sweating, and destroy domestic comfort, and the only way to avoid these evils is to work away from their homes in factories. Thus Mrs. Sidney Webb, in an address to the Women's Liberal Association in Oxford in February, told her audience (we quote from the *Queen*) that she held the real remedy to the evils of the sweating system to "be an extension of the Factory

Acts to small work-shops and to home work by including every small shop or home where his work is taken in the factory of the wholesale trader; the trader should be compelled to keep a register of these places and names, and the inspector would visit them, and where he found unsatisfactory conditions would hold the trader, not the workers, responsible." Mrs. Webb admitted that this system would, by degrees, drive home work out of the field, and that at once the "poor widow" who cannot leave her home would appear on the scene, but she hoped this argument would be pushed aside again as it had been before.

Some one else than the poor widow appeals to the thoughts of this present writer, and that is the wife and mother, who in the intervals of home work can earn a little which gives her that money power without which no one in our complex civilisation can have the independent standing which is essential to human dignity. This is a lesson the average man generally, and the average working man not less than others, is slow to learn in regard to women, however quick to learn it in regard to himself, and until men do learn it, their wives will want—and will rightly want—to earn something for themselves. Mrs. Webb went on to say she wished to abolish married women's work, except for their own families, because it has a tendency to pull down either the husband's industry or his wages, and it was her work to raise the standard of comfort and of intelligent interests in the home.

It is mockery to talk of raising the standard of comfort in the home, by lowering the status of the women who make the home. Yet every new restriction forced by law upon women lowers their status.

The law would reduce them to a level with children. Mrs. Sidney Webb would abolish home work.

Mr. John Burns would, in addition, obstruct outside work; speaking at a meeting in Bristol in September last, he said (we quote from the *Western Daily Press* of September 14th), "The best way to provide work for the workless was to reduce the hours of women and girls, who ought to be at home."

And all the while that economists are trying to crush

out work, Nature is calling on women to fulfil the duty of every human soul, and uphold their own independent individuality. The self-respect of every woman requires of her that if she has not independence by inheritance, or by the due respect of a husband who values her work at home at its worth, then she must acquire for herself. It is a law of human nature which will assert itself despite all modern economic theories.

At a conference in Glasgow, of which a report will be found elsewhere, Dr. William Smart laid it down that women should be paid by the value of their product, not by the standard of their wants, and that the idea of a "supplementary" wage must be got rid of.

But how? We repeat it again, not by lowering the status of women, not by doing as Professor Caird so earnestly advocated in the speech in which, following Dr. Smart, he gave his blessing to the efforts to diminish the freedom of women. That is only another way of teaching men to undervalue women's labour, another way of lowering yet further the scant respect working men too often show to their wives, quite unconsciously it may often be. We know that there are many exceptions amongst the first ranks of English artisans who are a law unto themselves. But for those for whom the law creates the standard the only remedy is—as a wife-beater said to the judge who condemned him for his ill treatment of his wife, "Make her my equal and I'll treat her as such."

When a deputation of the Trades Union Congress waited on the Home Secretary, Mr. Asquith, on February 14, in reference to the Factories and Workshops Acts, Mr. Asquith is reported to have said that he "was carefully considering whether it would be expedient to bring laundries within the scope of that Act."

Mr. Secretary Asquith is opposed to giving women the Parliamentary vote which would raise the respect of working men for the women who live alongside of them, now stamped by law as unworthy of the elementary right of citizenship. What cruel kindness to increase the present inequality of their position by the enactment of fresh restrictions on their right to work!

No one who carefully studies the report on laundries prepared after searching enquiry by the three ladies commissioned by the Women's Industrial Defence Committee* to enquire into the condition of laundries in London, can doubt that to include laundries under the Factory Acts will shut out thousands of women from a home industry which now gives them an honest livelihood. The work will be driven into steam laundries, and already where there are steam laundries the women are being forced out by the intrusion of men and boys into this hitherto essentially women's industry.

With curious irony, while the Home Secretary is being urged to gradually stifle this branch of women's work, the County Councils are everywhere seeking to have it taught to women on improved principles as a skilled industry. Which will prevail—the theoretical economist or the practical teacher?

But it is not industrial workers only who are threatened with the interference of a legislature so pressed with would-be reforms that it can hardly see the wood for the trees.

This is an age of combination as well as of competition. When a profession, like the journalists, for instance, form themselves into an institute in order to keep up a high standard for their profession, and to secure the observance of the needful etiquettes of the profession, it is a very different matter to the enactment of a distinct code of regulations for women by force of law, as is proposed in the Midwives Registration Bill. The correspondence which has appeared in these columns sufficiently shows there can be a right and a wrong way of bringing about the desired registration, a way which may give the woman midwife responsible recognised place in her profession, or lower her to a mere tool for the doctor. The Bill has not so far been introduced this session, but if when it comes forward it is still in the same form as that introduced in 1891, the latter result is the more probable of the two. That Bill proposes that the General

---

* To be obtained at the office of the Employment of Women, 22, Berners Street, W.

Council of Medical Education and Registration of the United Kingdom shall frame rules, to be approved by the Privy Council, regulating the conditions of admission to examination and the general standard to be attained by women as midwives, and that the County Council shall provide for the carrying out of the examinations and the registration of the women. The Bill further proposes " that no woman shall have any right to claim to be examined until after she has first produced a certificate from a registered medical practitioner practising in the district in which she is herself resident, that she is of good conduct and in good health."

That any one adult human being's claim should thus be at the option of any other one human being seems hardly consistent with the liberty of the subject. Nor is the closing paragraph of the report issued in August last by the Select Committee appointed to consider the question of compulsory registration of midwives, of a character to reassure those who fear that the proposed registration may be only a form of " abolition of midwives." That paragraph runs as follows (the italics are ours) :—

" In conclusion, your Committee desire to refer to the apprehension expressed by certain witnesses belonging to the medical profession, lest their interests might be injuriously affected by an improvement in the status of midwives. The great preponderance, however, of medical and other evidence, having regard to both the authority and number of witnesses, was to a contrary effect. Your Committee, therefore, whilst giving due consideration to the expression of such fears, believe that the suggested injury is not likely to prove serious, and they are *of opinion that medical men will not only be relieved of much irksome and ill-paid work*, but also that improved knowledge on the part of midwives will induce them to avail themselves more frequently and at an earlier stage than at present of skilled medical assistance in time of emergency and danger. On this point your Committee had full and substantial evidence."

Industrial or professional, the British workwoman

has reason to watch with serious alarm the plans of her would-be protectors, lest they seek to remedy the ills of unequal wages and unequal training by making her, not the equal before the law of the men by whose side she has to labour, but by making her more their unequal before the law than she is already.

ART. III.—LUCY STONE.

THE name of Lucy Stone is probably not so familiar on this side of the Atlantic as in America; yet among all the courageous and steadfast pioneers in the woman's cause, whose life and labours have made possible such reforms as we enjoy to-day, or such progress as we hope to make in the future, hers is deserving of special remembrance as one of the most truly brave and persevering. Her life is almost one unbroken record, at least in its earliest portions, of struggle against nearly every disadvantage it is possible to name; poverty, which in itself, seems as if it should have been prohibitive of all independent or non-remunerative work; prejudice, which it is not easy for us to imagine at the present day, and not seldom even personal risk. Few even of the early abolitionists—of whom she was also one—had a harder experience, or a harder battle to fight in support of the principles they felt it their duty to inculcate. It is, however, remarkable that with all this fearless courage, and perfect carelessness as to what personal consequences she incurred, she never allowed herself to be carried into any course of action doubtful, or ill-judged, as is too often the case with many possessing very likely an equal share of courage and principle, but less tact and discretion, alike in serious matters and in trivial ones.

Lucy Stone was born on August 13th, 1818, near

West Brookfield, Massachusetts, the youngest but one of a family of nine. Her father was a New England farmer, well-to-do in the world, and respected by his neighbours, but something of a domestic tyrant, maintaining, both in theory and practice, the alleged inferiority of women to men and the subordination of the wife to the husband. The sight of the tyranny endured by her mother and other married women early and deeply impressed the thoughtful little girl, who made up her mind quickly that the laws which permitted this ought to be changed. Coming across texts in the Bible appearing to justify this tyranny she at first wanted to die; then she determined that when she was grown up she would go to college, learn Greek and Hebrew, and see for herself whether such texts were correctly translated. She carried out this resolution without any help; her father, who had already assisted his son through college, only wanted to know if she was crazy, when she wished to go also. She had not the resource open to clever girls of our own day, in being able to win scholarships or exhibitions, but could only earn the money to buy books by gathering and selling wild fruits, and by teaching district schools. In this she was eminently successful, being once engaged to teach a "winter school," which had been broken up by the older boys throwing the master out of the window into a snow-drift. She, however, was able to manage this difficult school perfectly, and even to ensure devoted helpers in the boys who had previously been most unruly; but all the time she received only a small part of the same salary paid to her incompetent predecessor. Indeed, with the low wages received by women teachers, it took her some years, till she was twenty-five, even to earn enough to pay her fare to Oberlin, then the only college which admitted women students. She was then obliged to travel in the cheapest way, and when crossing Lake Erie, not being able to afford a cabin, to sleep on deck among horses and piles of grain. Most of the students at Oberlin were poor; but she was poorer than any others. She could not even afford to purchase board at the moderate rate of a dollar a week, but boarded herself at less than half a dollar, cooking her own food in her room, and earning most of her slender funds by teaching in the preparatory department, and doing housework in the Ladies' Boarding Hall at three cents an hour. During all the four years of her course she never once went home, and had only one new dress, that being a common print. She thoroughly succeeded, however, in the object for which she came, and also found time to engage in work among the fugitive slaves with which Oberlin, a strong abolitionist centre, was crowded. She was requested to take charge of a school for teaching the coloured people to read. Some of the men, only lately slaves, thought it beneath them to be taught by a woman; but she soon acquired the greatest influence over them. Her first public speaking was while still a student at Oberlin, having been invited to take part in a meeting got up by the coloured people to celebrate the anniversary of West Indian Emancipation. The next day, however, she found herself summoned before the Ladies' Board to answer for what they considered forward and unwomanly behaviour in venturing to get up on a platform, and speak in the presence of men in public, notwithstanding that these men were many of them the college professors, whom she was in the habit of meeting every day in the class-rooms! She was, however, at the end of her course appointed, as one of the most successful students, to write the essay to be read at Commencement; but only on the understanding that one of the professors should read it for her, as it was not proper for a woman to read her own essay in public. She therefore decided not to write it, as a kind of protest. Instances of this nature seem to remove us to an incredible moral distance from the forties, and we feel tempted to ask ourselves if it is possible that such dense prejudice could possibly have belonged to a time not more remote from our own.

After graduating in 1847, Lucy Stone immediately entered upon her career as a Women's Rights and Anti-Slavery Lecturer. It is a matter of history how early and inseparably these two stirring questions became interwoven with one another in America, so that very early in the Anti-Slavery struggle it appears practically identified with that for women's equal position. Whether this arose from the part played by such women as Lucretia Mott, Abby Kelly, the Sisters Grimke, and others, or from the fact that those who were constantly engaged in contending against one form of injustice could hardly fail to be awake to oppression in other forms, the pre-eminent example of William Lloyd Garrison became one generally followed by his friends, most of whom appeared in favour of the Women's Movement as a logical consequence of their sympathy with the wrongs of the slave. Lucy Stone, however, seems to have been a worker for women before she was an abolitionist. She was engaged as a regular lecturer by the Anti-Slavery Society, and soon became one of their most effective speakers; but she sometimes made the woman question so much more prominent than the slavery one in her speeches, that her friend Samuel May once remonstrated with her for this. She answered, "I cannot help it; I was a woman before I was an abolitionist." She wished to resign her position as Anti-Slavery lecturer in order to devote herself solely to her own specialty; but as she was one of their best speakers the Abolition Society refused to give her up, and it was finally arranged that she should speak for them alone on Saturdays and Sundays, and on the Woman Question during the rest of the week, on her own responsibility. In so doing she had a terribly uphill task, having no co-operation, no organisation to assist her, reduced even to the necessity of putting up her own posters in the streets with a parcel of tacks and a stone picked from the ground for a hammer. In doing this, she was often followed and annoyed terribly, and all sorts of devices were sometimes used against her while lecturing. On one occasion a pane of glass was broken in a window behind the speaker's stand, and she was suddenly deluged with ice-cold water from a hose, in the depth of winter. A certain minister, being one day asked to give notice of one of her lectures, did so in these terms: "I am asked to say that a hen will attempt to crow like a cock in the town hall at five to-morrow. Those who like such music will attend." She perseveringly, however, won her way by the power of quiet courage, simple eloquence, and unassuming ways, which surprised those whose previous idea of the woman's rights' woman was the mythical tall, angular, harsh-featured virago, who to this day appears to survive occasionally in the tradition of opponents. The personal character of Lucy Stone and her undaunted courage secured her in time its due respect; and it is recorded that as an abolitionist lecturer she was often listened to when other speakers were howled down. One notable instance of her courage and powers of quiet persuasion must be told in full. At an open-air Anti-Slavery meeting at Cape Cod a crowd collected, so evidently meaning mischief, that all the speakers gradually felt obliged to retire, excepting only Lucy Stone and Stephen Foster. She advised him to run; he replied, "But who will take care of you?" At this moment the mob made a rush for the platform, and a big man sprang upon it, brandishing a club. She turned and said quietly, "This gentleman will take care of me." Her fearless confidence so won upon the man, that he declared he would, and taking her under one arm, and swinging his club in the other, led her out through the crowd, who were roughly treating Mr. Foster and such of the other speakers as they had been able to lay hold of. She prevailed on her impromptu protector to stand by, while she mounted a stump, and addressed the crowd, moving them so by her speech that they not only refrained from further mischief, but took up a collection to pay for Mr. Foster's coat, which had been torn in pieces during the struggle.

In 1855 she was married to Henry B. Blackwell, the brother of Dr. Elizabeth and Dr. Emily Blackwell, a strong sympathiser with all her opinions, and ever since her faithful friend and co-worker. On their marriage, the two issued a joint manifesto, protesting against the then state of the law, investing the husband with the entire custody of the wife's person, the exclusive possession of her property, and the sole right to the control and guardianship of their children;

"investing him with legal powers which no honourable man would exercise, and no man should possess." The couple had some trouble in finding a minister who would consent to marry them, without using the formula requiring the bride to obey her husband. Such a minister was at last found in the person of the Rev. T. W. Higginson, of Worcester, Mass., since better known as Colonel Higginson, of the 1st South Carolina Coloured Volunteers. As part of the same protest against unjust laws, merging the identity of the wife in that of the husband, Mrs. Stone decided, with Mr. Blackwell's full concurrence, to be known after marriage, as before, by her maiden name. This step was, of course, widely criticised and discussed at the time; but did much to hasten the alteration of the laws of Massachusetts in regard to wives. We find it mentioned that on this subject Lucy Stone had the opinion of eminent lawyers, who agreed in telling her that there was no law requiring her to take her husband's name; it was simply a matter of custom. She, nevertheless, was in later years, refused the right of School Suffrage, because she would not consent to be registered as "Mrs. Blackwell."

The married life of the couple, under such happy circumstances, was one continued course of active work and effort towards securing equal rights, which it would be impossible to even attempt to record in detail; lecturing, writing, and agitating in behalf of improvements and amendments in the laws for women. A few years after being married, Mrs. Stone allowed her goods to be seized and sold for taxes, writing a protest against taxation without representation, with her infant on her lap. In 1866 she helped in organising the American Equal Rights Association, formed to work for such rights both for negroes and for women. In 1869 she arranged the American Women's Suffrage Association, in conjunction with Garrison, Colonel Higginson, Mrs. Livermore, and others. The *Woman's Journal* was started in Boston, in 1870, chiefly by her efforts. Of this, she and her husband, latterly also their daughter, Alice Stone Blackwell, have always been the associate editors.

Her death took place, after a short illness, on the 18th of October last. Throughout old age she had retained undiminished, the pure and lofty enthusiasm for the cause, which had distinguished her through life, and continued engaged in active work almost to the last. When her friends regretted that she should die without beholding the final triumph of the cause to which she had devoted her life-long energies, she replied that supposing she did not hear of it in the life beyond, it could only be because she would be busy with even better work. Her last words were: " Make the world better." And from the general tone of loving regret expressed by all who knew her personally, or in work, we feel that the world has been as fully blest in the personal influence of the woman herself, as in her actual labours. Even her most trivial actions exhibited a high tone of steadfast principle and wise judgment; and this was pre-eminently the case with such instances as in a woman of less well-balanced mind might have seemed needless, or even foolish, insistance on trifles. We may fitly borrow, in reviewing the results of incalculable value resulting from her action to all subsequent women workers in whatever branch, that epitaph placed in Westminster Abbey, over one of the greatest of our Indian statesmen : " Her works do follow her."

M. A. BIGGS.

Art. IV.—MARIA DERAISMES AND THE WOMAN'S MOVEMENT IN FRANCE.

FOR many years Maria Deraismes was looked upon as the sole and undisputed head of the Woman's movement in France. In 1879 she succeeded Mons. Léon Richer as President of "La Société pour l'Amélioration du Sort de la Femme," which in 1881 amalgamated with " La Société pour la Revendication des Droits de la Femme." She directed the societies combined until the day of her death, and until quite recently no other properly organised group for the defence of women's interests existed here.

As early as 1866 Mlle. Deraismes' name appeared, together with about forty others, in an appeal claiming civil rights for women, but it was not until 1870 that "La Société pour la Revendication" was organised. One of the first acts of the young society was the decision that the funds raised should be devoted to the establishment of a free school for girls, in which no religious teaching of any kind should be given.

This repelled the mass of French women and gave an excellent pretext for opposition; for, not without reason, this attitude was considered as an indication of what would be the future religious and political tendency of the woman's movement in France. The approbation of freethinkers and the support of extreme republicans was not sufficient to ensure success under Imperial Government, nor, indeed, since, for the matter of that.

Maria Deraismes was born at Paris in 1829, being sixty-five years old at the time of her death. Her parents were well-to-do middle-class people. Her father seems to have been a bright intelligent man, and to have taken great interest in the political events of his time, and they were numerous and manifold. Maria Deraismes' childhood and girlhood were passed in the Rue St Denis, in a quaint old house, long since pulled down and replaced by a modern building, which still, however, belongs to the family. The scenes she witnessed there made a deep impression upon her, and it is probable that her political fervour in after life was in great measure due to what she then saw and heard.

All who were intimate with Maria Deraismes remember her vivid descriptions of the insurrectionary period between 1835 and 1848. The excitement and emotion were felt throughout France, but Paris did most of the fighting, and the Rue St Denis was in the heart of the fray. Its inhabitants were kept in a perpetual tremor. Sometimes a barricade would be thrown up close to the Deraismes' house, and men, women and children killed or wounded within sight.

Here and there snatches of news would come—as news
flies in Paris no one knows how—that the Tuileries
were ransacked, the prisons opened, and frightful
disorders committed. Then came the flight of the
King, Louis-Philippe, and the proclamation of the
Republic.

In their joy at its advent many of the partisans of
the new regime were somewhat forgetful of the liberty
of those who, while perhaps quite as sincere republicans, were less demonstrative in their enthusiasm. A
favorite mode of celebrating the Republic was the
planting of a tree (*arbre de la liberté*). This ceremony,
in which all good citizens were expected to participate,
was performed with as much pomp as circumstances
allowed ; the local authorities presiding, a priest
being in attendance to bestow a blessing on the young
sapling, a band of music meantime playing the Mar-
seillaise, or other popular patriotic airs. If the ceremony took place at a certain distance, it often happened
—for the days are short in February—that it was
quite dark before the procession returned to its starting point, where it dispersed. On its return the company was much more numerous and noisy than when
it set out, and these boisterous crowds were the terror
of the quiet members of the community. Many a
peaceful evening meal in the Deraismes' household
was disturbed by the cry, " *Des lam-pi-ons ! des lam-
pi-ons !* getting louder and shriller as the crowd ap-
proached, which meant that every house must be
illuminated as they passed, or woe to those who did
not put " lampions " in their windows.

Maria did not share the irritation of her parents at
this too frequent interruption of their dinner, but
would be the first to seize whatever lights were in the
room, and delighted, put them well in sight of the
crowd outside on the window sill. She loved and
admired the people of Paris, and to the day of her
death she remained unflinchingly true to them and to
the Republic.

Maria Deraismes' early education was much that of
other girls in her station of life at that period ; neither
better nor worse than that of Englishwomen of the

same time; a little music, a little drawing, a little history, a little geography, indeed, but a *little* of everything (which, by the way, cannot after all have been such a very bad way of educating girls, for if it did not make geniuses, made " all round " sort of women, and gave them no pretext for being vain of their learning.) But Maria's tastes were literary and artistic, and she was an omnivorous reader. Her school days ended, she took lessons from celebrated teachers in drawing and painting, as well as in music and elocution. Some of her family and personal friends sat to her for their portraits, and she was a fair musician. She also wrote several short plays, and published a volume called " Le Théâtre chez soi." She was a clever journalist and a brilliant controvertist, but it was as a public lecturer that she was the most justly appreciated, for she had remarkable talent as an orator. The first time she spoke in public was in 1866, at the Salle des Conférences, Boulevard des Capucines, Paris, and the subject she chose was " L'Influence du Roman." Curiously enough she was induced to speak in public in order to refute an attack made by Barbey d'Aurevilly on women authors. Her success was immense, and it coincided with, and gave weight to, her support of the nascent woman's movement. From then till the end of the Empire Mlle. Deraismes was one of the regular and most popular lecturers of the Société des Conférences. During the Franco-German War she began a political campaign in Brittany, at St. Malo, in favour of the Republic, but the fatigue, under the cruel circumstances of her country's defeat, proved too much for her. Her health, always delicate, broke down, and she did not again speak in public till four years later. During those years of compulsory silence Maria Deraismes was not idle. Her house had become a political centre and the recognised headquarters of free-thought, and when she again appeared in public her lectures had therefore a significance beyond the subject treated, notwithstanding that those she generally chose were women's rights, children's rights, and being a member of the Antivivisection Society—the rights of animals.

In 1881 she canvassed most actively in the department of Seine and Oise in favour of the Radical deputies, and was successful in securing the election of the nine candidates she patronised. She had come to be looked upon as a political power, and this power she was induced to utilise in favour of women, and she was elected President of the Sociétés "pour l'amélioration du sort de la Femme," and that of "la Revendication de ses Droits" combined.

The Congress held in 1878 had demonstrated, if not the open hostility, at least the indifference of the majority of Frenchwomen to the question of women's rights. In order, therefore, to attract attention to, and arouse some interest in the subject, Maria Deraismes addressed a letter to women engaged in commerce, encouraging them to join their claims to those of the small shopkeepers and tradesmen who were at that time agitating to obtain the right of vote at the elections of the Judges of the Tribunal de Commerce.

Seventeen thousand copies of this letter were sent by post to as many women merchants, shopkeepers, and tradeswomen, but to this direct appeal the Committee received only two replies, one of which was slightly abusive. This was disappointing and embarrassing, so after deliberation it was decided not to let the state of the case be too widely known, but, inasmuch as a few Deputies and Senators were in favour of the movement, to proceed boldly and not be dismayed by present difficulties. So the work was undertaken, and the battle has been fought with hardly any help from those who were to be benefited by it.

A few days before her death Maria Deraismes had the satisfaction of knowing that success had crowned her long and patient efforts. The Bill admitting women engaged in commerce to vote at the elections of Judges of the Tribunal de Commerce passed the Senate* and became law just eleven years after the first reading in the Chambre des Députés, in 1883.

---

* The Bill had not really passed when Mlle. Deraismes was assured of its success. During the discussion in the Senate on January 19, its grammatical accuracy was called in question, and

Meanwhile a more friendly feeling was gradually growing up, chiefly among Protestants, doubtless inspired by accounts of what women were accomplishing in other countries, and fostered by the influence of women of talent like Madame Emilie de Morsier. This feeling was latent, and only somewhat attenuated the hitherto open opposition; still, while it did little to diminish the hostile attitude towards the recognised leaders in the woman's movement, it at least admitted the justice of some of their demands.

The effects of this feeling were visible when—long before the opening of the Paris Exhibition—plans began to be laid for an International Women's Congress, to be held in 1889. It was then proposed to Mlle. Deraismes that a vast women's congress should be organised, of which her special work should form a section—but only a section—and of which some celebrated person, say Monsieur Jules Simon, should be requested to become the President. Monsieur J. Simon's name was proposed as he was well known to be favourable to women, and his acceptance was thought to be likely to ensure recognition from Government and an official position for women in the exhibition, and this afterwards proved to be right. But Mlle. Deraismes would in no wise consent to this proposition. Her sense of the importance of her position as a freethinker—which to her mind made part of her republicanism—prevented her from seeing the advantages of this arrangement.

The result was that the Congress presided over by Monsieur Jules Simon, composed almost exclusively

---

it was returned to the Chambre des Deputies. Mr. J. Macé, Senator, was alive to the risk incurred by this measure when he wrote me " Who knows when and in what form the law will come back to us!" It was, however, returned rapidly, and the new wording not only satisfied the grammatical fastidiousness of the Senators, but was congenial to the general feeling, for the law stipulates the exclusion of women from being elected members of a Tribunal de Commerce, whereas hitherto this was merely understood from the tenour of other laws. So there is a new difficulty to be overcome when next the matter is brought before the French Chambers.

of charitable institutions, became the official Women's Congress ("Œuvres et Institutions Féminines"), while the Congress under the direction of Maria Deraismes represented the political side of women's questions, and held its meetings at the rooms of the French Geographical Society. The two Congresses were active and energetic, and did good work. Women came to know each other better, and with better knowledge came better feeling. Through the constant agitation of the woman's question during the summer of 1889 many women came to realize the vital importance of the work, and although no open reconciliation has taken place, severals guilds and associations for the amendment of laws concerning women have been founded outside Maria Deraismes' society, and are successfully awakening public opinion.

Unhappily, this new element received neither welcome nor approbation from Maria Deraismes, who, with most of her collaborators, looked upon this innovation as disloyalty to herself. For twenty years Maria Deraismes' supremacy had been undisputed, and it was painful to her to see what seemed to be the deviation of the women's movement.

Associations of no special political tendency, simply groups of men and women united on one point, viz., the amendment of the laws concerning women, and with perhaps no other point of contact; Catholics using their influence and their friends, Protestants theirs, as well as freethinkers to help women of all classes and denominations to obtain justice where it is denied them—this mode of work appeared to Maria Deraismes like so much energy diverted from what she considered the only true course of action, and likely, too, to be detrimental to the Republic itself.

She felt so strongly on this head that she made an effort to concentrate her forces and regain the position she had held so long. In 1882, in recognition of the services she had rendered in the political campaign of 1881, Maria Deraismes had been made a Freemason by the lodge at Le Pecq, Seine and Oise; she decided, therefore, in 1893, to inaugurate a Women's Lodge; but, saving her immediate surroundings, very few women have joined. The lodge is not recognised by the majority of Freemasons, and will doubtless not long survive its founder. It possesses no funds save the meagre subscriptions of its members, none of whom are wealthy. Maria Deraismes made no provision in its favour in her will, as she might have done if she had really considered Freemasonry likely to be a useful adjunct to the woman's movement in France.

JEANNE E. SCHMAHL.

THE WINTER IS PAST.

SPRING lights the earth's green altar!
   The birds their anthems sing,
In glad full-throated psalter,
   "The Spring! the Spring! the Spring!'
We, too, may join the chorus,
   With glad hearts, too, may sing,
"The future lies before us,
   And lo! it is the Spring!"

Look up! where flights of swallows
   Wheel circling through the air,
We know that Summer follows
   With beauty everywhere;
The damp, chill woods are dreamy,
   With violets' perfume;
Grey orchards, gnarled and seamy,
   Are white with promise bloom.

Look round! where green blades thickly
   Are covering every sod,
Where hedgerows bare and prickly
   Burst forth like Aaron's rod.
Soon comes the scent of clover!
   Though East winds yet may blight,
The Winter's past and over!
   Day climbs the stairs of night.

WARNER SNOAD.

WOMEN'S SUFFRAGE.
NOTES OF THE QUARTER.

The expectation that the Registration Bill will be one of the foremost measures introduced by the Government in the Session of 1894, has given the Parliamentary friends of the movement hopes of being able to introduce a motion for Women's Suffrage as an amendment to that measure.

The difficulty of securing time in Parliament for the passage of any measure introduced by a private member has so enormously increased of late years, that the opportunity of raising the question on a Government measure has become of the utmost value, and the friends of the movement should watch the progress of the Registration Bill, so that when the opportunity arrives they may urge their members to give their support to such amendments as our Parliamentary friends decide to bring forward.

Under these circumstances much activity has been shown by various of the Women's Liberal Associations, and resolutions urging on the Government that women should be admitted to the register on the Registration Bill have been passed at several representative meetings, as will be seen by the reports given below.

The Central Committee of the National Society for Women's Suffrage have forwarded a request to Viscount Wolmer, M.P., that he will repeat the notice for an instruction which he gave last year on the Registration Bill going into Committee.

Since the last issue of this Review a little monthly paper entitled *Women's Suffrage News*, has appeared. The first number was issued on January 25, and the enterprising editor, who writes under the *nom de plume* of A. B. Louis, proposes to bring it out regularly on the 25th of the month, and to render it a means of communication amongst the workers in a common cause. Communications for the editor should be sent to the care of Messrs. Bale, 106, Great Titchfield Street, W.

The price is one halfpenny. We would heartily commend this bright little publication to all who are taking active interest in the Women's Suffrage work.

The admirable speech by the Ven. J. M. Wilson, M.A., Archdeacon of Manchester, at the annual meeting of the Manchester Women's Suffrage Society, has been reprinted in pamphlet form, and can be obtained of the Secretary of the Manchester Committee, Miss Roper, B.A., at the office, Queen's Chambers, John Dalton Street, Manchester.

A work will shortly be published by Mrs. Carmichael Stopes on "British Free-women and the History of their Privileges." It is the result of much careful research amongst original sources, both printed and MS., and will present a number of historical facts, little known or wholly forgotten, yet having very important bearings on the present status of women.

The book is likely to prove most valuable to all students and workers in the women's movement.

Work for the Women's Suffrage Appeal has extended steadily, as the list of meetings in the past three months will show. Signatures should all be sent in without delay to the Appeal office, 47, Victoria Street, or to the Women's Suffrage offices, at 29, Parliament Street, S.W., and 10, Great College Street, Westminster.

RESOLUTIONS AT MEETINGS OF LIBERAL ASSOCIATIONS.

At the annual council meetings of the Southern and South Western Counties Union of Women's Liberal Associations, held in the Victoria Rooms, Clifton, on March 15, Mr. W. Dove Willcox moved: "That this meeting is of opinion that the new Registration Bill affords an opportunity that should not be lost to do away with the anomaly by which many ratepaying citizens, although duly qualified, are excluded from registration because they are women." This was seconded by Mr. J. Pembery, supported by Miss Conybeare. Miss Latimer moved as an addition to the resolution that a memorial embodying its terms be sent to Mr. Shaw-Lefevre, with a request that women be included in the new Registration Act. The resolution and rider were then adopted.

On March 19, at a special Council Meeting of the London Liberal and Radical Union, held at the National Liberal Club, Mrs. Maitland moved : "That this meeting of the Council of the London Liberal and Radical Union urges the government to include the enfranchisement of duly qualified women, when they bring in their measure of Registration Reform." This was seconded by Mr. Leech (Marylebone East), supported by Mrs. Sheldon Amos. A motion to adjourn the debate having been rejected by 75 votes against 45, Mrs. Maitland's resolution was adopted by 88 votes against 30.

At the Annual Meeting of the Welsh Union of Women's Liberal Associations, held at the Town Hall, Rhyl, March 14, a resolution in support of Women's Suffrage was passed, on the motion of Mrs. Viriamu Jones, seconded by Mrs. D. A. Thomas, and supported by Mr. McLaren, M.P., and Mrs. E. Lloyd Jones.

The Council of the Scottish Women's Liberal Federation held their Annual Meeting on March 20 in the Association Rooms, George Square, Glasgow, Mrs. Lindsay presiding, when amongst numerous resolutions adopted was the following, moved by Miss Helen Waddell and seconded by Miss Burton :—"That this Council expresses satisfaction that the Government proposes to introduce a measure of registration reform, and trusts that this opportunity will be taken for dealing with the question of the Parliamentary enfranchisement of women."

A circular has been addressed by Miss Priestman, president of the West Bristol W.L.A. to Women's Liberal Associations, urging them to memorialise the Government in favour of introducing provisions in the Registration Bill to secure to women the right of voting on equal terms with men.

AUSTRALIA.

New South Wales.—At the January meeting of the Primitive Methodist Conference in New South Wales a resolution in favour of full Women's Suffrage was passed unanimously.

Queensland.—The Australian *Christian World* of February 8, states that steps are being taken to bring the question of Women's Suffrage to the front in Queensland. A strong committee has been formed, and a public meeting is to be held.

South Australia.—The Woman's Suffrage Bill again failed to obtain the absolute majority necessary for the amendment of the constitution. This is very disappointing to the friends of the cause. However, the success in New Zealand will powerfully re-act upon opinion in Australia.

NEW ZEALAND.

The *Times* of April 6 states that : "Returns which have been prepared giving the number of women who voted at the last general election in New Zealand show that the women were prompt to exercise the newly-created franchise. Dunedin had 7,644 women on the roll, and only 1,338 failed to record their votes. Many of the absentees were no doubt deterred by the heavy rains which fell on the polling day. In Auckland, out of 6,660 on the roll, 5,283 voted; in Wellington 6,146 out of 7,280 voted; and in Christchurch 5,989 out of 6,710 went to the poll. In the country districts women whose names were on the roll exercised their privilege in large numbers. Waitemo, where the Minister of Lands was a candidate, has the best record, for in that constituency only 90 out of 1,327 failed to vote.

WOMEN'S SUFFRAGE IN NEW ZEALAND.

An article by Dr. Bakewell in the *Nineteenth Century* full of reckless statements and self-contradictions, has been much quoted amongst the opponents of Women's Suffrage, but if it seemed to them to come like the proverbial "nuts and ale" to strengthen their prejudices, facts seem to qualify their feast.

We are happy to be able to present our readers with some passages from a paper with which we have been favoured by a resident in New Zealand, Mr. C. P. Newcombe:—

This measure, which has been advocated in New Zealand for 20 years, was passed in the House of Representatives by a considerable majority, but in the Upper House by a very small one. Then the beer interest got up a great petition to the Governor, praying that he would not give his sanction to a bill which Dr. Bakewell affirms "no one but a few fanatics and a few Conservative politicians really desired, and which at the very least 95 per cent. of the population neither desired nor approved of." I propose to lay before your readers the opinions of a few of these fanatics, that they may judge of the statements of Dr. Bakewell. The report of the National Association of New Zealand, presented September 28th, 1893, says : "Undoubtedly the great event of the year under review is the admission of women to the franchise. The effect of this reform cannot yet be estimated, but it cannot fail to have a beneficial influence upon politics, provided the ladies exercise their right of voting. The earnestness with which the work of registering has been entered upon augurs well for the intention to make their newly acquired powers effective. The Council have a strong conviction that the measure will result in great good. Especially beneficially should the women's influence act in improving the *personnel* of our parliaments."

* * *

The Rev. Dr. Cowie, Bishop of Auckland, on September 25th, said he believed the women of this colony would select honourable men of independent means and self-denying lives, and men actuated by a Christian spirit. But whilst attending to these points, they would not forget the special qualifications necessary for a wise and successful legislator. The women, and the poor it had been said, had in all countries and in all ages suffered from the brute strength of men. He believed this saying would become less and less applicable in this country.

* * *

The Rev. S. F. Prior, a leading Wesleyan minister, said in his opinion women were better qualified to vote than three-fourths of the young men who attained twenty-one, and were entitled to vote by virtue of their manhood. A man reasoned out a matter by the slow process of logic, but a woman got to the same goal by an instinctive sense of right and wrong.

* * *

Sir G. Grey, in a speech on the "Female Franchise," said he felt certain that the step taken would spread throughout the whole English-speaking population. The utility of it and the certainty of it depended on the women of New Zealand. He saw now that the force of human intellect brought to the management of human affairs was to be doubled. The privileges that one-half of the world enjoyed were to be enjoyed equally by the whole world, and the greatness and the goodness of the female would be recognised by the manner in which she used the power that formerly was accorded to man alone.

* * *

Dr. Bakewell asserts that two questions influence the women's vote—prohibition and secular education. He says: "You have probably the same class of rabid fanatics as we have here—people who are dangerous monomaniacs. The immense majority are either reformed drunkards, and who dread even the smell of alcohol, or those whose relatives are or have been drunkards. If the millions of male members of teetotal societies have been reformed drunkards, that is an unanswerable argument in the favour of that movement. But neither in England nor in New Zealand can this be said of one-tenth of their number." He asserts that the women wish to conserve the present secular system, because "in every family there is a child who is either a teacher, or hopes to be." Your readers will have a high opinion of the intellectual *calibre* of the children of New Zealand, when they learn that in every family there is a student who either has, or aspires to be able to pass a succession of difficult examinations to qualify him or her to be a teacher! The education of New Zealand is free and secular. As a result, Dr. Bakewell asserts that the children "never read the Bible in school, and there is no such book at home. They are as destitute of any religious sentiment as a horse or a cow. They are not heathens, they have no religion at all." Now I affirm that this statement is as false as it is mischievous. The Doctor is a champion of the denominational system, because the Roman Catholic Church (of which he is a member) claims "that the Government should give grants to private schools which comply with the rules, and follow the standards of the Education Department." One of the best observed holidays in the year in Auckland is St. Patrick's Day, which, falling at a time when the summer is at its best, gives opportunity for the excursions of the Sunday Schools. And there is no prettier sight throughout the year than the long procession of Catholic children, well dressed, well fed, and thoroughly happy, their priests and teachers walking with them, and going to the public domain for a day's enjoyment; scarcely less numerous are those connected with the Church of England and the Wesleyan Methodists. The Band of Hope numbers its thousands. All these are employed in the moral and religious instruction of the children. Few, if any, escape the attention of the hundreds of workers, who with their ministers do that

Concluded at page 106.

SECOND RECORD OF MEETINGS AT WHICH THE APPEAL HAS BEEN ADVOCATED.

Date.		Place.	Description.	Chairman.	Speakers.
Jan.	10	Ilfracombe	Drawing Room Meeting, by Inv. of Miss Tickell.		Miss Down, Mrs. McMichael
,,	18	Upper Berkeley Street, London	Drawing Room Meeting, by Invitation of Mrs. John Hollond	Mr. John Hollond	Mrs. Fawcett, Rev. C. J. Ridgway, Mrs. Holah
,,	25	Wilton Place, London	Drawing Room Meeting, by invitation of Mrs. Algernon Joy	Mr. Joy	Mrs. Fawcett, Mrs. Westlake
,,	,,	Sale	Drawing Room Meeting by inv. of Mrs. Rooke	Miss Atkinson	Mrs. Sheldon Amos, Rev. Carey Bonner
,,	26	Guilden Morden	Public Meeting	Mrs. E. O. Fordham	Miss Friend
,,	,,	Gorton (Old Endowed Schoolroom)	Public Meeting in connection with the Manchester W.S. Society	Mr. H. P. Ilderton	Mrs. Sheldon Amos, Hon. Mrs. A. Lyttelton
,,	,,	Rochdale (Parish Room)	Annual Meeting of W. L. A.	Mrs. Wilson	Mrs. Sheldon Amos
,,	,,	Royston		Mrs. E. O. Fordham	Miss Friend
,,	29	Wellingboro'	Meeting of the Primrose League	R. Orlebar, Esq.	Miss Friend
,,	30	Bloomsbury (Vestry Hall)	Public Meeting	Rev. A. B. Boyd-Carpenter	Mrs. Fawcett
,,	,,	Penge	Meeting of W. L. A.	Mrs. Leeds	Mrs. Holah
Feb.	8	Niddry Lodge, Campden Hill	Drawing Room Meeting by kind permission of Miss Mabel Holland	Mr. Richard Shore	Dr. F. A. Abbot, Mrs. Fawcett
,,	12	Ealing	Meeting of W. L. A.	Mrs. Atherley Jones	Mrs. Holah
,,	,,	Wandsworth	Drawing Room Meeting by Inv. of Mrs. Shillington	Mr. Shillington	Mrs. Fawcett
,,	14	Pioneer Club	For Members and Friends	Mrs. Massingberd	Mrs. Fawcett
,,	,,	Henley-on-Thames	Lecture organised by W. L. A.	Mr. Council	Mrs. Stanbury
,,	15	Palace Court	Drawing Room Meeting by Invitation of Mrs. Purdie	Mrs. Pearsall Smith	Mrs. Wynford Phillips, Mrs. Cottrell Tupp
,,	16	Cheyne Walk	By kind permission of Mrs. Hawels	Mr. Whitmore, M.P.	Mrs. Fawcett, Mrs. Wynford Phillips, Mrs. Stuart Menteith
,,	,,	Haverstock Hill	Drawing Room Meeting by invitation of Mrs. St. Osyth Eustace Smith	Mr. E. K. Blyth	Miss Louisa Bigg, Miss Blackburn
,,	19	Wimbledon	Drawing Room Meeting by invitation of Mrs. H. W. Lawrence		Mrs. Fawcett
,,	21	Birmingham (Priory Rooms)	Public Meeting in connection with W. L. A.	Councillor R. F. Martineau	Miss Friend
,,	22	Wolverhampton	Drawing Room Meeting by inv. of Miss Langley	Mrs. Major	Miss Friend, Miss Southall
,,	26	Leytonstone (Iron Room)	Public Meeting arranged by Rev. W. Manning	Rev. W. Manning	Mrs. Fawcett
,,	27	Bloomsbury Square	Drawing Room Meeting by inv. of Mrs. Stapley	Dr. Alice Kerr	Mrs. Ormiston Chant
,,	,,	Birkenhead	Public Meeting		Mrs. Mallet, Miss Mellor and others
,,	,,	Norwood	Drawing Room Meeting by inv. of Mrs. Byrne		Mrs. Stopes
,,	,,	Battersea	Public Meeting	Mrs. Homan, M.L.S.B.	Miss Clementina Black, Mr. Willis, L.C.C., Mrs. Gray and Miss Griffin
,,	28	Stamford Hill	Meeting at the Skinner's School for Girls, arranged by Miss Page		Mrs. Fawcett
,,	,,	Carnarvon	Lecture in connection with the Primrose League	Mr. Charles A. Jones	Mrs. Stopes
Mar.	2	Bangor			Mrs. Stopes
,,	,,	Rhyl	Lecture in connection with W.L.A.		Mrs. Stopes
,,	,,	Battersea	Polytechnic Lecture	Mrs. Lloyd Jones	Mrs. Fawcett

Date.	Place.	Description.	Chairman.	Speakers.
Mar. 8	Aberystwith	Meeting at the Hall of Residence for University College	Miss Carpenter	Mrs. Stopes
,, 5	Newtown, Montgomery	Lecture in connection with W.L.A.		Mrs. Fawcett, Mr. W. McLaren, M.P., Mr. L. R. Everett, M.P.
,, 7	Ipswich (Public Hall)	Public Meeting arranged by Local Committee	Captain Pretyman	Miss Whitehead, Mrs. Gordon
,, 8	Regent's Park	Drawing Room Meeting, by inv. of Mrs. Logan		Mrs. Fawcett
,, 9	York Place, (Baker Street)	Meeting for Teachers, arranged by Miss Franks	Mr. Francis Storr	Mr. and Mrs. Josselyn, Mrs. Haweis, Miss Conybeare
,, 10	Colchester	Drawing Room Meeting by invitation of Mrs. Josselyn	Captain Lacon	
,, 12	Highbury (New Park)	Drawing Room Meeting by kind permission of Miss Mallett	Mrs. John Hullah	Mrs. Benjamin Clarke, Miss Griffin, Miss Blackburn
,, 13	Cheltenham, (Corn Exchange)	Meeting arranged by Local Committee	The Mayor	Mrs. Fawcett
,, 14	Bath (Guildhall)	Meeting by invitation of Ladies	Lady Blaine	Mrs. Fawcett, General Coningham, Dr. Bedloe, Mrs. Hallett, &c.
,, 21	Anderton's Hotel	Address to a meeting of the "Cemented Bricks"	Mr. John Hobson	Mrs. Fawcett
,, 21	New Cross	Public Meeting arranged by Mrs. Norfolk	Mrs. Greenwood	Mrs. Stanbury, Rev. Brooke Lambert

THE FOLLOWING MEETINGS HAVE BEEN HELD IN SCOTLAND IN CONNECTION WITH THE SCOTCH APPEAL COMMITTEE.

Date.	Place.	Description.	Chairman.	Speakers.
Dec. 17	Edinburgh (85, Drummond Place)	Drawing Room Meeting by invitation of Mrs. Balgarnie	Mrs. Balgarnie	Miss Clapperton, Miss Lees, Miss H. B. Thomson
,, 18	,, (West End Cafe)	Drawing Room Meeting arranged by invitation of Women's Suffrage Appeal Committee Social Gathering, W.L.A.		Miss Wigham, Miss Flora Stevenson
,, ,,	,, (Literary Institute)		Mrs. Steel	Mr. Shaw, M.P., Miss Wigham, Miss L. Stevenson
,, 20	,, (Great King Street)	Drawing Room Meeting	Mrs. Lang Todd	Mrs. Stopes, Miss Lees, Miss F. Stevenson
,, 21	,, (Canongate Institute)	Public Meeting	Miss Burton	Miss H. B. Thomson, Mr. Campbell Irons, Mr. Councillor Watterson
,, ,,	,, (Roselea Grange)	Drawing Room Meeting by invitation of Mrs. Lewis	Miss Burton	Miss Wigham, Miss Clapperton, Miss H. B. Thoinson
,, 22	,, (Brompton Hall)	Lecture in connection with W.L.A.	Mrs. Shaw	Miss Balfour, Miss Thomson
Jan. 5	,, (Haddington Assembly Rooms)	Meeting by invitation		Miss Wigham, Miss Balfour, Miss Burton, Miss Lees, Miss Dowie
,, 12	,, (Gartshore Hall)	Tea Meeting by invitation of W.S. Executive Committee	Miss L. Stevenson	
,, 19	,, (York Place)	Drawing Room Meeting by invitation of Mrs. Millar	Mrs. Millar	Mr. Shaw, Miss L. Stevenson, Miss Wigham
Feb. 12	Dumbiane (Overdale)	Drawing Room Meeting by invitation of Miss Cochran	Miss Cochran	Miss E. S. Kirkland
,, 16	Grief (Hydropathic Establishment)	Drawing Room Meeting by inv. of Mrs. Turnbull	Rev. Mr. Wylie	Miss E. S. Kirkland
,, 28	Selkirk (Ettrick View)	Drawing Room Meeting at Russell's Hotel		Miss H. B. Thomson
Mar. ,,	St. Andrew's (Suffolk Road)	Drawing Room Meeting by invitation of Mrs. Meikle	Miss Burton	Mrs. Muir Dowie, Miss Lees, Mrs. Watson, Mrs. Craig
,, 21	Costorphine (Public Hall)	Public Meeting	Miss Foulds	Miss Lees, Mrs. Watson, Miss H. B. Thomson

which the law of New Zealand declares not to be the work of the State school teacher. And whatever other changes are made, this practice is the least likely to be altered.

ELECTIONS AND APPOINTMENTS.

ROYAL COMMISSION ON SECONDARY EDUCATION.

Mrs. Henry Sidgwick, Mrs. Sophia Bryant, D.Sc., and Lady Frederick Cavendish have been appointed to serve on the Royal Commission to inquire into Secondary Education.

This is the first instance of which we find any record of women being appointed as Royal Commissioners, the nearest analogous case being the ladies who acted as Assistant Commissioners to the Labour Commission.

POOR LAW GUARDIANS ELECTION.

In consequence of the New Local Government Act, which comes into force in November, the Local Government Board have issued an instruction that the usual elections in April will not take place this year, but the guardians elected last year will continue in office until November.

Meantime those interested in promoting the return of Women Guardians should endeavour to be ready with suitable candidates, and all desiring help or information will do well to apply to Mrs. Angus Hall, secretary of the Society for Promoting the Return of Women Guardians, at 4, Sanctuary, Westminster.

The *Local Government Chronicle* of February 14, states that the Board of Guardians of the Bromley Union, Kent, have unanimously appointed Miss Ellen Grimsey, the matron's daughter, to be master's clerk.

SCHOOL BOARDS.

The following ladies have been elected on to school boards since the new year:—
Barrow-in-Furness—Mrs. L. T. Foll and Mrs. M. Mallagh.
Chiswick—Mrs. A. Grant.
Northreppe (Norfolk)—Mrs. S. E. Gurney.
Rawtenstall—Miss Worswick (bye election).
Redruth—Mrs. M. Dungey.
E. and W. Rounton (York) Mrs. M. F. Johnson.
Scredington (Lincoln)—Mrs. H. A. Clarke.
Walthamstow—Miss M. L. Carter and Mrs. S. Ellison.
Wymondham (Norfolk)—Mrs. H. L. Cubitt.

INSPECTORS.

The Home Secretary has sanctioned the appointment of two more women as Factory Inspectors; the names of these ladies have not yet been announced.

OVERSEER.

Mrs. Julia Towhill has been appointed Overseer for the parish of Tellisford, near Freshford, Bath.

MEDICAL APPOINTMENTS.

Mrs. De la Cherois, M.D., and Miss Baker, L.R.C.P. and S.Edin., have been appointed on the medical staff of the Butler Boulton Provident Dispensary, a large municipal charity in Oxford. Its funds are supplemented by the payments of members, who are nearly 8,000 in number. These are the first ladies who have held any appointment on the staff.

A new post has been created at the Royal Free Hospital, London, that of assistant anæsthetist, to which Miss Aldrich Blake, M.B., and B.S., Lond., has been appointed.

Miss Drew and Miss Stuart were elected members of the London District Committee of the Journalists' Institutes, at the annual meeting held in the Memorial Hall, Farringdon Street, on March 17.

The Keighley Co-operative Society have decided that married women may in future be admitted members of the Society, though their husbands be already members.

NEW ZEALAND.

Mrs. Yates has been elected Mayor of Onehunga in New Zealand, which appears to be the first occasion on which this office has been held by a woman in the British Empire.

RECORD OF EVENTS.

THE LOCAL GOVERNMENT ACT.

CLAUSES AFFECTING WOMEN.

Clause 3 (2).—No person shall be disqualified by *sex or marriage* for being elected or being a member of a parish council.

Clause 20 (2).—No person shall be *disqualified by sex or marriage* from being elected or being a guardian.

The above clauses effectually set at rest the uncertainty which has hitherto attended the election of married women as guardians, and any woman is now eligible as a parish councillor or as a guardian, who is on the Local Government Register of Electors, or has resided during the whole of the twelve months preceding in the parish or within three miles thereof.

After November 8, when the first elections under the Act will take place, not only all the duties now performed by guardians will be liable to devolve on women, but also all the multifarious duties of the national housekeeping, so to say—all (other than ecclesiastical) performed by vestries and churchwardens and sanitary authorities—care of street paving and lighting, of wash houses, public libraries, recreation grounds, allotments, water-courses, drains, public ways, &c.

Clause 22.—The chairman of a district council, *unless a woman* or personally disqualified by any Act, shall be by virtue of his office justice of the peace for the county in which the district is situate.

Although several instances occur in history in which women have held the office of justice of the peace, it is not remarkable that the Legislature was unwilling to change existing precedents by a side issue. Accordingly Parliament has adhered to the modern precedent created by the service of women on the Poor Law Boards, but has declined to revert to ancient precedents in regard to the magisterial bench.

Clause 43.—For the purposes of this Act *a woman shall not be disqualified by marriage* for being on any local government register of electors, or for being an elector of any local authority, provided that a husband and wife shall not both be qualified in respect of the same property.

This clause was added in Committee of the House of Commons, by the President of the Local Government Board, the Hon. H. H. Fowler, in deference to an instruction, which was moved for by Mr.

M'Laren, and carried on November 16, by a majority of 21, viz., 147 to 126.

This is the first statutory recognition of the electoral right of a married woman. At the same time it preserves the practice of one vote for the household by not allowing any double voting of husband and wife as joint occupiers.

THE ASSOCIATION OF IRISH SCHOOLMISTRESSES.

The Association of Irish Schoolmistresses held their annual meeting at Alexandra College, Dublin, on February 8, Miss White, vice-president, presiding. The annual report contains a significant instance of the value of such an association, and the ease with which rights may be ignored where there is not some such body to keep watch and ward.

The Royal University of Ireland last year instituted new junior fellowships of the value of £200 a year each tenable for four years. The Association was informed by the secretaries of the University that the Senate had not decided to throw open their Fellowships to women. A memorial was at once addressed to them which was signed by 140 graduates—all the women graduates up to 1893, with the exception of about eighteen, who could not be reached. The Senate decided in favour of the women graduates, and moreover it was ascertained that by the Act of Parliament founding the University, every appointment, including the permanent Fellowships, is open to women, and cannot be legally closed against them. The report also states that the question of the admission of women to Trinity College is now being practically considered by the Academic Council of Dublin University.

THE ALEXANDRA SCHOOL, DUBLIN.

The annual distribution of prizes at the Alexandra School, on February 27, was made the occasion of the opening of the new Drill Hall, which has been added to the School. This Hall is 69 ft. in length by 29 ft. in breadth, and the height is 39 ft. from the floor to the ridge of the open timber-work roof.

The report of this School, which was read by the head mistress, Miss Mulvany, referred to the loss that they had had in the death of their vice-warden, Rev.

Percival Graves, D.D. After the prizes had been distributed by the Archbishop of Dublin, his Grace declared the Hall open, with a few words in commendation of the special purposes of the Hall, in the course of which he said he might supplement Miss Mulvany's report by expressing the universal pleasure of those interested in the progress of the school at having amongst them Miss Mulvany—a lady to whose indefatigable zeal and signal ability the institution mainly owed its success. Looking at that meeting and remembering how this school formed but a part of a larger institution for the higher education of women, he could not help thinking of that wonderful process of emancipation as regarded woman and as regarded her higher education which had taken place within the last century. They had had many emancipations during that time. They had had the emancipation of the slaves in the British dominions, and that was a very good thing. They had had what was called Catholic emancipation, and that he ventured to say was a good thing, too; and they had had emancipation of trade, and other emancipations, but amongst them all there were few of greater importance than that to which he had already referred—he meant the emancipation of woman, as regarded her higher education, from the thraldom by which she had been hitherto bound—emancipation from those mere trivialities and conventionalities and insipidities as regarded her social position, which, until lately would seem to have been regarded as almost the vocation of womankind. Now woman had been called upon to come out, as it were, into the open and to show that she as well as man had something to do, something to learn, and something to win in public life. He also meant—in addition to this emancipation from what might be called intellectual torpor—emancipation from physical lassitude, by the encouragement that had been given of late to woman to engage in healthful exercises, in lawn tennis, and even in golf and other such pursuits. The proceedings closed with the benediction.

LADY MARGARET HALL, OXFORD.

An influential meeting was held on March 15, at 7, St. James' Square, the residence of Lord Egerton of Tatton, in support of a special appeal for funds in aid of the extension of Lady Margaret Hall, Oxford. The Rev. E. S. Talbot, D.D., vicar of Leeds, presided and described the extension required. They wanted to put up buildings which should be able to contain more students. They had had a chapel from the first; but it had somewhat of that queer anomalousness which characterised the whole building, and they ought now to have a larger hall and a real chapel. They must also look forward to something in the way of a larger hall for meals and for different kinds of meetings, if Lady Margaret Hall was to gain the weight that it ought to have in women's education at Oxford. The opportunity was still open to them of requiring a large freehold site suitable to their requirements, and for that they asked assistance that day.

A resolution affirming that the education of women deserves the support of English churchmen, was moved and seconded by Lord Cranbrook and the Bishop of Ely.

Mr. A. J. BALFOUR, M.P., in supporting the resolution, said that he conceived that those who framed it meant something more than the bare and abstract statement which it contained, and that they intended their words to be interpreted by and in accordance with the general objects which had called them there together. He supposed he had been called upon to take part in those proceedings because he was among the earliest of those who at Cambridge—which began that movement—took some practical steps towards securing educational advantages for women, and the opinions which he held more than twenty years ago, the experience of those twenty years had only served to strengthen and confirm. He remembered perfectly well that when the movement was started there were not a few critics who thought that it was not calculated to do much good to the women, and that it might do some harm to the men ; that the character of University society might be altered for the worse by introducing into the University buildings devoted to the higher education of women. He did not say that the arguments used by those critics were intrinsically absurd or unreasonable, but looking back over the many years that had passed since the experiment was first tried on a small scale, he thought they might say with confidence that even the most anxious critic would hardly now be prepared to assert that any of the fears originally expressed had been shown to have the slightest foundation in fact. They had seen, both at Cambridge and at Oxford, colleges for women flourishing exceedingly, doing an admirable work for those for whom they were called into existence, and in no sense disturbing the even current of masculine education, which had been going on side by side.

He was not sure that there was not more need for some colleges in the case of women having a distinctly religious quality than there was in the case of men. He could imagine that there must be existing in different parts of the country many quiet and remote parsonages in which the vicar or rector, anxious to give his children, his daughters, the full advantages of a sound education such as could only be obtained in the neighbourhood of our great Universities, where teaching facilities could alone be obtained in sufficient quantity and quality—that such a man would be reluctant, nevertheless, to allow his daughter to go to any college where she might be subjected to influences with which she had little sympathy, and where the continuity of home education and tradition might be rudely broken. For people circumstanced as those whom he had described, was it not desirable, even necessary, that something should be done? The work appeared to him to be more than legitimate, and he could not imagine any object which ought to commend itself more to their liberality and their energies than that which they had met that afternoon to further.

The resolution was carried unanimously.

Mr. G. W. E. RUSSELL, M.P., moved, "That Lady Margaret Hall, Oxford, has exceptionally strong claims on the sympathy of the meeting." This was seconded by Mr. SPOTTISWOODE, and carried.

Dr. INCE (Regius Professor of Divinity) moved " That the contemplated enlargement is at the present time indispensable." Sir JAMES PAGET, in seconding this resolution, said he thought hard work was good for men and women, and tended to prolong rather than to shorten their lives. When people complained of overwork they sometimes did so when they really tried to work hard and play hard as well, and it was that which injured them.

The resolution was carried, as also a resolution "That a fund be opened and efforts made to raise money for the purpose," proposed by Dr. BAKER, Head Master of Merchant Taylors' School, and seconded by Canon SCOTT HOLLAND.—Abridged from the *Times*.

THE GIRLS' PUBLIC DAY SCHOOL COMPANY.

Her Royal Highness Princess Louise, Marchioness of Lorne, attended the twenty-first annual meeting of the Girls' Public Day School Company at the Royal Albert Hall, on March 2nd, and distributed the prizes to the successful competitors in the examinations of the pupils attending the London schools of the Company. The arena and the stalls were occupied by between three and four thousand pupils, while the remainder of the building was filled by parents and friends. The company now possesses some 36 schools scattered over London and the provinces, with 7,134 pupils. The company's paid-up capital amounts to £92,086, and the shareholders, who number 2,101, receive a dividend of 5 per cent. on the capital. The interests of the teachers have not been overlooked, a provident fund, with a capital of £32,000 having been established.

The prizes and certificates having been distributed, Lord ABERDARE, in moving a vote of thanks to the Princess, said it was now about 23 years since a number of distinguished men and women met in the rooms of Her Royal Highness at Kensington to found the Girls' Public Day School Company. There had been a great stir in education, and powerful commis-

sions had sat upon the Universities, the great public
schools, and the endowed schools, the last of which
had been most fertile in results. All those applied to
the education of the men and boys of the country.
The ladies who founded the company were determined
to work a revolution in the education of women.
Among those beneficent revolutionists he was glad to
see the Dowager Lady Stanley of Alderley and
Miss Shirreff. He could understand critics saying,
when they heard that the company had just attained
its majority, that, after all, for 21 years' work, 36
schools and 7,000 scholars did not form a very
great achievement. But that was only a portion of the
work which was being done. The sight of the schools
rising throughout the length and breadth of the land
had had a beneficial effect upon the general system of
female education. A vast number of the very best
schools in England had been founded upon the same principles which had directed the operation of the company.
The schools were started upon fresh principles; modern
ideas on education were applied; and the result was
a breadth and thoroughness which could not be found
in any of the best boys' schools. Looking at the
part now taken by women, how imperfect would be the
education of this country if it were confined to men!
It was always admitted that women were a most
useful element in the governing of the school boards,
boards of guardians, and other institutions, and he was
not surprised to see that upon the commission to
inquire into intermediate education, the members of
which had just been appointed, there were three ladies.
One of those ladies, Lady Frederick Cavendish, had
been for many years a member of the council of the
company.

Sir JOHN LUBBOCK, M.P., in seconding the vote of
thanks, said that even the most inveterate grumbler
must admit that within the last few years our country
had made great progress, especially in the education
of women. It had done so against great difficulties and
much opposition. They had found that a wise education was the best safeguard against the evils of the
world.

THE NEW WELSH UNIVERSITY.

The New Welsh University, which at present includes the Colleges of Aberystwith, Cardiff and Bangor, is in advance of every British University in regard to women. Its charter enacts that "Women shall be eligible equally with men for admittance to any degree which the University is by this our charter authorised to confer. Every office hereby created in the University, and the membership of every authority hereby constituted, shall be open to women equally with men."

The University Court—the supreme governing body of the University—held its first meeting at the Privy Council Chambers, Downing Street, on April 6th. This Court consists partly of persons appointed by the Lord President of the Council, partly of persons appointed by the County and Borough Councils of Wales, each of which may appoint one representative and an additional member for every completed 100,000 population in the district of the Council; in addition to these, four members are appointed by each of the associated colleges, and others by the guild of graduates, and by the head teachers of intermediate and of elementary schools. In the last two cases one of the members must in each instance be a lady.

CONFERENCE OF WOMEN'S PROTECTIVE AND PROVIDENT LEAGUE (SCOTLAND).

A conference, promoted by the Women's Protective and Provident League, was held in Glasgow, for the formation in Scotland of a National Federal Council to consider the conditions of women's work. The following report is abridged from the *Scotsman* of March 3rd. The proceedings took place in the hall of the Co-operative Restaurant, 62, Renfield Street, and were taken part in by about 100 delegates from Trades Councils and other trade organisations. Dr. William Smart presided, and among those present were Professor and Mrs. Caird, Councillor Hunter, and Miss Irwin.

The CHAIRMAN, in opening the proceedings, welcomed the delegates to Glasgow. It was evident, he said, that the economists had never given sufficient thought to the question of women's work as distinct from men's work. There had been a strange silence on the subject, the bright exception being Mill, who openly advocated the opening of industrial occupations freely to both sexes. Now at last they recognised that ; but as regarded wages, the position of women was strangely indeterminate. In most occupations they were willing to take her work ; they were by no means clear upon paying her her proper wage. And indeed it was not a problem of capital against labour. The most enlightened of them were puzzled how to secure her her fair share of what her industry helped to produce. The serious thing was that women had brought with them the tradition of a customary wage, and were entering into competition generally with no higher expectation than that wage. They should never see clearly till they swept away the fallacy that women's wage was a "supplementary" one. The only economic conception of wage was that it was determined by what the worker produced, not by what she lived on. But even if it were not so, could they allow the "supplementary" conception to keep down wages when women were demanding a career that should not make them look to marriage as the sole escape from life-long struggle with starvation ? Now, what required to be emphasised was that women were pressing into all occupations, dragging with them that traditional wage, while the public was firmly convinced that it was all a woman was entitled to. He concluded by saying their principle was that women should be paid by the value of their product, and not by the standard of their wants, they did not ask that women should have equal wages, but that they should have equal rates of wage when they did similar work ; and that, where their labour could not be measured by men's, their weakness should not be taken advantage of. With that in view, there was no reason why they should not make the organisation of women an object in which all good people, working people and capitalists alike, might join.

The MASTER OF BALLIOL (Professor Edward Caird) said he had come there to express, as one of the earliest members of the Council of the Protective and Provident League, his great sympathy with the movement initiated that day. He believed it might do a great deal of good, and he considered a very valuable part of the programme was the collecting of minute information as to the employment of women and the conditions under which their labour took place. He referred to Miss Irwin's labours in this direction. She had not only drawn up many reports for the Labour Commission, which, he thought, had not been put before the public in the way they ought to have been, but, on the motion of the Protective and Provident League, she had prepared a most excellent report upon the work of laundresses. That report had shown its usefulness already, for, in communicating with the various members of the House of Commons, the members of the League had found that the work was practically done. Now, it was absolutely certain that what was proposed in Miss Irwin's report—that the establishments in which these laundresses were employed should be brought under the Factories Acts—would be an accomplished fact. All that was needed to be done to redress such wrongs was simply that the facts should be made known, and he had no doubt there were many other occupations in which similar improvements could be made. Once the facts were fairly stated, no party—neither Liberals nor Conservatives—could possibly resist them; and consequently they found that the members on both sides were quite ready to promise their support, whereas the matter had been put aside in the previous Parliament, simply because the facts had not then been stated.

Miss MARGARET H. IRWIN then submitted the scheme for the formation of the proposed National Federal Council. It had for its objects the promotion and protection of women's industrial interests and the systematic investigation of the conditions of women's employments. The work suggested to be dealt with by the Council covered the following departments :—Trade organisation, special and systematic inquiry into the conditions of women's work in the various trades, the collecting and publishing of statistics, and the holding of meetings for discussing questions affecting women's trade interests. With regard to organisation, she suggested that steps should be taken to assist local agencies, and to bring about an understanding among workers in the same trade regarding the establishment of a standard rate of wages throughout that trade, and a uniform rate of paying for the same work where it was carried on under the same local conditions. They thought that special and systematic inquiry should be made into the employment of women as shop assistants and barmaids, the employment of children as message boys and girls, the labour at home by married women and children, the steadying of the supply of work and procuring continuity of employment among the women workers of season and fashion trades, the sanitary condition of workshops, the system of wages payments in textile industries and subcontracting in potteries and other industries, and an inquiry into the desirability of providing in the various industries abstracts of the Factory and Workshop Acts, which should be drawn up in such a form as to be comprehensible to the average worker. It was suggested that the Council should be composed of representatives of Scottish Trades Councils, each Council sending not more than two delegates, who need not be members of trades employing women, and representatives of women's unions and men's unions in trades employing women. Conducted on strictly non-political and non-sectarian lines, it was suggested that it should be regarded solely as a consultative body, as a centre for considering all questions affecting women's labour interests.

Mr. JOHN WILSON, Edinburgh Trades Council, moved :—

"That this Conference, agreeing to the general principles of the scheme now before it, expresses its opinion that it is desirable to establish a National Council, composed of labour representatives from the various districts in Scotland, to consider the conditions of women's employments, and resolves that the delegates present do, in their representative capacity, constitute themselves into such a body."

Mr. ALEXANDER WHYTE, Kirriemuir Mill and Factory Workers' Union, seconded, and the resolution was adopted unanimously.

The Conference then proceeded to discuss in detail the various points suggested in the scheme, and on the question of the trade organisation of women.

Mr. H. M. MILLOY, Greenock Trades Council, moved:—
"That it be a recommendation from the N.F.C. to all delegates present to bring before their local unions and Trades Councils the necessity of taking steps to establish women's unions in their several districts, and for rendering every assistance to women's unions where they are already established."

Mr. COOPER, Scottish Tailors' Society, in seconding, said the girls in his trade often put them in a very unfortunate position. Only last week the executive of his society had voted £50 for the organisation of the girls in his trade. There were very few trades, he believed, more directly affected by the labour of women than that of the tailor's. It was only the unscrupulous employer who prevented the girls from getting a decent wage. He mentioned that whereas a man was paid 5s. for a certain piece of work a girl only got 1s. 6d.

The motion was carried.

Mr. WILLIAM DICKSAN, Glasgow Trades Council, moved:—
"That where men and women are employed in the same trade, an effort be made by the members of the men's unions to obtain an equal or approximate rate of payment for women where their work is of the same nature and efficiency as men's."

The Rev. HENRY WILLIAMSON, Dundee, said that owing to the establishment of the union among the mill girls of that city the wages had increased by 20 per cent. since 1885.

Mr. COOPER, Glasgow, moved as an amendment that the word "approximate" should be deleted from the motion.

A long discussion followed, the contention in favour of the amendment being that where women's work was equal in quality and quantity they should have the same wages. In favour of the motion it was pointed out that if wages were identical employers would prefer men before women.

The motion was carried by 27 votes to 3.

Mr. GALLOWAY, Glasgow Trades Council, moved:—
"That efforts be made to establish a standard rate of wages in all trades, and a uniform rate of payment for the same work when it is carried on under the same local conditions." Miss IRWIN seconded.

Objection was taken to the motion, as it was held to be covered by the previous motion carried. On it being pointed out that it was of great importance in trades where women alone were employed, the suggested motion was carried.

Mr. BOND, Glasgow Trades Council, moved:—
"That the W.N.F.C. recommends that in trades which employ both sexes the men's union should make an effort to federate the women's union with their own." Miss M'GREGOR, Glasgow, seconded, and the motion was adopted.

A number of other points regarding the objects of the Council were discussed in detail. A Central Executive having been appointed, the proceedings terminated.

Having given the above account of the proceedings of

the conference, it will be well to give also some criticism of those proceedings which appeared in the *Glasgow Herald* of March 17th, in a letter from Mr. Cree, well known as a strong supporter of the employment of women in that city, pointing out that interference in trade questions from the outside, tends to make matters, which are already difficult, yet more difficult than they were before.

"Dr. SMART says that prices once down, the step is all but irrecoverable, and he adds, 'that if they must lay the blame somewhere, let them lay it on the middleman who pits maker against maker, and tempts with cheap goods, made in anticipation of demand, those who would have been quite willing to pay a price sufficient to allow a decent wage.' Now, as a middleman myself, I say, that apart from the fall from monetary reasons and improved processes, prices are just as ready to rise as to fall. And so far from the harmless, necessary middleman being to blame, it is he who keeps up prices. If there were no middleman and little demand prices would go down with a vengeance at once, and many works would stop. It is the middleman who tides over the bad times. And the competition is not all the one way, as the new economists seem to think. The maker pits middleman against middleman to get prices up, and the middleman pits consumer against consumer for the same purpose.

"And if the people are quite willing to pay a higher price, how does the middleman require to tempt them with a lower? He does not sell one farthing cheaper than he can help. And if anybody pays more for coats to please the tailor, has he not just so much less to spend on boots? And if he has more than enough for all his wants he will just save so much less, and there will be so much less capital wanting employment in the hiring of labour."

* * *

"About 18 months ago a pottery works was started for the manufacture of jam pots, with women turners. After three months' working the employer got a letter from the union, calling upon him to dismiss the women and employ men instead. He refused, and his work was stopped by the union. Thinking that a Women's Protection League would be willing to protect women, he wrote to the secretary and a lady called. She heard his story, and then said—'I suppose this trouble would not have arisen if you had been paying the women the same rate as the men get?' He replied, 'I am paying them 16 to 22 shillings a week; do you suggest that I should pay them 50 shillings?' 'Well,' she said, 'it is a large wage, but the principle is correct.' So there was no help there. The strike continued, and I do not think the work was ever re-opened. Now, was the principle correct? Is it good economy to employ highly skilled men at 50 shillings a week to do work so simple that girls at 16 shillings can do? I do not think so. Here the Women's League sympathise with those who turned the women out of their employment. It has simply been made a tool by the men's unions. The men used to object to the employment of women at all in their trades. Finding public opinion against them, they now profess an anxiety that women should get the same rates as themselves, knowing that if that demand is made the women will be quite as effectually excluded as before.

THE ROYAL COMMISSION ON THE EMPLOYMENT OF WOMEN.

A brief account is given by the Press Association of the forthcoming Report of the Royal Commission on the Employment of Women. This Report is founded partly on the inquiries made by the four Lady Assistant Commissioners, and partly on the evidence given before itself. The report will state that while the wages of men have increased much during the last fifty years, the wages of women have scarcely increased at all, excluding domestic servants. In speaking of the sweated trades, chiefly the making up of cheap clothing, the Report attributes the low wages earned by women to the competition of the various shops with each other, each trying to sell the cheapest, and to the competition of women with each other, there being more women than there is work for them to do. The Report also speaks of the long hours of work in certain trades, such as shop assistants, barmaids and laundresses. It also refers to unhealthy trades, such as the white lead industry.

All that is said appears to be very true and sensible, but when the Report comes to the remedies for these evils it is less satisfactory. The remedies, according to the Press Association, are to shorten the hours of work for women in these trades by Act of Parliament. By this means it is evident that many thousand shop assistants would be turned out of work, also a good many barmaids, several thousand laundresses, and a few hundred lead workers. Most of these would of course crowd into the cheap clothing trade, as every woman can use a needle more or less well. We must hope the Press Association is mistaken as to the plans of the Commission. Should these plans be correctly reported, and should they be carried out, the wages of needlewomen will fall lower than ever.

ROYAL IRISH ASSOCIATION FOR EMPLOYMENT OF WOMEN.

The annual meeting of the Royal Irish Association for Promoting the Training and Employment of Women was held at 21, Kildare street, Dublin, on March 20th. The chair was taken by Greenwood Pim, Esq.

Among those present were:—Lady Victoria Hamilton, Lady Ferguson, Mrs. Power Lalor, Mrs. Maurice Brooks, Mrs. Fane Vernon, Mrs. G. Stewart, Mrs. Charles Martin, Mrs. Browne, Mrs. Lawson, Miss Margaret Stokes, Miss MacDermot, Miss M'Donnell.

The report, which was read by the Secretary, Miss Croker, referring to the formation of the Society in June, 1883, remarks:—" It is gratifying to be able to state that the council, in sending out their tenth annual report, feel they can confidently say that the work begun ten years ago is now established, and that the importance of providing women with suitable training to fit them for remunerative employment is now fully recognised. Many difficulties presented themselves when the association first began its work, and some still exist, but as each year goes by it is seen that many hindrances and obstacles have been removed, and, no doubt, before long the way will be much clearer. The training given to the pupils in the various classes is one of the principal features in the useful work undertaken by this association, and the council are glad to report that a marked improvement has taken place during the year as regards the regular attendance of the pupils."

The scrivenery shorthand classes continue to be the largest. The fact that the profits in the classes have increased is encouraging; on the other hand, it is unsatisfactory to hear that subscriptions have fallen off, for the society has not yet reached a self-supporting basis.

In addition to the ordinary work of the society, " the council have much pleasure in stating that the hopes expressed in their last report as to the establishment of cookery and laundry work classes have been realised, the Municipal Council of Dublin having granted a sum of £100 for the holding of such classes, which were opened in June, and have so far been well attended. By the means of these classes educated women can now train in both subjects, so as to qualify as teachers, and will at the end of their training be granted diplomas, if they pass the necessary examinations. It is hoped, therefore, that when more technical classes for women are started throughout the country that constant employment will be given to the staff of teachers now training in this school of cookery and laundry work."

EDINBURGH SCHOOL OF MEDICINE FOR WOMEN.

Two scholarships, tenable at this school, have just been given by a lady for the benefit of students of small means who desire to qualify themselves as medical missionaries. One is of the value of £100, and will give a free education both at school and hospital; and the other will reduce the fees for education by half. The selection of candidates has been placed in the hands of a committee of ladies specially interested in mission work. Application should be made to the Secretary of the school, Surgeon Square, Edinburgh.

LONDON SCHOOL OF MEDICINE FOR WOMEN.

The annual report of the London School of Medicine for Women states the number of students now attending the school and hospital are 162. Twelve of the students became registered medical practitioners in 1893.

ORIENTAL STUDENTS.—In the proceedings of the ninth Congress of Orientalists, just published, we notice two papers by women. One is the very interesting paper by Caroline A. Foley, M.A., giving an account of the distinguished part played by women in the intellectual awakening in India in the sixth century B.C. (which we now call Buddhism), and of the very enlightened and healthy tone which animated the women communities of the Buddhist order at that time. The other is Mrs. Mabel Bode's paper, giving a translation from an ancient Pali work, of the lives of several of these women leaders in the Buddhist reformation. We notice that Miss Cust was one of the honorary secretaries of the Congress. The "Proceedings" contain only an abstract of Mrs. Bode's paper which has been published in full in the *Journal of the Royal Asiatic Society*, where there are also papers by Miss Mary Ridding and Miss Duff on other points of Indian History. It would seem from the two papers first referred to that the position of women in early Buddhism was very remarkable. While the actual government of the order as a whole was left in the hands of the men, the sisters were teachers of philosophy and ethics, and their essays and poems have been included in the sacred books.

M.A.B.Y.S.—We have again to record the good work done by the Metropolitan Association for Befriending Young Servants, a Society which does not progress by leaps and bound, but which never goes back. The number of young servants in personal communication with lady friends is 8,624, of ladies actively befriending girls, 1,050; of district committees, 31; of training and lodging homes, 19; of unions working in connection with the Association, 32; of other schools 9. In the notice in these pages in April last year, the opening of Scott House for feeble-minded girls was mentioned. This has now been working for eighteen months, and a distinct improvement in the girls is reported. The main business is laundry work, but knitting, basket making, needlework, house and kitchen-work are taught, as far as the capacity of the girls allows. One girl has improved as far as to be able to take a place as laundry-maid in a gentleman's family, where she is doing well. At an Industrial Exhibition held at St. Martin's Town Hall, Charing Cross, on July 5, 1893, the M.A.B.Y.S. was well represented, and the exhibits of the girls in needlework of various kinds, laundry work and cooking reflected great credit on them. A great number of prizes for good service have been given during the year, thirty-one being for seven years' service and over. The Report, from which we have extracted the above particulars, finishes " with a lament over the state of the funds" in which there is a deficit of £386. It "has suffered," says the Chairman, the Rev. Brooke Lambert, "because those who were applied to seemed to think that a Society with a balance could not want money"—an idea which is not conducive to the satisfactory working of charitable societies!

NATIONAL HEALTH SOCIETY.—Dr. C. G. Shelley lectured in the Committee Room of the National Health Society, 53, Berners Street, on Feb. 14, on "The Feeding of School Boys and School Girls," a theme on which, in his capacity of consulting medical officer for Haileybury College, he was particularly qualified to speak. His words were followed with intelligent interest by the audience, which was chiefly composed of ladies. Among the gentlemen present it is noticeable that the majority were medical men. Dr. Shelley's subject included sanitary feeding in general, with special reference to the infant and the growing child, and he insisted on the importance of certain forms of diet, notably milk, to the value of which as the chief nutriment of early childhood up to the age of eight, he gave some striking testimony.

WOMEN'S TRADES UNION LEAGUE.—The League is now established in the new offices to which it has moved, in concert with the Club and Institute Union, in Clerkenwell Road (close to Gray's Inn Road). A fine portrait of Mrs. Emma Paterson—a crayon enlarged from a photograph—adorns the walls of the new offices. The portrait has been presented to the League by Mr. Hodgson Pratt, one of the earliest workers with Mrs. Paterson.

CLUBS.—Owing to the increase of members, the University Club for ladies has removed from 31, New Bond Street, to larger premises at 47, Maddox Street, W.

The Writers' Club find their premises at 190, Fleet Street, inconveniently small, and will remove early in May to more spacious rooms at Hastings House, Norfolk Street, Strand.

The Pioneer Club is also compelled to seek more spacious quarters, those to which it removed in Cork Street last spring already proving too small. On May

3 it will move to 22, Bruton Street, a large mansion formerly the residence of Lord Hastings.

THE ASSOCIATION OF WOMEN PIONEER LECTURERS (4 Caroline Place, W.C.), has arranged short courses of lectures on "Natural History for Children," followed by "Rambles in the Museum," to be given in the Natural History Museum during the summer, by kind permission of the Trustees. Mrs. Rose, certificated in zoology by Roy. College of Sc., Lond., will lecture in April on " Some Typical Mammals."

In connection with the Association of Women Pioneer Lectures, Miss March Phillipps has been giving a course of six lectures on "Early Italian Painting," at 132, Queen's Gate, by kind permission of Miss Wyatt. The lectures embraced the period from the first rise of Italian art to the Bologna School.

THE QUEEN OF PORTUGAL, having been asked to write a few lines for a national album, to be published at the forthcoming *fêtes* in celebration of the 500th anniversary of the birth of Prince Henry the Navigator, has, says a Reuter telegram from Oporto, sent the following contribution:—" As a mother and as a Queen, my greatest ambition would be to endow my country —the Portuguese nation—with a group of children like those of Philippa of Lancaster, and that among them there should be one who should do great deeds for Portugal and for the world like Prince Henry." The Queen Philippa alluded to by her Majesty was the daughter of John of Gaunt.—*Times.*

REVIEWS.

The Rights of Women, a comparative Study in History and Legislation, by M. Ostrogorski, translated under the author's supervision. Swan, Sonnenschein & Co., price 2s. 6d.

THE English translation of M. Ostrogorski's work, *La Femme au Point de Vue du droit Publique*, has now appeared, forming one of the Social Science Series, issued by Messrs. Swan, Sonnenschein & Co.

The notice which appeared in this Review (January, 1892), when the original work was published in Paris, has already indicated the character of this work. But it may be well to remind our readers that it is the most complete compendium of the status of women in all countries that has appeared, and has been prepared with the utmost care and accuracy.

There is, however, one matter of regret in regard to the English edition, and that is the title. A book always becomes known by its first rather than by its subordinate title, and to call it *Rights of Women*, does not convey an adequate idea of the contents of the book; the expression is not only in itself too vague and indefinite, but it has a connotation of aggressiveness. It is too like that exasperating phrase "women's rights," a phrase which all who actually work in women's movements in England, studiously avoid. The "Public Status of Women" had been a better title to our thinking.

But title apart, we have nothing but welcome for a work which should find a place on the bookshelves of all students of women's questions.

The translation has been enriched by an appendix on the civil condition of women on the Continent, which shows what a grip the Code Napoleon still holds on all countries where it has been introduced, how tardily it has been slightly relaxed in some—Italy for instance, how unchanged it remains in others—Holland and Belgium for instance. In Germany the civil laws of the several states of the empire are about to be consolidated into a single code. The draft of this code is now in preparation, and its scheme extends the contractual capacity of married women, and secures her the profits made in carrying on a trade or profession. It also proposes to allow women to be testamentary witnesses. Russia, whose political institutions are the least liberal in Europe, possesses the most liberal laws as regards the civil capacity of women.

Adventures in Mashonaland, by two Hospital Nurses, Rose Blennerhasset and Lucy Sleeman. Macmillan & Co.

" The White Rabbit put on his spectacles. 'Where shall I begin, please your Majesty?' he asked. 'Begin at the beginning,' the King said, gravely, ' and go on till you come to the end: then stop.'" Such is the advice we should give to anyone who is fortunate enough to get hold of this book. It is the story of two nurses who undertook to open a hospital in the pioneer camp of Umtali, in Mashonaland, and it gives a lively picture of the hardships and difficulties they endured; of their cheerfulness and high spirits under adverse circumstances; and their patient courage and perseverance in the most monotonous work. To arrive at their destination they journeyed in a cockleshell of a boat for sixteen hours up the river Pungwé, which swarmed with crocodiles. "One or two, disturbed by our passage, dropped sullenly into the water. They filled us with horror. Out of such evil-glittering eyes might lost spirits and condemned souls look forth." The rest of the journey, about 160 miles, was performed on foot, and a graphic account is given of the difficulties of making a start. The Vice-Consul and the Doctor did their best to dissuade them from going. "No women he had known had ever walked in Africa; even men found it trying, and sometimes died on the way. We told our excellent advisers that we could only die once, and that dying was just as disagreeable in a room as on the veldt." About seventy miles from their destination they were deserted by almost all their carriers, " but lamentations were useless," and leaving part of their party with the baggage, the remainder set out, and accomplished their journey in four days, the first half of the walk, from Chimoio to Masse Kesse

being accomplished in the shortest time then on record,
" so we were inclined to give ourselves great airs, as of
'African travellers.'" No wonder! for this walk was
through an almost pathless " veldt " infested with lions
and hyænas, who prowled round their shelters at night.
But their difficulties were not over. At Umtali nothing
was ready—even the site of the hospital was not
decided on, but in a short time, by their persistent
efforts, hospital huts were erected, and their work
began—work which was interrupted only by occasional
attacks of fever until the two years of their engagement
were over, and, weakened by fever, but with their
hospital thoroughly organised, they were able to hand it
over to their successors in working order, and to return
home. Not the least striking parts of the book are the
descriptions of men and women and manners. We
obtain a clear idea (clearer than perhaps the authors
intended) of Bishop Knight Bruce, who induced them to
undertake their enterprise, with his charming manners
and careful dress, his vacillating councils, swayed by the
last speaker, and his extraordinary want of judgment in
choosing his male coadjutors ; of the jovial but untrust-
worthy Johnson, with his "habit of romancing on all
occasions "; of Mr. Selous, "known throughout Africa
as the man who never tells a lie"; of the pleasant and
plucky young explorers, so many of whom, alas! dis-
appeared into the heart of the country to be seen no
more; of the savage queens, Maquaniqua and Chiconga,
with their attendant and obsequious husbands, and
their love of "fire-water"—"what was good for men
was good for women too, at least for chieftainesses!"
—of the kind and generous, if not too sober police, and
of many others.

We had marked many passages for quotation, but
selection is impossible ; and we must content ourselves
with recommending everyone to read for themselves
how two women, who for many months appear to
have been the only women in a camp of men, could
bring an element of order into chaos; insist on
necessary reforms ; win the respect of those among
whom they lived ; maintain their courage in a country
infested with wild beasts, and a camp invaded by

lions ; and their cheerfulness amid the most depressing circumstances, and the hardest and most monotonous work. With many higher qualities they were, fortunately, endowed with a sense of humour, which enabled them to extract amusement out of incidents from which many women would have extracted only worry ; and this quality not only lightened their labours at the time, but has helped them to write an exceedingly entertaining book, and one which does not depend for its interest on mere amusement, but on qualities of a more solid kind.

We cannot close without referring to the number of interesting people mentioned in the book. Mr. Rhodes, Mr. Selous, Mr. and Mrs. Theodore Bent visited Umtali during their stay there ; and on their journey home they met Mr. Eugen Wolf, the German explorer ; Bishop Smythies of Zanzibar ; and poor little Ferida, the daughter of Emin Pasha ; " a melancholy-looking coloured child, only redeemed from positive ugliness by a pair of magnificent Eastern eyes, large, lustrous, and solemn." She was under the charge of a German lady, and must have been a strange contrast to her " unusually fair, fat children." It is not a picture of happy childhood. " She said little or nothing, made no noise, and moped about in corners."

The Story of Two Noble Lives—Countess Canning and Lady Waterford, by A. J. Hare.

"This is going rather far back," we are inclined to exclaim on opening this book, which begins with the great-grandparents of its subjects. But the early beginning is justified by its interest, and the book would have been marred by the omission of any link in the chain of persons and events. The great-grandparents, the Earl and Countess of Balcarres, were remarkable characters in their day. They had a large family, of whom Lady Elizabeth—who as a child suggested to her sister, the authoress of Auld Robin Gray, Jeanie's culminating misfortune, " Steal the coo', sister Anne " —became the wife of Philip Yorke, Earl of Hardwicke. Her daughter Elizabeth, who married Sir Charles Stuart, afterwards Lord Stuart de Rothesay, ambassador at Paris during the Bourbon restoration, was the mother of the subjects of this memoir, the two beautiful and accomplished sisters, Charlotte, Lady Canning, whose husband was General-Governor of India throughout the Mutiny, and Louisa, Marchioness of Waterford, whose beautiful drawings won for her a high place in the Palace of Art, while her amiable and unselfish character earned the affection and esteem of all who knew her. The book extends over a period of nearly two centuries, from the Jacobite Rising in 1715, in which Lord Balcarres was "out," to the death of Lady Waterford in 18. It is composed chiefly of letters from Lady Hardwicke, Lady Stuart, Lady Canning and their friends, skilfully woven together by the editor, and when we say that these comprise letters from Ireland during Lord Hardwicke's Lord Lieutenancy, 1801-1806, from Paris from 1814-1824, and in 1830 and 1848, and from India during the terrible time of the Mutiny, we have said enough to show that they contain matter of the deepest interest. But much more may be said. All these ladies were clever, nay brilliant, letter writers, and their letters give a vivid picture of the events during these years of the principal actors in them and of society in England, Ireland, France and India. Perhaps the most brilliant letters of all are those of Lady Hardwicke, who, to the end of her long life, which terminated in 1858 at over ninety years of age, retained her vivacity and freshness of mind; but these yield in depth of interest to Lady Canning's, written during the Mutiny, in which we find ourselves admiring more and more her husband's stedfast and consistent attitude in the midst of unparalleled difficulties, never yielding to panic, and persevering in the course of what he felt to be his duty in spite of the clamours of the press, now for more severity, and now for greater leniency, and the ill-support of the Government at home. There are three thick volumes of this most interesting book, but there is little or nothing of it which one would wish to be omitted. It is illustrated with some excellent and some very indifferent engravings and photogravures, and it contains much of interest to which we have not space even to allude.

Ladies at Work. Edited by Lady Jeune.

The above is a collection of very interesting papers on some of the principal occupations of a professional nature now open to ladies, or, as we might otherwise say, those in which the peculiar qualities of women of culture and refinement are most distinctly of advantage to themselves or others. Perhaps "Ladies in Professions" would have been a more distinct and descriptive title of the book, since technical occupations and other miscellaneous work which might very well have been included in the more general term, are hardly touched upon. The several papers, which appeared originally as essays in the *Monthly Packet*, are all written by experts in the several branches, and treat of such subjects as journalism, art, authorship, the stage, medical work, with special reference to India, nursing, teaching, and work among the poor. They contain for the most part directions how to prepare for each of the careers described, not omitting, while holding out every encouragement to those who are willing to work, all the special difficulties and discouragements that may lie in the way of the aspirant, nor witholding what in these days of over-competition and pressure it would be cruelty to withold, the knowledge of the relative chances of making a living in each profession. An intending actress, for instance, is fairly warned that not only is the profession one involving much heavy work and severe physical strain, but that it is very much of the nature of a monopoly; so that an outsider without theatrical friends or connections, finds herself at a disadvantage compared with the child of a super or scene-shifter. If, however, she has a fair amount of talent, is hard-working and persevering, she may work her way up by slow degrees, but should on no account resort to the stage unless she can "afford to wait," and is not immediately obliged to earn her daily bread. Similarly, a teacher of music is told that the number of these being numerous out of all proportion to the demand, no one should in prudence rely on this profession who has not private means to fall back upon. Miss Fanny L. Green, the professional journalist, while describing the fascinating nature of the craft, and its manifold interests, informs us that it is also one of the most exacting, and any woman who should enter it with the idea of making money by a light, easy calling, would find she had made a huge mistake. As yet but few of the prizes of journalism have fallen to the lot of women; yet the craft compares favourably with many others, in that for the same work the same wages are given to women as to men. Miss C. M. Yonge, from her long experience, contributes some very valuable and very kindly hints to young writers—we may add distinctly encouraging to those who feel themselves irresistibly drawn to authorship. The chapter on art by Miss Florence Reason will go to the heart of all artists or art-students who love their work, and feel in it that exquisite joy that alone can carry them undaunted over the long drudgery of learning, or the struggles of their early career. The paper on nursing fully sets forth the blessings of the work as they appear to those who have a true vocation; but is calculated thoroughly to dispel the illusions of the too numerous class, who think they can be nurses because it is "so sweet," and fail at the outset before the very stern realities of a probationer's training.

We could wish that in her remarkably well-written introduction the editor had not expressed herself doubtful (though scarcely hostile) as to the value of the still to be conceded boon of the suffrage, and its necessity in constituting women the actual as well as the theoretical equals of men before the law. Until women are to all intents and purposes really citizens, it is to be feared that no amount of education, professional status, or character, will suffice to ensure them their due estimate of worth and dignity, so closely are the ideas of political and individual worth inwoven in the British mind, consciously or unconsciously. In these days, too, when the suffrage is fast becoming extended to all men, irrespective of character or capacity, it becomes doubly important that women should no longer be content to form a class apart, whose interest legislators may safely disregard; nor their patriotism suffer them to be indifferent to the possession of a vote, by which they can most effectively modify the counsels of their country for good.

The whole of the papers, however, apart from the valuable indications which most of them contain, are especially to be commended for the distinct tone of hope and courage which they convey. While the writers all alike candidly state the disadvantages as well as advantages of their chosen vocation, never seeking to palliate or disguise the former, they breathe nothing but the most welcome encouragement to willing workers. Though such workers are told that even the brightest talents and most highly-trained intelligences must be prepared for inevitable disappointments and difficulties, they are also brought to feel that persevering and conscientious work must win the day at last, and secure some, if not an overwhelming, measure of success. *Avec les braves il n'y a rien d'impossible* might well have been the motto of the book; the watchword throughout is "be brave;" and Lady Jeune does full justice to the wonderful courage of the early pioneers in the woman's movement, which captured the strongholds of medicine, of education, and to a large extent of the political world, and set free the imprisoned intelligence of women to work its destined career of good. "Much has been done, but more remains to do," and it depends on ourselves if we are faithful and have spirit enough to carry on the work of our predecessors, and do all it lies in us to do.

We have not space to linger over the remaining papers, though many of these contain valuable hints on trained teaching, the life of a lady doctor in India, with Miss Sophia Lonsdale's valuable suggestions on work among the poor, and the importance of securing well qualified—and well paid—professional workers for this purpose. A chapter by Lady Clifford deals with the profession of lady attendants for the insane. This is hardly a branch of nursing, as nurses of a lower grade and a staff of servants are employed in all mental hospitals; the attendants spoken of act rather as lady-companions to patients of their own social grade, and receive six months' training as the sole preliminary to their profession. They receive a salary of £25 a year,

with all found, and wear a gray uniform when on duty.
We cannot either quite pass by Miss Coleridge's concluding paper on " The lady of all work," by which she
signifies the energetic, capable being, who without
being tied down to any visible profession of her own, or
ostensibly living any but a family or a society life, is
nevertheless actively engaged in work of various kinds,
on councils and committees, organizing, directing, helping, acting as a kind of centre of encouragement and
assistance to other workers, the "free lance," so to
speak, of the woman's movement. At the same time she
must neglect no duty, whether domestic or social, and
must always be ready to decide which of her many
occupations must, if need be, go to the wall, in favour of
the most important. She is as much the product of
the latter end of the nineteenth century as the lady
doctor or trained nurse, and an account of her activities
and vocation seems a very fit conclusion to the volume.

A. B.

OBITUARY.

Mlle. Maria Deraismes died in Paris, February 6.
Of this eminent worker in the cause of women, the
following appreciative account appeared from the pen
of their Paris correspondent in the *Daily News* :—

"The deceased, who was a member of the Société
des Gens de Lettres, and of the Grand Orient masonic
lodge, was a woman of singularly great and brilliant
gifts and acquirements, and not only of powerful inteltect, but of great heart and moral nature. Look at her
from whatever point one might, she was a splendid
being. Fortune could not shut her in or cramp her
broad sympathies. The highest culture did not make
her fastidious or separate her from the working women

of Paris, of whom she was the spokeswoman for thirty
years. Her conversation beamed with wit, and was
rousing from its originality. She was entirely free
from vanity. Her deep earnestness of purpose, her
passionate love of justice, were kept out of sight,
though they were always directing her conduct, and
were the source of inspiration when she wrote and
spoke for the public. She was as good-tempered as
she was kindly. Her tact was never at fault on the
platform or elsewhere. She had a merry way of dis-
posing of an adversary which placed all the laughers on
her side. It often was said that nobody of her time so
thoroughly possessed the French language or was able
to be trenchant with so light a hand. For long years
she defended the rights of childhood. Any ill-used
child, whether in a slum, a school, an asylum, or a
penitentiary, was sure to find in her an active and sym-
pathising advocate and protectress. Her house was a
meeting-place for practical reformers of all countries.
She was hospitable, wealthy and animating. It was,
perhaps, the most delightful house in Paris. Those
publicists who entered her circle were bound not to
speak of it in the press. Maria Deraismes died of
cancer. She struggled heroically through her long
illness to hide her sufferings from her only sister, who
always lived with her. She also continued to lead the
campaign in favour of the claim of Parisian tradeswomen to take part in the election of the judges of the
Tribunal of Commerce. The last consolation of her
life was to receive a collective visit from her friends in
the Senate to assure her that the petition in favour of
civil rights being extended to women had been well
received. It was preparing the way for a Bill that
would give her every satisfaction. The *Débats* gives a
long obituary notice of Mlle. Deraismes. It says of
her that during thirty years she worked to give woman
as high a place as man in the statute book and in society
and human life. It cites among her writings, which
were chiefly controversial, her witty pamphlet, 'Eve
contre M. Dumas fils,' and her critique on the Théâtre
de M. Sardou, in which, with a light touch, and in a
style at once sober and glowing with humour, she finds

MM. Sardou and Dumas guilty of befouling her sex to amuse the public. The *Débats* calls particular attention to a volume published under the title of "L'Epidémie Naturaliste" in art and literature. She was the enemy of a school which seeks exclusively to deal with the baser instincts of human nature, and to give the seasoning of talent to pictures of gross or refined vices. Mlle. Maria Deraismes was an active journalist, contributing to the *Epoque*, the *Grand Journal*, the *Nain Jaune* in De Villemessant's time, and to the *République Française* in its early days. She seldom signed her articles. The shadow of a scandal never passed over, much less settled on, her great and good life."

GEORGIANA LADY WOLVERTON passed away from among us on January 10th last. The daughter of the Rev. George Tufnell, of Uffington, Berks, she married in 1848 George Grenfell Glyn, who in 1873 succeeded his father as second Baron Wolverton, and was left a widow in 1887. To the outside world she was, perhaps, best known as the foundress of the Needlework Guild, of which H.R.H. the Duchess of Teck is patron, and which extends its helping hand to so many charities and poor parishes in London and the country, but she was identified with almost every charitable and benevolent work in the districts in which she resided, and was also the founder of the House Boys' Brigade, an orphanage at Iwerne, and the Barmaids' Guild. In truth her life was lived for others, her purse being always open, as far as was in her power, to help those in need, while her sympathy and kindness were even more far-reaching. But Lady Wolverton was gifted not only with the sympathy, kindness, and generosity which are not seldom met with, cheering poor mortals in their struggles and sorrows; she combined with them in an unusual degree qualities which greatly enhanced their value, a keenness of perception and power of organisation which enabled her to extend their effect far beyond the sphere of her personal influence. She could see the work needed, the way of doing it, and the people by whom it could be done. Her wish was that her *work*, not her *name* should last. "We want," she said, speaking of the Needlework Guild, "the guild to last and grow, and not to die out anywhere. Of course if personal feeling is the motive, the removal of the person means the collapse of the work." Herself one of the women who find distraction and comfort in the use of the needle, she was convinced that there were many others with like tastes whose lives would be far happier if they had an object to work for. This conviction took a definite shape through a sudden demand for clothes for her orphanage. Unable to supply the demand by her own work, Lady Wolverton appealed to people staying in her house to help her. "No one," she says, in her own account of the incident, "'seemed to have anything particular to do,' and gladly set to work. It then occurred to me for the first time that there must be hundreds of women in England working aimlessly, many uselessly; and, on the other hand, there were thousands of men, women, and children wanting clothes. If only a little bridge could be thrown over from the Island of Waste to the Island of Want how both would benefit!" This was the beginning of the Needlework Guild, which was founded in 1882 and has now spread into almost every county in England, into Scotland, Ireland, America, France, Italy, Switzerland, and Australia. It numbers 116 groups, and last year sent up 48,050 articles of clothing for distribution. Being in earnest herself, she inspired her fellow workers with her own spirit, and set them a wonderful example of industry. "We must," she said, "'gather up fragments' of time, as well as material, as in our guild nothing must be lost." And again, "Is it not enough to make us vow to waste no precious moment, when, by gathering them up we can do so much to lighten heavy hearts?" An invalid herself for the last years of her life, she still worked and found that "illness is not of necessity an inactive state." Almost her last words and thoughts on earth were for "the dear guild."

Lady Wolverton died at 73, South Audley Street, and was buried at Iwerne Minster, near Blandford, on January 16. A memorial service was held on the 15th at St. Mary Abbott's Church, when, among the numerous mourners were a hundred boys of the House Boys' Brigade, and a deputation from the Eastern Central Institution for Telegraph Boys. Among the many wreaths and crosses placed on the coffin was one little cross with a card inscribed "From one to whom she was kind."

MISS SOPHIA DOBSON COLLET.—The death is announced of Miss Sophia Dobson Collet, so well known as a writer on religious movements in India. Miss Collet was engaged at the time of her death on the life of the great Indian religious reformer Rammohun Roy, which she has left unfinished. She edited the lectures given by Keshub Chunder Sen during his visit to England in 1870, also the "Brahmo Year Book," besides writing many contributions to periodical literature. Although a victim all her life to complicated physical troubles, her disposition was one of the greatest cheerfulness, and she gathered round her a large circle of intellectual and devoted friends.

MRS. MENZIES.—We regret to have to record the death of Mrs. Menzies, of 24, Carlton Hill, N.W. During several years she assisted in the publication of this Review. Her good judgment made her a valuable co-operator, and her loss will be felt by those who are interested in the employment of women.

FOREIGN AND COLONIAL NOTES.

AUSTRALIA. (*See also* p. 100.)

At the commemoration of the Adelaide University held December 21 last, Miss Marian Chapple was awarded the John Howard Clark Scholarship for English Literature. The Chancellor said the John Howard Clark Scholarship had been awarded twelve times, and for eleven years in succession it had been won by men. Miss Chapple's success was a victory for her sex as well as for herself. He congratulated the lady. On the same occasion two ladies took the degree of B.Sc.—Stella Howchin and Violet May Plummer.

A system of instruction in the primary principles of agriculture and horticulture has been instituted in connection with the public primary schools of South Australia. The colony has been divided into six divisions, and there are prizes for the children. At the recent examinations, taking the six divisions as a whole, the girls were quite equal to the boys.

NEW ZEALAND. (*See* p. 100 and 108.)

FRANCE.

The Senate, on Jan. 19, by 132 votes to 84, agreed to give votes to women engaged in business at elections of the tribunals of commerce.

The Regulation of the Employment of Women and Children in France.—The *Labour News* states that : " The district inspectors appointed to administer the law of November, 1892, regulating the employment of women and children in factories and workshops, have made their first report. The clauses of the law were not rigorously enforced until October 1, 1893, and the reports are made up to November 15. From a summary of these reports it appears that the prohibition of the employment of children under 13 has roused little opposition, except that a few glass works have asked permission to retain in their employment children engaged before the passing of the law. The provision limiting the working day to ten hours for children under 16, to eleven hours a day and sixty hours a week for young persons from 16 to 18, and to eleven hours a day for women, has been followed by protests in every district in all trades employing adults, young persons and children together. The manufacturers complain that they are practically obliged either to fix the hours at ten a day for all employed, or to organise relays of children and young persons, or to dismiss children and young persons altogether. This third course is often impossible, owing to the difficulty of obtaining enough adult labour. The first, in the opinion of the manufacturers, would entail increased cost of production and a reduction of wages, and the second makes the proper regulation of the work-room difficult, removes the children from the control of their parents, and likewise makes it difficult to secure conformity with the law. There has been but little opposition to the provision prohibiting the employment of women, and of young persons and children at night work, except from a few newspaper printing offices, wool carding works and small industries. With reference to the exceptions allowed in various industries, the factory inspectors lay great stress on the great difficulty in enforcing the law if they have a great variety of details to superintend."

SWITZERLAND.

Female Factory Inspectors.—The united Workwomen's Unions and Women's Leagues of the canton of Zürich have addressed a petition to the Government, praying that the enforcement of the recent Cantonal Law for the protection of female and child workers should be entrusted to female factory inspectors. The petition has been refused for the present.

UNITED STATES.

COLORADO.—A copy of the Proclamation of the Governor of Colorado, issued on December 2nd, after the passing of the Women's

Suffrage Bill, appears in the *Worcestershire Echo* of January 24, sent by a correspondent in Denver *àpropos* of some remarks in that paper on the political education of women. The proclamation may also interest the readers of the ENGLISHWOMAN'S REVIEW:—

PROCLAMATION
BY
THE GOVERNOR OF THE STATE OF COLORADO.

WHEREAS, The Ninth General Assembly of the State of Colorado passed an Act, approved April 7, 1893, entitled "An Act to submit to the qualified electors of the State the question of extending the right of suffrage to women of lawful age, and otherwise qualified, according to the provisions of Article 7, Section 2 of the Constitution of Colorado," and

WHEREAS, The said question, as provided in Section 2 of said Act, was submitted to the qualified voters of the State of Colorado, at the general election held on Tuesday, November 7, 1893; and

WHEREAS, After canvass of the official returns of said election by the State Canvassing Board, it appeared that of the votes cast—

35,798 votes were cast for "Equal Suffrage Approved," and 29,451 votes were cast for "Equal Suffrage Not Approved," and that the majority for "Equal Suffrage Approved" was 6,347 votes.

Now, THEREFORE, I, DAVIS H. WAITE, Governor of Colorado, do hereby proclaim, as provided in Section 5 of the said Act, that every female person, a resident in Colorado, shall be entitled to vote at all elections in the same manner in all respects as male persons, and subject to the same qualifications.

"GOD AND LIBERTY."
Done at Denver, December 2, 1893.

DAVIS H. WAITE,
Governor of Colorado.
NELSON O. McCLEES,
Secretary of State.

KENTUCKY.—*The Women's Tribune* says: "The Husband and Wife Bill was signed Thursday, March 15, by the Governor. The measure is a radical change in laws governing marital relations, so far as property is concerned, and gives the wife exclusive control of her separate estate. The general effect of it is to make every married woman owning property, separate and apart from her husband, practically a *femme sole*, and empowers her to sell and convey, to contract and be contracted with and transact all business as though she were a single woman. It also equalises courtesy and dower. We have been working for this for six years, and this bill gives us all we ask for."

MASSACHUSETTS.—The Municipal Women's Suffrage Bill passed second reading in the Massachusett's House of Representatives on March 14, by 122 to 106, including pairs. The third reading, which was to have taken place on March 17, was adjourned to the 29th.

OHIO. —The Ohio Legislature has just removed one of the disabilities of married women in that State by passing a bill providing that the marriage of a woman shall not disqualify her from acting as administratrix or executrix, "whether such marriage occur before or after her appointment or qualification."

The Bill to extend School Suffrage to Women in Ohio was defeated in the House of Representatives by 46 to 44.

PASSING NOTES.

WOMEN AND PRESS REFORM.

THE *Woman's Journal* of January 13 states that more than twenty thousand California women have signed the following petition to the San Francisco newspapers:—

We, the Women of California, present you this petition, which we believe represents the convictions of many times the number of those whose names are subscribed. We recognise that the newspaper is indispensable in our homes, and as the guardians of family purity we make this appeal.

We approve of our papers in their energy and enterprise, but we believe the time has come for them to take a higher stand on the question of public morals. We deplore in them "sensationalism," not the exposure of crime. We deplore "personalities," not the public announcement of personal acts. We believe that it is a minority of your readers who demand sensational, personal or immoral details, rather than the clean statement of facts and truth. There is too often a minuteness of detail in the reports given of crime, wickedness and sensuality, which can gratify only prurient and vulgar curiosity, or awaken such curiosity in innocent and inexperienced minds. We feel that spreading broadcast vicious and debasing news in our homes and among our children, and the consequent knowledge and easy familiarity with crime in all its forms, has a tendency to lower the tone of thought among the best of our people, and to strengthen the worst instincts among the morally lower classes.

We, therefore, most earnestly and respectfully petition the press at this time to make a concerted effort to elevate the moral tone of their columns, and to give us newspapers free from the evils we deplore, feeling confident that the majority of the public will encourage such an effort, and promising you our heartfelt co-operation and support.

The beneficial results of this protest have been visible and gratifying. The following is quoted from a private letter:—

"As direct proof of the immediate effect of this effort on our local press, a reporter on ———, one of the two most offensively and enterprisingly sensational of our dailies, told me that since this movement he and his kind were under special instructions to treat their details in a restrained and cleanly manner." . . .

"This movement," says the *Tribune*, "originated with the Pacific Coast Women's Press Association, and has been heartily welcomed and supported by all respectable people in California." In a long article on the subject, it justly remarks that journalists ought to remember that their "end in life is so to serve humanity as to raise its general level," and that they ought not to be found "justifying error by its pecuniary profitableness." It maintains also that it is a mistake, even from a pecuniary point of view, to cater only for readers of low tastes. "Thousands of readers are honestly disgusted every day by the needless parade of vice and crime in our daily papers, but not one in a thousand takes the trouble to write a private letter to the editor and remonstrate. Hence silence is taken to imply consent, and, perhaps, even secret approval."

May we hope that a similar movement to that inaugurated by the California women may be set on foot in England.

MISS MASON'S REPORT TO THE LOCAL GOVERNMENT BOARD FOR 1892-3.

During the year 1892-3 Miss Mason visited forty-three committees, having under their care 640 children boarded out in twenty-one of the English counties, and attended five conferences of committees, guardians and others interested in the boarding-out system. The result of her experience, which now extends over some years, is that she remains of the same opinion as to the excellence of the boarding-out system, if well administered, within certain limits. She does not "find that elder children, or those of feeble intellect, or exceptionally bad habits or disposition are, as a rule, benefited by it. But for suitable cases, if placed in suitable homes and well supervised, nothing can be better." The general report of the condition of the children is extremely satisfactory, and where abuses occur, the cause can usually be traced to defective supervision on the part of the boarding-out committee. The committees, however, generally take real interest and trouble in their work, and are more awake than they formerly were to the necessity of effective supervision and inspection.

WOMEN DENTISTS IN RUSSIA.

By the courtesy of Mrs. Bolton Lacey, the first Englishwoman to have practised the art of dentistry, we have been furnished with the following particulars of the school for the art of dentistry, opened in St. Petersburg on September 25, 1893, by Madame Helen Vongl de Svydersky, D.D.S. of the Dental College of New York:—

After completing her studies in New York, Madame Svydersky started in practice at St. Petersburg. She was at that time the only woman dentist in all the Russias. Their number has since rapidly increased. A dental hospital, founded by Madame Svydersky in St. Petersburg some years ago, has made excellent progress, and she has now founded the College, which was opened last September, and admits persons of both sexes between the ages of 17 and 40. The College is under the *surveillance* of the Inspector General of Medical Administration in St. Petersburg. The course of study extends over two years and a half, and students who pass through the course with success will obtain a certificate entitling them to apply for a diploma as Surgeon Dentist, on condition of passing an examination before the Examining Committee of the University or of the Academy of Medicine.

The Editor wishes to intimate that "Inquirer" will be glad of any information on the subject of her letter in the January number on Foreign Homes for Women. Any communications sent to the office of this REVIEW would be forwarded to her.

London School of Medicine for Women.

IN ASSOCIATION WITH
THE ROYAL FREE HOSPITAL.

THE Course of Study includes a complete preparation for the Medical Examinations of the University of London, the Royal University of Ireland, the Conjoint Examinations of the King and Queen's College of Physicians and the Royal College of Surgeons, Ireland, and the Conjoint Examinations for the Scottish Triple Qualification of the College of Physicians and College of Surgeons, Edinburgh, and the Faculty of Physicians and Surgeons, Glasgow. Also for the Diploma of the Society of Apothecaries, London, in Medicine, Surgery and Midwifery. For information respecting Scholarships, &c., apply to the Dean, Mrs. GARRETT ANDERSON, M.D., or to Mrs. THORNE, *Honorary Secretary*, 30, Handel Street, Brunswick Square, W.C.

EDINBURGH SCHOOL OF MEDICINE FOR WOMEN,

SPECIALLY RECOGNISED AS

Qualifying for the University of St. Andrews.

President:
H.R.H. The Duchess of Fife.

Vice-Presidents:
The Marchioness of Tweeddale. The Lady Helen Munro Ferguson. The Lady Reay.

This School forms an integral part of the Extra Mural School of Edinburgh. Its five years' curriculum is specially adapted to the requirements of the University of St. Andrews and of the Conjoint Scottish Colleges, but qualifies for all other examining Boards. Winter Courses, 100 Lectures each; Summer Courses, 50 to 60 Lectures each. Clinical instruction in the Royal Infirmary, with special cliniques in the Eye, Throat, and Ear, Skin, Gynæcological, and Lock Wards, with Clinical Lectures in Medicine and Surgery. School Fees, £75 in four instalments; or total Fees for qualifying course in School and Hospital, £95 in one payment. For information as to Scholarships, &c., apply to Dr. JEX BLAKE, *Dean;* or Miss BLACK, *Secretary*, Surgeon Square, Edinburgh.

THE UNITED SISTERS' FRIENDLY SOCIETY
(SUFFOLK UNITY).

"Work and Leisure" Court, No. 15.

The object of the Society is threefold; to afford
 1. A weekly allowance in sickness.
 2. An annuity commencing at the age of 65.
 3. A sum of money (£6 or upwards) payable at death to the duly nominated representative of a Member.

All single women and widows of good health and character, between the ages of 16 and 45, are eligible for Membership in the "Work and Leisure" Court, subject to election by the Committee, and to a satisfactory Medical Certificate from a duly qualified Medical Practitioner. A further examination by one of the Physicians of the Court may be required by the Committee.

President: Miss L. M. HUBBARD, Editor of "Work and Leisure."
Secretary: Miss EDITH M. MASKELL, 7c, Lower Belgrave Street London, S.W.
(To whom all communications should be addressed.)

THE NEW HOSPITAL FOR WOMEN,
144, EUSTON ROAD. N.W.

THE PHYSICIANS ARE WOMEN.

Treasurer:—Mrs. WESTLAKE, The River House, 3, Chelsea Embankment, S.W.
Hon. Secretary:—Miss VINCENT, 6c, Hyde Park Mansions, N.W.
Physicians and Surgeons to the Patients:—Mrs. MARSHALL, M.D.;
Mrs. DE LA CHEROIS, M.D.; Miss COCK, M.D.;
Mrs. SCHARLIEB, M.D., B.S.Lond.
Physicians and Surgeons to Out Patients:—Miss WALKER, M.D.;
Miss WEBB, M.B.; Mrs. STANLEY BOYD, M.D.
Ophthalmic Surgeon:—Miss ELLABY, M.D.
Assisted by a Consulting Staff of Physicians and Surgeons.

This Hospital is established to enable poor women to be attended by FULLY QUALIFIED WOMEN DOCTORS.

A Report and further information may be had on application to MISS MARGARET M. BAGSTER, *Secretary.*

Bankers:—BANK OF ENGLAND (Western Branch), Burlington Gardens, W.

Crown 8vo.   **One Shilling** (Post Free).   In the Press.

BRITISH FREEWOMEN:
THEIR HISTORICAL PRIVILEGE.

Showing the Historical Aspect of the Women's Suffrage Question.

BY CHARLOTTE CARMICHAEL STOPES.

Of all Booksellers, or at 10, GREAT COLLEGE ST., WESTMINSTER, S.W.

SWAN, SONNENSCHEIN & CO., LONDON.

Society for Promoting the Employment of Women.
22, BERNERS STREET, OXFORD STREET, W.

Established 1859.   *Incorporated* 1879.

This Society was established for the purpose of finding openings for girls to learn different kinds of trade and business. Also for aiding those already trained to procure employment. A register is kept for experienced and certificated Bookkeepers, Saleswomen, Matrons, Sick-nurses, Engravers, Law Writers, Printers, Gilders, and other assistants. Orders for copying MSS., circulars, &c., and for directing envelopes, are promptly executed.

Bookkeeping.

A class for training young women as Clerks and Bookkeepers is held on the evenings of Monday and Thursday.

PRICE ONE SHILLING.

New Series—Vol. XXV. No. III.   July 16th, 1894.

THE
ENGLISHWOMAN'S REVIEW

OF

Social and Industrial Questions.

EDITED BY HELEN BLACKBURN.

CONTENTS FOR JULY, 1894.

ARTICLES.—More Dangers to the British Workwoman. Report on the Employment of Women by the Lady Assistant Commissioners *(continued)*, by Miss J. BOUCHERETT. With all my Worldly Goods I thee Endow, by Mrs. STOPES.

WOMEN'S SUFFRAGE.—Notes of the Quarter. Annual Meeting of the Central Committee. Report of the Appeal Committee. Results of the Election in New Zealand. Australian Women's Suffrage Society in Melbourne.

ELECTIONS AND APPOINTMENTS.

UNIVERSITY INTELLIGENCE.

RECORD OF EVENTS.—Deputation to Home Secretary on Factory Bill. London County Council Domestic Economy Scholarships. Ladies' Committee of Chicago Exhibition. British Silk Association. Swanley Horticultural College. Society for the Employment of Women. Memorial to Jenny Lind.

REVIEWS.—British Freewomen. Letters of Harriet, Countess of Granville. A Plea for Appointment of Police Matrons. The Relation of Women to Municipal Reform. Le Grand Catechisme de la Femme. Woman and her place in a Free Society.

PASSING NOTES.—Technical Teaching for Girls in Ireland. Registration of Midwives.

CORRESPONDENCE.—Progress of Women in Germany. The Deceased Wife's Sister. L'avant Courrière.

CHARACTERISTICS OF WOMEN'S PICTURES.

LONDON

PUBLISHED AT THE OFFICE OF THE "ENGLISHWOMAN'S REVIEW,"
22, BERNERS STREET, OXFORD STREET, W.

AND FOR THE PROPRIETOR BY

WILLIAMS & NORGATE, 14, Henrietta Street, Covent Garden, London
and 20, South Frederick Street, Edinburgh.

PUBLISHED QUARTERLY on the 15th January, April, July, and October.

ENGLISHWOMAN'S REVIEW.] *Advertisements.* [JULY 16th, 1894.

WOMEN'S SUFFRAGE.

APPEAL
FROM WOMEN IN FAVOUR OF WOMEN'S SUFFRAGE

All enquiries and communications to be addressed to Miss Helen Blackburn, 10, Great College Street, Westminster, or Miss Gertrude Stewart, 29, Parliament Street, S.W., by whom books for signatures will be supplied on application.

Central Committee of the National Society for Women's Suffrage.

Hon. Sec.: Mrs. FAWCETT.   *Secretary:* Miss HELEN BLACKBURN.

Office: 10, GREAT COLLEGE STREET, WESTMINSTER.

MARRIAGE LAW DEFENCE UNION.

An Appeal from the Women of England	1d.
The Woman's View of the Question	1d.
A Letter to English Wives. By Edith Mary Shaw ...	6d.
A Lady's Letter to a Friend, on behalf of those who do not wish to Marry their Brothers	½d.
What Miss Lydia Becker says	½d.
A Sister-in-Law's Plea for Mercy	½d.
A Woman's Opinion on the Wife's Sister Bill	½d.

MAY BE HAD AT
1, KING STREET, WESTMINSTER, S.W.

PERIODICAL PUBLICATIONS received during the Quarter:—
  AMERICA—*Woman's Journal; Woman's Exponent; The Woman's Tribune; Demorest's Monthly Magazine; The Cycle.*
  AUSTRALIA—*Dawn.*
  AUSTRIA—*Mitheilungen; Volkstimme.*
  BELGIUM—*Revendication du Droit des Femmes.*
  FRANCE—*Le Journal des Femmes.*
  SWEDEN—*Dagny.*
  NORWAY—*Nylaende.*
  DENMARK—*Kvinden og Samfundet.*
  SWITZERLAND (Zurich)—*Frauenrecht.*
  The Indian Magazine; Woman; Concord; The Lady of the House; Women's Union Journal; Review of Reviews; Threefold Cord; The Spinning Wheel; Nursing Notes.

A FAIR FIELD AND NO FAVOUR!

*Office for the Employment of Women as Compositors.
Girls trained and employed for the past twenty years.*

Ladies and Gentlemen are invited to place their orders for

PRINTING

WHERE THEY WILL BE EXECUTED BY

Women

IN A STYLE

EQUAL TO THE BEST.

NO SLIPSHOD WORK!
NO EXORBITANT PRICES!!

Estimates for Book and Magazine Work with Specimens.

JOHN BALE & SONS,

Steam Printers,

87-89, GREAT TITCHFIELD STREET,

OXFORD STREET, LONDON W

Englishwoman's Review.

CONTENTS FOR APRIL 16th, 1894.

ARTICLES:
>The Report on the Employment of Women, by the Lady Assistant Commissioners, by Miss J. Boucherett (continued). The British Workwoman in danger. Lucy Stone, by Miss M. A. Biggs. Maria Deraismes and the Woman's Movement in France, by Madame Schmahl. The Winter is Past (Poem), by Mrs. Warner Snoad.

WOMEN'S SUFFRAGE:
>Notes of the Quarter. Resolutions of Liberal Associations. South Australia. New Zealand. Second Record of Meetings.

ELECTIONS AND APPOINTMENTS.

RECORD OF EVENTS:
>The Local Government Act. The Association of Irish Schoolmistresses. The Alexandra School. Lady Margaret Hall. Girls' Public Day School Company. The New Welsh University. Conference of Women's Protective and Provident League (Scotland). The Royal Commission on Employment of Women. Irish Association for Employment of Women. Edinburgh School of Medicine. London School of Medicine. Oriental Students. M.A.B.Y.S. Clubs, &c., &c.

REVIEWS:
>The Rights of Women. Adventures in Mashonaland. Two Noble lives. Ladies at Work.

OBITUARY:
>Mdlle. Maria Deraismes. Georgiana Lady Wolverton. Miss Dobson Collet. Mrs. Menzies.

FOREIGN AND COLONIAL NOTES.

PASSING NOTES:
>Women and Press Reform. Miss Mason's Report. Women Dentists in Russia.

ated of the Home Secretary, which, though in so many words ex-

THE
ENGLISHWOMAN'S REVIEW

(NEW SERIES.)

No. CCXXII.—JULY 16TH, 1894.

ART. I.—MORE DANGER TO THE BRITISH WORKWOMAN.

THE British workwoman is in even greater danger than we anticipated when we wrote on this subject in the last issue of this REVIEW, for since then the new Factory and Workshops Bill has been printed, and we now know that it proposes to pursue further the policy of treating adult women as children—which has been the blemish on all factory legislation hitherto—and also that it proposes to put new powers in the hands of the Home Secretary, which, though in so many words extending equally to men, would in fact press much more hardly on women. With the recent experience of the efforts made to stop the work of the pit-brow women and the nail and chain makers fresh in our memory, it is impossible to avoid the conclusion that the Home Secretary would have much pressure brought to bear on him to declare as dangerous, and to forbid trades in which women work, wholly irrespective of the needs and wishes of the workers themselves, and that the pressure of the voting portion of the community might easily outweigh any opposition which women—at least as long as they lack the power of the vote—could bring to bear.

Mr. Asquith will surely meet with disappointment if he expects that his reply to the deputation which waited on him at the House of Commons on June 26—a report of which is given elsewhere—will reassure those who believe that the clauses in the Bill affecting women, however kindly meant, would operate to the great disadvantage of the workers. He has in truth only deepened the serious alarm with which many persons, earnestly interested in labour questions, regard his Bill. Those who attended the deputation knew full well already that the whole existing legislation in regard to factories "rests on the assumption that public safety and public interest require that women should be treated in some matters, and among others in the hours of labour, on a different footing from men." It is precisely that assumption which they dispute. True, the deputation did not seek any alteration of the existing law—what is done is done, and for good or for ill the conditions of work have adapted themselves to the dislocations caused by past legislation; what they deprecate is any further legislation in the same direction.

It is easy to believe that the minister who has charge of this Bill does not aim at the destruction of home work, but only at preventing the evasion of the law. But that the aims of the Home Secretary are not the aims of the persons who are urging on this legislation is rendered only too apparent by the many indications of a growing desire amongst labour leaders and trade unionists to put an end to home work. Working women know this by their own experience. Living in the midst of the labour atmosphere they can perceive currents at work which are imperceptible to those outside, and assurances that the Bill will not hurt them and does not intend to limit them to eight hours are no proof that the Bill will not strike a serious blow at home work.

Women must have some command of money in order to secure their own dignity and self respect. Rich men know this, and insist on marriage settlements for their daughters. Poor women know this, and seek to earn some addition to the family income which may be within their own control. The married woman who is industrious and thrifty finds she can do best by her family if she takes work to do at home and can choose her own times and seasons—let the thriftless and feckless say what they please; no matter what the law, such will remain thriftless and feckless still.

Unless, and until, husbands recognise the value of the domestic work of wives, the power of earning will be a necessity—it is in fact to the poor woman what marriage settlements are to the rich, and every interference with her freedom of action in the matter is a blow at her effectiveness in life. The struggle that is going on now in the labour world lies between this natural desire of women to have some control of their surroundings, and the desire of men to retain all within their own hands. The instincts of the women were perfectly right, which led them to desire to place their views before the Home Secretary; they can perceive threatenings invisible to him, they hear mutterings of this trade and that being called unsuitable for women, and though the present authorities may not heed such mutterings, what guarantee have voteless women against future efforts?

Had Mr. Asquith cross-questioned the women less and listened to their causes of apprehension more, he would have found that they did not misunderstand the nature of his Bill. They came to protest against interference in their labour, not for themselves only, but for women generally. They know well that there are multitudes, like the embroidress who said she gladly worked overtime beyond the limits proposed by the Bill, at one season without pay, to take it out in holidays with pay, at another; and very many also like the shirt maker, who freely admitted, until Mr. Asquith's cross-questioning frightened her, that she habitually worked beyond the legal hours of overtime for five months in the year, in order to earn sufficient for the slack months. Even the boot closer, who dreaded lest her trade should be considered injurious, was not so much out of order as she seemed; for she had already heard her trade so stigmatised at a meeting—supposed to be a meeting of laundresses, in support of the Bill, but where no laundresses were present. Had Mr. Asquith, instead of trying to confuse and confound the women, listened to their perhaps not too articulate representations, he would have perceived that his effort to protect the poorest workers from over-pressure was the cause of very serious and reasonable alarm amongst a large number of steady, industrious women, who dread to have the rough arm of the law thrust in between them and their employers.

Certain laws of general guidance there must be, but to compel the intervention of law in every mutual arrangement is not the way to encourage a growth of friendly feeling in transactions between individuals, into which all human relations must finally resolve themselves. Moreover, the constant intervention of law is a sure way of calling out ingenuity in its evasion, and the effort to substitute protection for control of their own affairs will either become a dead-letter law, or it will undermine respect for those so protected.

The crying need of the day is for more respect for women workers, and this Bill offers them less. Respect is the only true protection for any human being. None injures another whom he respects.

Art. II.—REPORT BY THE LADY ASSISTANT COMMISSIONERS ON THE EMPLOYMENT OF WOMEN.

(*Continued.*)

Miss Collet continues her report and enquires into the condition of *shop assistants and dressmakers* in provincial towns.

She met with an instance of extraordinary long hours—the longest on which evidence was given her anywhere—in a small shop in which wool, shirts, tobacco and snuff were sold. The shop was kept by a widow and her daughter, with one assistant. The hours of the assistant were from 8.30 to 8.30 on ordinary days, and until midnight on Saturday. On Sunday morning she had to clean the shop and arrange the shop window, so that Sunday afternoon was her only holiday time except bank holidays. The food was good, though she had scarcely time to eat it, but the wages were only 4s. 6d. a week the first year, which was raised to 5s. the second year, and 5s. 3d. the third year. The assistant made no complaint of loss of health, which confirms my impression that when women get plenty of good food they can do a surprising amount of work without suffering, and that half the illness supposed to be caused by hard work is really caused by the combination of hard work and poor food. The work of an ordinary servant girl in a lodging house is far harder than the work of this exceptionally hard-pressed shop assistant, the hours being usually from six in the morning till ten at night, during which time the poor slavey is almost constantly on her feet going up and down stairs, sometimes carrying heavy trays. Yet it does not very often happen that the girls break down under the strain. They are sustained by the good food. This shows, I think, that the aim of persons interested in improving the condition of women, should be directed to obtaining for them higher wages and consequently better food, rather than towards shortening their hours of work.

Miss Collet is of opinion that factory women are much

better off than shop women, both as regards length of hours, comfort and health. She reckons that the wear and tear of mind of a shop assistant counts for a good deal, and that the comparative freedom from care of a factory hand makes her life happier as well as healthier. She is also of opinion that factory women are better off than dressmakers as regards hours of work, health and wages. She considers *dress and mantle makers* a specially ill paid class. They do not earn enough to obtain good food. She mentions several instances of "improvers" in dressmaking who only received 5s. a week, and had to find their own food; in one place improvers only had 3s. 6d. a week, without meals. One woman over 30 had 8s. a week, but paid 2s. a week for her room. She only brought dry bread or cold potatoes with her for lunch.

Wages are not rising in the dressmaking trade, but rather the contrary. This is a matter for regret, but not for surprise. The restrictions on women's work already imposed by the Factory and Workshops Act have turned a good many out of their trades, and prevented young girls from entering them. These dispossessed women, and young girls starting in life naturally crowd into needlework of all kinds, and by competition bring down wages.

Miss Collet, in reporting on *Miscellaneous Industries* in London, states that tailoresses desire more efficient inspection as to sanitary conditions in domestic workshops. There appears to be a division among the tailoresses. Those engaged in factories wish to put an end to domestic workshops and home work. Those engaged in domestic workshops or home work desire to be left alone.

At the *Army and Navy Clothing Factory*, Pimlico, the average wages during the last twelve years were 14s. 6d. This includes women who are upwards of 60, and girls of 16. Out workers employed in the same work earned about 1s. a week less until last year, when they earned 14s. 11d., which is 1½d. a week more than the amount earned by the factory hands during the same period.

The number of women employed in London as

printers is small (the Census gives the numbers as 1,316), but the wages are good, ranging from 28s. a week down to 11s. 10d., the usual thing being from 24s. to 17s., according to skill. The girls are healthy, they sit at their work on high stools if they like, and they do not suffer from handling the lead type, as they wash their hands before meals; and as they earn good wages they doubtless provide themselves with good food.

A *hat trimmer* complained of the interference of the Factory Inspector with their hours of work in his workshop. They worked from 9 till 8, but the inspector told him the women must not work later than 7, and that if he wanted longer hours he must begin earlier. The women complained, and said they all liked coming late and working late. Their fingers were too cold in winter to work early, they said. Wages average about 10s. a week, ranging from 8s. to 18s., and a few earning more.

Artificial flower makers are rather well paid. The lowest wages of cutters are 7s. a week, the highest 14s., the majority earn from 9s. to 12s. Shaders get more; the maximum wage was 20s., usual wages from 12s. to 16s. Rose makers—elderly women generally—earn from 25s. a week down to 12s. Leaf makers—young inexperienced girls—earn from 8s. to 10s. but skilled hands earn more. Mounters from 12s. to 25s. The work is very irregular. When there is a pressure the manufacturer employs out-workers, generally married women, probably persons who had been engaged as girls in the trade, but had ceased to work after marriage except on special occasions. By this means the in-workers are kept pretty regularly employed. The war in France in 1871 threw the trade of London in flower making into the hands of English manufacturers, who have contrived to keep it ever since; before then artificial flowers came from France chiefly. The French are now trying to regain the trade by making a cheaper kind of flower.

Feather curling is chiefly done in factories, but if there is pressure the workers often take feathers home with them to make up there. The majority of the girls earn from 10s. to 17s. a week, but some earn more by working at home. The hours are short, from 9 till 7, with an hour for dinner and half an hour for tea. In another factory no work was taken home, but overtime is worked when there is pressure.

A poorly paid kind of work, considering its disadvantages, is that done for the *aerated water* manufacturer. The bottles are liable to burst. When that happens the glass often cuts the faces of the girls—they wear iron spectacles to protect their eyes—and the water wets them. The work is fatiguing. The girls struck in one factory three years ago and their wages were in consequence raised from 10s. to 12s. a week. In the other factories they go on at the old wages. Now I hope that it will occur to no philanthropist on reading this bad account of the trade to try to get the work prohibited to women. It is so natural when a bad trade is heard of to say, "Let us get this trade prohibited to women, and so deliver them from this slavery that they may live free and happy ever after." But will they live happy ever after? What would really happen to them is that a good many would go to the workhouse, and they can do that now if they like. They work at the bad trade because they prefer so doing to living in the workhouse. Thus by forcing them into the workhouse you will not, oh, philanthropist, make them more happy, but less happy. Those who do not go into the workhouse will strive to get into other trades, and by competition will bring down wages generally. Just think what that means. It means less good food, less fuel, less warm clothing, less of every comfort to all working women. The wages of women have not risen as much as the wages of men have of late years.

The reason, or at least one chief reason, is the action of philanthropists in putting restrictions on women's work. They must not work at night, they must not work long hours, they must not do this, they must do that, and the consequence is that wages do not rise. There is even reason to think they are now falling in needlework trades. The limitation of hours in the cotton and woollen factories introduced by Lord Shaftesbury fifty years ago having been a successful measure, people think the same principle applies to all industries and not to factories only, but even to workshops.

The *fur pulling trade* is a very disagreeable one, dirty, of doubtful salubrity, and not well paid, the ordinary earnings being 1s. 8d. a day, but very poor people are glad of the work. *India rubber working, i.e.*, the making of tennis balls, tubing, bicycle tyres, waterproof garments, etc., is very disagreeable because of the smell, but is not unwholesome. The wages are good, usually from 10s. to 15s. a week; some earn more, even as much as 25s. a week, a few earn less. The wages being so good it is to be feared that it may before long be discovered that the trade is unhealthy for women, and that it ought to be prohibited to them.

Miss Collet concludes her report by remarking that the sanitary accommodation is almost everywhere very defective, and is specially so in shops, even in good shops in fashionable streets in London.

REPORT BY MISS M. ABRAHAM ON THE TEXTILE INDUSTRIES OF YORKSHIRE.—Miss Abraham arranges her report differently from Miss Collet. Instead of giving a separate account of each place visited, she classifies the complaints made against all. The cause of the most frequent complaints is the fines. If a worker does not appear within five minutes of the proper hour in the morning or after dinner time she has to pay a small fine. It seems that factory hands generally prefer being locked out and losing the half day's work to paying even a penny fine. This seems hardly reasonable on their part. A more reasonable complaint is that fines are inflicted for work that is spoilt, but that the work being spoilt is not always the fault of the worker. Some firms fine often, others very seldom. Deductions are also made for cleaning the lavatories and for hot water, also for a compulsory subscription to the Infirmary. Under the head of "Deductions," Miss Abraham says, "may be classed the money fraudulently stopped from wages earned by means of a false length of warp, or a false number of picks stated upon the weaver's card; the weavers being paid by the length of the warp and number of picks. I have received evidence upon this point from weavers who have given me satisfactory proofs of their statements about several firms." In a note Miss Abraham adds: "A case has recently been decided at Leeds in which a conviction was obtained on such a charge." This is a tremendous accusation. It is difficult to believe that a master manufacturer could be guilty of such dishonesty. Possibly some overseers have cheated both the employers and the employed in the matter.

In disputes between employers and employed, the subject is usually wages. When there are strikes, sometimes one side, sometimes the other, is successful. At Halifax the men employed in weaving Brussels carpets struck on receiving notice of a reduction in wages, and persisting, were replaced by women, who are now receiving 20s. a week wages. As women are continually being turned out of work by law, and replaced by men, it·is fortunate that they sometimes get a chance of replacing men.

Manufacturers are often in the position that they must reduce wages or give up their business, for business cannot be carried on at a loss, and a reduction in the price of goods is often forced upon them by foreign competition. It is far better that an industry should be carried on by Englishwomen, than that it should pass away from England altogether, like the Coventry watch trade.

Miss Abraham thinks that there is a tendency to substitute women for men in many trades in Yorkshire.

With regard to the effect of the labour of women on their health, Miss Abraham says that *wool combing, rag sorting and picking, rug weaving and silk gassing* are all more or less injurious. The heat in the wool-combing sheds is extreme. The smell of the foreign rags and the dust arising from them are most offensive. In rug weaving the atmosphere is offensive, Miss Abraham says, but she gives no reason for this, and though she has included rug weaving in the list of injurious occupations, she admits that no disease results from it. In the gassing process of silk weaving the rooms in which the process is carried on there is a strong smell of gas. She thinks the women employed there looked unhealthy.

Imperfect sanitary accommodation exists in almost all mills. In some the arrangements are so defective as to be a serious cause of ill-health to all the workers. Evidently more sanitary inspectors are required to see into this matter. The only accidents peculiar to women's work in mills arises from the shuttles flying. Injuries to the eye sometimes occur from this cause. A "wing guard" is sometimes put up to protect the worker; this is effectual as far as her neighbour's shuttle is concerned, but is no protection from her own. The bar guard is effective, but is inconvenient to the weaver; there seems, however, to be a kind of guard in use at some mills which is effectual and not inconvenient.

Miss Abraham is not of opinion that employment in mills in Yorkshire has a bad effect on the morality of the women, but thinks that the coarse and violent language sometimes used by the overlookers may have a bad effect on the children.

Miss Abraham writes in a reasonable manner about the employment of married women. Their absence makes the home less comfortable. Single women, she says, are generally opposed to the employment of married ones, as they wish to be relieved from their competition, but married women wish to be at liberty to work when convenient to them to do so. It comes to this. If all married men were perfectly industrious and sober, and so deeply attached to their families that they gave their wives the whole of their wages, it might be possible without cruelty to forbid the employment of married women, though even then there would be cases of sick husbands and of unskilful men unable to get work, but until this happy millennium comes to pass it is better for married women to go to work when they find a want of food in the cupboard and of money in the purse. The wife who is fortunate enough to have a husband who punctually brings home his wages, and who is skilful enough to earn good pay, is pretty sure not to wish to go to work.

It must be left to the woman's own discretion, and depend on the circumstances of the family.

The wages earned by women in factories in Yorkshire are good, rarely being so little as 10s. a week, and often rising to 15s. and sometimes to 18s. and even 20s.

Miss Abraham also reports on the *Cotton Industry* of Lancashire and Cheshire. The complaints about fines, deductions and cheating in measurement are the same as in Yorkshire. There are also disputes about the length of time which ought to be taken for cleaning the weaving frames. The wages of women are very high in some parts. Miss Abraham believes that many women weavers can earn 24s. a week all the year round. Men and women in Lancashire being paid by the piece and on the same scale it becomes a matter of individual skill, and the work being of a kind well suited to women, women earn as much as men. This delightful condition of affairs does not extend to all Lancashire, as at Wigan the wages are, Miss Abraham says, very low. In some places men are employed at mule spinning, while women spin with a different machine. These men earn 35s. a week, the women only 14s. or 15s. The sanitary condition of factories seems to be abominable, and Miss Abraham says that the sanitary inspectors take no notice. Shuttle flying causes frequent accidents. The steaming of the cotton is excessive, probably unavoidably, as it is the custom to use a great quantity of size, which is supposed to improve the cotton cloth, and the more size the more heat and steam is required. Why this idea exists that size improves calico one does not understand. Purchasers generally complain of the size and would prefer to have the calico without it. The component materials of the size are unwholesome and disagree with the workers. The morality of the women in Lancashire is less good than in Yorkshire. The wives of cotton operators do not often work in factories; about half the married women are the wives of miners and other workmen.   JESSIE BOUCHERETT.

Art. III.—"WITH ALL MY WORLDLY GOODS I THEE ENDOW."

Since my earliest youth I have tried to understand the meaning of things and the import of words and propositions. On my coming from Scotland, many things in English life struck me sharply as worthy of note, to which my English sisters' senses had become dulled through custom and authority. One such appears in the marriage service of the English Church. The man says to the woman, " with all my worldly goods I thee endow." What does he mean? What do his words mean? Taken singly as parts of speech, the words themselves are clear, incapable even of a double or secondary meaning. In their full verbal sense they ought to mean that everything on marriage becomes the wife's, and that the husband intends to throw himself on her grace in his own estate. Allowing for exaggeration natural to men in states of high exaltation, in regard to the extent of the word "all," we might take it as having the natural meaning, " I give thee all I have to use and choose, but you and I being now one, are equally possessors, spenders and inheritors of the estate, heretofore mine only, now devised for the use of us two, whilst the life of either lasts." Does it mean this? or anything like this? Did it ever mean this? From a careful perusal of old laws, charters and wills, I am inclined to think that in the old marriage service men did endow their wives with their property in this second sense in which I have translated their oath. The husband and wife stood before their property, equal sharers in its rights and enjoyments, half being for the one and half for the other, until a third party appeared, and the children's share was obtained equally from the share of either parent. One natural distinction came in when death broke the bond. The wife had no power to will away her half or third, because her husband's grant to her was a personal grant. She had no need to will her share back to him, for at her death it returned to the donor. At his death, however, he might will his half to her

estate, she retaining her own half, unless there were
children, when the division was in thirds. For she
held her own at his death, as through his life. This pre-
supposes that *all* the property originally belonged to
the husband. If the wife had the property, she also
endowed her husband with it to share when she was
alive. If there were children, her husband retained
her property at her death, "by the courtesy of England," that, recognising in him the guardian of his
children, and their supporter, left him their inheritance
as well as his share for his life only. If there were
no children, the devolution on the husband could only
work on different lines. He had no power to will away
his wife's inheritance from its rightful heirs. He was
no freeholder, but "tenant in courtesy." In Kent and
other places where the old Saxon laws lingered, the
half only came to the husband till he married again ;
as the half of her husband's property fell to the woman
till she married again.

In old transfers of land and property we find the
husband and wife appearing and signing together. I
have just come upon a new repertory of reference in
Mr. W. H. Stevenson's "Records of the Borough of
Nottingham." In vol. i., page 123, "November 29,
1335, To this court came Robert de Crophill and
Elizabeth his wife, and by their unanimous assent and
equal will, they have given, granted, and by their
charter have confirmed, &c. . . . . And the
aforesaid Elizabeth, in the absence of the aforesaid
Robert, her husband, was examined, according to the
custom of the liberty of the town of Nottingham, if
the aforesaid grant and confirmation of the aforesaid
charters had been made under the coercion of her
husband or not. The said Elizabeth says that she
had confirmed the said gift, grant, and confirmation of
charters, without the coercion of her husband or of
anyone else."

I am aware that this, and other similar cases, may
have reference to the woman's own property. But it
may not. The charters granted by Saxon kings were
confirmed by their queens, and it is quite possible that
the same custom prevailed among the propertied
classes in later times.

These "Records" make the question of "dower" quite clear. In 1335, Agnes, wife of Richard de Grimston, applies for her dower, which is different in proportion, as the property of her late husband lies in the French or the English Borough of Nottingham, a half being her right in the English borough, a third in the French borough (vol. i., page 125). "On March 28th, 1358, John de Perdon, of Brikelsworth, knight, and Matilda his wife, claim from Walter de Gotham a moiety of four messuages, and of a rent of a hundred shillings, as the dower of the said Matilda from Ralph de Crophull, knight, late her husband. Whereupon the said Walter comes and says that whereas she seeks dower of a moiety, it is clear that this is against the common law, without any special reason being assigned, and therefore he demands judgment. And the aforesaid John and Matilda say that the aforesaid messuages and rent are in the English borough of the liberty of the town of Nottingham, within which English borough women should be dowered with a moiety of the lands and tenements of their husbands." A jury of eighteen swear that they are in the right as to their statement of the law of dower in the English borough, and they are awarded half the messuages, though there is some mistake about the 100 shillings, not clearly expressed (page 169, vol. i.). This proves, as many other cases do, that consequent marriages, in general, did not take away the right of dower. The famous Elizabeth of Hardwick, ancestress of the Cavendishes and the Duke of Devonshire, grew rich through her successive marriages and accumulating dowers. The same laws or customs prevailed among meaner mortals —the clear recognition of the wife's share in life, and the wife's share in inheritance.

Therefore, we may acquit the framers of the English marriage service of having inserted a phrase absolutely meaningless into the man's oath. But the usages of later centuries have worked out new law channels, and this phrase of the Prayer-Book has been left stranded high and dry, something more deadly and dangerous than a skeleton of what was once a living being.

When the man swears "With this body I thee

worship," he swears to honour, to reverence, to be faithful unto death. He *may* honestly mean this at the time, and however his after life may belie his matrimonial oath, there is nothing in the oath itself false or impossible. Good men are encouraged by it, wavering men are strengthened by it, though bad men are made the worse, through having falsely sworn. The Church, by its banns and its service, may presuppose that all who seek its blessing in matrimony intend to lead godly and pure lives. But the Church ought to know better regarding this phrase of endowment; not one man for a very long time has come before the altar without being forced therein to commit perjury. Not only does he know that he does not endow his wife with all his goods—not even with her reasonable share of them—but till 1870 he knew that he took possession of all his wife's unsettled chattels too. The words till then should have been put into the woman's mouth, and not into the man's. It is possible that a man, before uttering the oath, made it true for himself by drafting a marriage settlement, or salved his conscience afterwards by a liberal will. But that does not redeem the action of others, who, knowing the law, and determining to abide by it, swear still.

Dr. Goudy, as Regius Professor of Civil Law in the University of Oxford, delivered his Inaugural Address at All Souls College on "The Fate of the Roman Law North and South of the Tweed" (just published). He there stated that it has been the common law of England for two or three centuries that a man can disinherit his children even from temporary irritation or any frivolous cause. "In Scotland the law is different. If he has disinherited any, the law treats such a will as *testamentum inofficiorum* and gives them a right of succession *contra tabulas*. Their share depends on the survival of a widow. If a widow survives she takes the third as the *jus relictæ*, the children take one third as *legitim;* the man's will has only power in determining the use of his own third. Each child is entitled to his or her equal share of the one-third or the one-half, as the case may be. Thus the present law of Scotland is the same as the old law of England, stated in Glanville L. 2. c. 5, (see Blackstone's Commentaries, ii. 443), and so it existed in the time of Littleton. Each party held its share, and that share was called the *rationabilis pars* of each. From Glanville this rule of *rationabilis pars* was copied into the *Regium Majestatem*. It is said in both works 'Cum quis in infirmitate positus testamentum facere voluerit. . . . omnes res ejus mobiles in tres partes dividentur æquales. Quarum una debetur hæredi, secunda uxori, tertia reservetur testatori.' Since the Reformation, however, this has died out in England, partly through desuetude, partly through the action of the Courts, after having lingered in some districts till the seventeenth century. Note.—One or two statutes were passed in order to get rid of it in those districts where it lingered as a custom, the last of these being 2 George I., c. 18."

In such a lecture Dr. Goudy naturally is not liberal of dry dates, or of exact illustrations. I merely transcribe some of his passages and give the sense of others, to show the reason why, coming from a country where men do not promise at the altar to endow their wives, but do it in obedience to their common law, it strikes me so powerfully that in this country men should be forced to swear what the law does not make them perform, and that neither they themselves, nor the clergymen before whom they swear, seem to recognise it as perjury. Macqueen's "Law of Husband and Wife, ed. 1885," which was revised after the passing of the Married Woman's Property Bill, Chapter i., discusses "The Rights arising from Marriage," and opens thus : "It may be observed at the outset, that the wife did not, under the old law, and does not under the present law, take any estate or interest in the property of her husband ; while on the other hand, the husband acquired under the old law, rights and interests absolute or qualified in the property of his wife." "Under both the old and present law, chattels or estate personal, which before the marriage belonged to the husband, continue to belong to him exclusively *after the marriage.*" "The statute 21 Hen. VIII., c. 5, sec. 3, enacts that if a husband dies intestate the Ordinary shall grant administration to the widow or to the next of kin, or to both, at his discretion. But the practice of the courts was to appoint the widow. She also secured her dower. Difficulties in alienating land when burdened with dower made men desirous of escaping its duties, and of finding means to "bar the dower." "Hence a carefully worked out "Act for the Amendment of the Law relating to Dower" came into operation January 1, 1834, 3 and 4 Will. IV. c. 105.

It is worth while noting that this "*Amendment*" came two years after the Parliamentary "*Reform*" of 1832, which threw women out of the Parliamentary Franchise, and one year before the *Reform* in the Municipal Franchise, that took their ancient borough rights from British Freewoman. Coming at the time it did, the "Amendment" made by men could only be expected to be in favour of men. Superficially considered, it seems in some clauses to benefit women. As Macqueen says, "it conferred upon widows the right to dower out of equitable estates, but this extension of right was more than counter-balanced by the provisions of the Act, which left the dower of the widow completely at the mercy of her husband during his life." "A devise by a husband of all his real estate upon trust to sell was such a disposition by will as deprived a widow of her dower. . . The fourth section decides that no widow is entitled to dower on any land disposed of by her husband during life or by will. . . No wife therefore can be safe under this law, but by settlement. . ." "Whether that is a fit rule for an enlightened people to adopt in the most important of all contracts is left for others to discuss; only observing that if husbands were uniformly wise, just and generous, the enactment might pass without comment." But stating that he was aware that husbands are sometimes weak, selfish, tyrannical, whimsical, that they sometimes dictate an unjust will on their deathbeds, he concludes by saying that "it is the most unsatisfactory and inexplicable act in modern legislation." If anything can rouse a *lawyer* to speak thus of *law*, it must indeed be bad ! It must be time for others to speak out too ! The future of a wife, however good and industrious, is left in England at the mercy of a wicked or whimsical husband, who swore before the Church, "with all my worldly goods I thee endow," who never meant to keep his word; but the Church blessed him, and the law supports him.

Unlike our Scottish Clergy, the Archbishop of Canterbury has a temporal as well as a spiritual power over the lives and consciences of men. He can find opportunities in Parliament to make this oath stand at least on its old footing. Failing this effort of his temporal power, he has clearly the right of his spiritual power to screen the generations of men from committing further known perjury by omitting this phrase. If he cannot make facts accord with this worthy oath, he can so modify the oath as to let it harmonise with the facts.*

The tide in women's fortunes began, it is true, to turn after reaching its lowest ebb in 1868. The Municipal Franchise was restored them in 1869; the Married Women's Property Bill passed in 1870. But if women come of families too poor to leave anything to inherit; if they are too infirm or too old to earn, or too absorbed in their husband's service, to go forth to labour on their own account—what to them is the rendering of the Married Women's Property Bill? They dimly see, but clearly feel, that they have toiled more than their husbands, and if through their common toil there may be some savings at the bank, that they should share while living, and inherit at their husband's death. But the law gives the husbands power to keep it all in their own name, and to will it away to whom they please, reserving not even to the hard-working and faithful partners of their toil the *rationabilis pars* that the old law allowed, and that in their marriage vow they promised. That a large majority of those men who do not make marriage settlements recognise the rights of their wives in their common property, is no argument to support the modern usage of leaving them

---

* Nevertheless, it is surely good that the Church, by a settled and enchaining service, hold up a standard which law should aspire to reach, and which every man is conscious exists, however far both law and practice fall short.—EDITOR.

absolute power regarding it. A small minority of husbands do abuse this power, make threats of exercising it an instrument of coercion, and indulge their whims, their temper or their vices, by not only spending during life, but by willing away at their death, the *rationabilis pars* of their wives and children, who are thus left pauperised to a hopeless life of toil, or the care of a heavily burdened state. *One* such case should be argument enough against an evil law. The *possibility* of it, in *every marriage without settlement*, is a source of national danger.

In the name of the poor wives and widows of the country, I commend this question, in both its aspects, to the consideration of Churchmen, Law-makers, and Women that work for Women.

CHARLOTTE CARMICHAEL STOPES.

THE DOWERLESS WIDOW.
AN EPIGRAM.

" With all my goods I thee endow,"
He promised in his marriage vow;
But either words are *never* plain,
Or *men* may swallow them again,
For wedded dowment, widowed dower,
Neither *assoiled* that perjured hour."

C. C. STOPES.

WOMEN'S SUFFRAGE.

NOTES OF THE QUARTER.

The following extract from the report presented at the Annual Meeting of the Central Committee will sufficiently indicate the position of affairs, further confirmed by Mr. Courtney's speech as chairman of the meeting, given at page 167.

"As soon as the Bill had passed second reading on May 4, Viscount Wolmer, M.P., gave notice of an Instruction in the same terms as last year:—' On order for Committee on Period of Qualification and Elections Bill being read to move, That it be an Instruction to the Committee that they have power to provide for the Registration of duly qualified women to vote at Parliamentary Elections.'

"Mr. W. S. B. McLaren, M.P., also set down a motion :—' On order for Committee on Period of Qualification and Elections Bill being read to move, That it be an Instruction to the Committee that they have power to insert provisions in the Bill to extend the Parliamentary Franchise to women.'

"As a preparation for all further contingencies, Viscount Wolmer also gave notice of an Amendment:—
'Clause 2, page 2, line 33, after "qualified," insert, (3) It shall be the duty of the overseers to include in the Parliamentary Register, whether under this section or otherwise, the names of all women, who, if men, would be duly qualified, and every woman so registered shall be entitled to vote at any Parliamentary Election for the county, borough, or other division where the qualifying property is situate.'

"As the session advanced, however, it became increasingly doubtful whether the Bill would reach the stage for either Instruction or Amendment, so that all the preparations made by your Committee for direct support of Viscount Wolmer's motion were necessarily held in abeyance."

During the past quarter three mass meetings have taken place, each illustrative, in its own way, of the rapid extension which the movement is undergoing. The first of these was in the Queen's Hall, Langham Place, on June 9th, when Lady Henry Somerset presided over an overflowng audience consisting very largely of members of the British Women's Temperance Association, by whose exertions, aided by the Committee at 29, Parliament Street, the meeting had been organised.

The next was on June 19, in St. James's Hall, organised by the Women's Liberal Federation, Lady Carlisle in the chair, when a resolution was passed urging the inclusion of Women's Suffrage in the Registration Bill.

The third was in Manchester Free Trade Hall, the scene of the first of the series of great demonstrations of women, inaugurated by Miss Becker fourteen years ago. On this occasion the vast Hall was again crowded to overflowing by an enthusiastic audience. The Hon. Mrs. Alfred Lyttleton presided.

It is also gratifying to record a unanimous vote in favour of women being included in the Registration Bill, at the Annual Conference of the Women's Co-operative Guild, a body rapidly growing both in numbers and in influence amongst the industrial portion of the community.

The Conference, which was held at Doncaster on June 26, was composed of delegates from the members all over the kingdom. Miss Ethel Wheeler attended as a deputation on behalf of the Women's Suffrage Societies.

ANNUAL MEETING OF THE CENTRAL COMMITTEE OF THE NATIONAL SOCIETY FOR WOMEN'S SUFFRAGE.

The Annual Meeting took place on July 6, at the Westminster Town Hall, the Rt. Hon. Leonard Courtney, M.P., in the chair. A letter of regret at absence was read from Mrs. Sheppard, of New Zealand, who had been announced to speak, and who wrote from the country, greatly regretting she was prevented reaching London for the meeting.

"It would have given me great pleasure to have been present, and to have heard the report of your work for the year, and to learn something of your proposed methods for future work. As Sir George Grey will be present, New Zealand will be well represented. He was from the first one of the warmest supporters of Women's Broad Suffrage in our country. When he spoke on the subject it was with no uncertain sound, and his vote was invariably given on our side.

"If I might be permitted a word to your meeting from this distance, it would be to urge women, on no consideration whatever, to work for or support a Parliamentary candidate who refuses to uphold Women's Suffrage. "In New Zealand we always considered that when a candidate was not sound on this question there was a 'screw loose' somewhere; at all events, we knew that the wishes of one half of the community would be ignored by him, and so judged that he was not a fit or proper person to enter Parliament."

Letters regretting absence had been also received from Sir John Hall and from Miss Tod, who wrote she hoped the meeting "would lead to a determination on the part of all the members of the Society, to press the claims of women to the Suffrage upon the members of both Houses of Parliament, as a matter of the most instant necessity —not only for themselves but for the State."

Mr. COURTNEY, after some preliminary remarks, said :—The House of Commons is naturally anxious about what would affect its own members, among whom there is some doubt whether it is expedient to allow women to vote. But as to their voting for parish, town, or county Councils, there is no doubt whatever. Though the Government thus goes some way, it does not go far enough for some of us, and the House rose against the Government, and insisted that it should go further. Whenever the Government hesitates some sturdy friend, like Lord Wolmer or Mr. Walter McLaren, says to it, " you must not shiver on the brink, in you must go." The Government will have to go a step further. The one Bill which did become law last year was a Bill which the advocates of Women's Suffrage may regard with great satisfaction. It is wonderful how the present Government endeavoured to avoid this question of Women's Suffrage, and in introducing their Registration Bill they tried to shut out the possibility of having Women's Suffrage considered. But though they exercised their utmost ingenuity so that no possibility should exist of an instruction or amendment being raised, yet it had to be admitted by the authorities that it had come to the length of making Women's Suffrage correlative. Thus if the Registration Bill does come on, Women's Suffrage will be heard of before the measure is considered in detail. I say *if* it does come on—for there is a doubt whether it will. The Session is coming near the end, the weather is very hot, and it is possible the Bill may not make much further progress. I should give a hint to the Government that if they want the Bill to progress, they had better not make two bites of a cherry, but boldly incorporate Women's Suffrage in their Bill. A good deal of opposition would be appeased, and by thus making a merit of necessity, they would save a great deal of time.

After referring to the success of the Franchise in New Zealand, Mr. Courtney concluded:—We are nearing success, but that is no reason for relaxing our efforts. It inspires us with gratitude and thankfulness to think that the time of fruition is so near, and I ask you to join with me in an expression of congratulation on our prospects. I now call upon Sir Geo. Grey, the Grand Old Man of the South, to move the first resolution, which is as follows :—

"That this Meeting adopt the Report and Financial Statement, and direct that they be printed and circulated."

Sir GEO. GREY said:—It is with some diffidence and with rather agitated feelings that I get up in the capital of the greatest empire in the world to reason on this important subject of giving the franchise to women. Undoubtedly the steps taken by Great Britain will be copied elsewhere ; for there is a feeling throughout the world that the trained statesmen of England have more knowledge than any others of the matters with which nations deal, because they rule many nations having various laws, and are brought into contact with many nations holding different views to those of civilized men. The decision of this meeting may help statesmen in determining the course to be adopted. Allow me to call your attention to the position of women in the world. They are endowed by Providence with tastes of various kinds, and with various gifts of sight, hearing and touch. All these qualities and talents should enable them to judge what is right. We find these gifts concealed in the machine of the human body which can use them, for in it is the gift of reasoning upon every one of the actions performed, and thus bringing the machinery into play to carry out what has been determined upon. Can it be otherwise than right for beings so endowed to use such gifts for the benefit of their fellow-men ? Is it not the greatest delight of the human mind to do some great service to a human being which shall induce him to go forward in the highway of virtue? Women are well fitted to achieve this end. They are gifted with gentleness of manner, persuasive power, and they take delight in succouring misery. Is it right that they should be deprived by men of almost every opportunity of exercising the great powers they possess ? If we could know the feelings of many millions of women in passing out of this life we should find they regretted that they had never had fair opportunities given them. For reasons, to me incomprehensible, they have been treated as reasonless beings, incapable of following a course of action that would be of benefit to humanity, and they are guided by the judgment of men when they should follow their own opinions. Sisters, wives and mothers have a right to demand that the gifts which have been bestowed upon them by their Maker should not be arbitrarily taken away, simply because they are called women, and that they should not be shut out from what is great and good in the world. We are justified in saying that women have a right to the fullest exercise of the inestimable gifts which their Maker has bestowed upon them. Will you, the eldest of the English-speaking races, will you submit longer to be shut out from such important rights ? Will you submit any longer in patience and without complaint to be deprived of the means of exercising the mighty gifts with which you are endowed? I would not have recourse to violent language, but I would say to you, it is your duty to work conscientiously onward and to use every faculty it is your privilege to possess. Further argument is unnecessary, compared with this great one of women's rights upon earth. It is needless to dwell longer upon this, but I can assure you the experiment in New Zealand of granting female franchise has been successful. It seems incredible that so great a change should have taken place, and that every one should have fallen into rank without a murmur. The conduct of the people at the hustings was such as had never before been seen. The women took up their proper places in the ranks quite naturally, and no one would have believed that rights from which they had been shut out for centuries had been given to half the human race in New Zealand. What was natural to women was naturally assumed by them; they were delighted to shake off the old and enter on the new course. If the women of Great Britain do attain this holy privilege, they will use their power in a way that will greatly benefit the country. They will bring about temperance and better laws, and their influence on their husbands and children will be greater than ever. This new species of modes of action will undoubtedly stir men up, and those who oppose women doing these things are enemies of their country and not friends to the human race in whatever part of the world. Let an example be now given by women of patient long-suffering and I feel sure success will come, and a new epoch will dawn for mankind, and the world, in many respects, will be purer and better than it has ever been.

Miss IRBY seconded the resolution, which was carried *nem. con.*

Mr. COHEN, M.P., moved the election of the Committee for the ensuing year. He thought they were approaching the time when it would no longer be necessary to have a Woman's Suffrage Society at all. He did not wish to see women in Parliament or on the County Council, but he did strongly believe that in the selection of candidates—in judgment on character—what he might call the robustness of women's minds was equal, if not superior, to that of men. Wherever the experiment—he would prefer to call it a reform—of Woman's Suffrage had been tried, it proved a triumphant success.

The CHAIRMAN then called on Miss Spence, from South Australia, as one who has worked in that colony for many years for this and many other good causes.

Miss SPENCE said that the names on the Committee list were nearly all familiar to Suffragists at the Antipodes, as those of persons full worthy of the confidence, not only of women, but of men. In South Australia the cause had been lost on side issues, and between the Conservative and the Labour party had fallen to the ground. Miss Spence did not regard the opposition as the result of ill-will, but of ignorance, prejudice, and false kindness.

The resolution having been carried, Mrs. FAWCETT moved and Miss FLORA STEVENSON seconded—

"That this Committee, while regretting that the course of Parliamentary business has been such as to render it impossible for their

Parliamentary leaders to bring forward any motion for Women's Suffrage in the House of Commons this session, earnestly entreat all friends of the cause to co-operate, whether by money or work, in extending the Appeal from women in favour of Women's Suffrage, and thereby strengthen the hands of their supporters in the legislature."

WOMEN'S SUFFRAGE APPEAL.

The Special Appeal Committee have issued the following report :
When the plan for a General Appeal from women in favour of Women's Suffrage was brought forward in June, 1893, it was expected that the Appeal would be presented to Members of the House of Commons early in the session of 1894, as it was the intention of the Parliamentary friends of Women's Suffrage to move an amendment to include duly qualified women on the list of Parliamentary voters in the Registration Bill.

Accordingly, when notice had been given by Viscount Wolmer, M.P., and Mr. W. McLaren, M.P., to move an instruction to that effect on the Registration Bill going into Committee, the Appeal Committee prepared a petition to the House of Commons, setting forth the nature and object of the Appeal, and signed by the members of the Committee in London, and also of the Appeal Executive in Edinburgh. It was intended that this petition should be presented before the instruction came forward. The Speaker gave permission that the Appeal itself should, at the same time, be placed in the Library of the House of Commons for inspection by Members.

However, as it now appears that hope of the Registration Bill reaching the stage when any instruction or amendment can be moved in the present session, is extremely remote, all these arrangements for dealing with the Appeal will have to be put off to another session. The Appeal Committee have given up their special office at 47, Victoria Street, and will adjourn until the time comes to consult on how to proceed next year.

Meantime the signatures—pasted on sheets and stitched in volumes according to their constituencies—will be deposited, for safe keeping, at 10, Great College Street, Westminster, and 29, Parliament Street, Westminster. Signatures will continue to be received by the Secretaries of the various Women's Suffrage Committees, and it may be hoped that by next year the number of signatures will have largely grown.

The total number of signatures received to the present time is 248,674—of these 50,913 are from Scotland ; 6,830 from Ireland ; 51,136 from London ; the remainder are distributed throughout England and Wales, but special mention may be made of the following places, whence the largest numbers have been received: Bristol, 3,775 ; Brighton, 1,732 ; Cambridge Borough, 2,025 ; Bodmin (Cornwall), 1,304 ; Croydon, 2,108 ; Torquay (Devon), 1,139 ; Southport (Lancs), 1,306 ; Manchester, 2,145 ; Harrow (Middlesex), 2,098 ; Newcastle-on-Tyne, 3,109 ; East Northampton, 2,030 ; Hexham (Northumberland), 2,513 ; Oxford Borough, 1,845 ; Penryn and Falmouth, 1,526; Eastbourne (Sussex), 2,089; Wolverhampton, 2,574; Keighley (Yorks), 2,968; Brecknock, 1,509; Cardiff, 2,102; Carmarthen Boroughs, 1,514.

The Committee are satisfied that the Appeal has fulfilled their original hope and has received the support of women of all classes, parties and occupations. It is difficult among such numbers to trace all the special names of note, but they rejoice to know that the signatures include the heads of nearly all the colleges for women, and of a large proportion of the head mistresses of high and other public schools for girls, and of women serving on Boards of Guardians and School Boards. The leading women in the medical profession have signed, and a number of the most eminent in literature and art, besides many of wide social influence, and leading workers in the many movements for general well-being.

More than 8,500 persons have assisted in collecting names, to all of whom the Committee desire to tender most hearty thanks, especially to those who have organised work in their respective neighbourhoods.

By Order of the Committee,
MILLICENT GARRETT FAWCETT,
President.

N.B.—Enquiries and communications in regard to the Appeal should now be addressed to Miss Blackburn, 10, Great College Street, Westminster, S.W.; or to Miss Gertrude Stewart, 29, Parliament Street, S.W.

RESULTS OF THE ELECTIONS IN NEW ZEALAND.

By the kind courtesy of Mrs. Sheppard, Superintendent of Franchise Petitions, we are enabled to give the following extracts from an early copy of the Franchise Report of 1893, *of the New Zealand Women's Christian Temperance Union, describing the results of the Elections in New Zealand.*

" In attempting to deal with the results of the Elections, we feel that some explanation is necessary, lest the effect of the women's vote should be misunderstood. Prior to the granting of the Franchise a question much —and we think foolishly—debated, was as to whether women would be Conservative or Radical in their politics. At this election the old Conservative party received a most crushing defeat. We think several causes operated to produce this effect. In New Zealand there has been for some years past a strong trend towards pure Democracy. At the previous election a compact Labour Party was returned, the members of which, by their moderate and intelligent action, won general respect from both sides of the House, and throughout the colony. They were thus able to hold their own at this election. Then the change in the incidence of taxation materially lightened the burden borne by the small farmers, who form a very large class in this country. The attempts of Government to encourage the sub-division of large estates by means of the graduated land-tax also met with the approval of those who wish to settle on the land. For years past the Government has introduced a number of measures, ostensibly for the amelioration of labour, and whatever opinion may be held as to the wisdom of those measures, yet it is certain they were received with approbation by the working classes. In a country where every poor man has a vote, and no rich man has more, too much importance cannot be attached to this fact, especially when it is remembered that the Conservative Party, which is mainly composed of large land and property holders and their friends, persistently opposed these measures. Another important factor in the election was the Liquor Law.

"For several years a strong agitation has been going on to secure for the people in each licensing district the power to close public houses by a direct veto. The Government, although not in thorough sympathy with the movement, had recognised to some extent its strength, and tried to prevent a split among their supporters by passing a Bill, which, although unsatisfactory, still admitted the right of the people to a direct voice in the suppression of the liquor traffic. On the other hand, with but few exceptions, the Conservative party threw its weight and influence with the publican party.

"The position, therefore, stood thus: on the Liberal side were the small farmers, the working classes, and the greater portion of the Temperance party. On the side of the Conservatives were the large landowners and their representatives, and the satellites of the brewery companies. The result could scarcely be deemed doubtful, as so far as the balance of power between the two parties is concerned, the women's vote has made no important difference. We hold the opinion that we expressed prior to the election, that, all things being equal, women would vote in the same direction as their male friends. Every enquiry that we have since made confirms this view."

From this report we learn that the number of voters were as follows:—

	Men.	Women.
On the Register	177,701	109,461
Voting at the Poll	124,439	90,290

AUSTRALIA.

FORMATION OF A WOMEN'S SUFFRAGE SOCIETY IN MELBOURNE.—The *Melbourne Argus* for April 21 states that: " A meeting of ladies interested in the extension of the suffrage to women was held yesterday afternoon at the Melbourne Town Hall. The meeting was the outcome of several private meetings which have been held during the past month, and was the first duly constituted committee meeting of the 'Central Committee of the National Society for Women's Suffrage.' The name of the powerful English organisation, of which Mrs. Henry Fawcett is honorary secretary, has been adopted, and the purpose of the Australian society is the same as that of the English one—to obtain the Parliamentary franchise for women on the same terms as it is extended to men. This is the sole 'plank' in the society's platform. A large committee has been formed, and at yesterday's meeting Mr. Wynne, M.L.C., was elected president. Lady Murphy, Mrs. Gurner, sen., Mrs. Balcombe, Mrs. Stewart Smythe, Mrs. Gresswell and the Rev. Dr. Strong were nominated as vice-presidents. Miss C. H. Thomson was elected hon. secretary, and Mr. T. Atherton was nominated as hon. treasurer. The appointment of auditors, solicitors. and bankers was deferred until the next meeting of committee on Friday, 27th inst."

FOR AND AGAINST WOMEN'S SUFFRAGE IN NEW YORK STATE.

The fact that the Constitutional Convention of the State of New York was to meet this year has drawn forth unusual activity amongst the workers for

Women's Suffrage, and has also evoked a protest on the opposite side. Two meetings of Brooklyn ladies opposed to the extension of the Franchise to women were held at the house of Mrs. A. W. Putnam, for the purpose of forming a Committee, and circulating a protest and appeal against the question. The protest is as follows :—

We, American women, citizens of the State of New York, protest against the proposal to impose the obligation of suffrage upon the women of this State, for the following among other reasons :—

(1) Because suffrage is to be regarded, not as a privilege to be enjoyed, but as a duty to be performed.

(2) Because hitherto the women of this State have enjoyed exemption from this burdensome duty, and no adequate reason has been assigned for depriving them of that immunity.

(3) Because conferring suffrage upon the women who claim it would impose suffrage upon the many women who neither desire it as a privilege nor regard it as their duty.

(4) Because the need of America is, not an increased quantity, but an improved quality, of the vote, and there is no adequate reason to believe that women suffrage, by doubling the vote, will improve its quality.

(5) Because the household, not the individual, is the unit of the State, and the vast majority of women are represented by household suffrage.

(6) Because the women not so represented suffer no practical injustice which giving the suffrage will remedy.

(7) Because equality in character does not imply similarity in function, and the duties and life of men and women are divinely ordered to be different in the State, as in the home.

(8) Because the energies of women are engrossed by their present duties and interests, from which men cannot relieve them, and it is better for the community that they devote their energies to the more efficient performance of their present work than to divert them to new fields of activity.

(9) Because political equality will deprive woman of special privileges hitherto accorded to her by law.

(10) Because suffrage logically involves the holding of public office, and office-holding is inconsistent with the duties of most women.

This was signed by Mrs. William A. Putnam and twenty other ladies, and the Committee invited all women citizens of the State of New York to join in sending up the following protest to the Convention at Albany :—

"We, women, citizens of the State of New York (21 years of age), believing that it will be against the best interests of the State to impose the obligations of the ballot upon the women of the State, protest against striking out the word 'male' from Article II., Section 1, of the Constitution."

The activity of the women suffragists, on the other hand, will be apparent from the following account, abridged from a letter by Mrs. Howland in the *Women's Tribune* of June 2.

Now that the Constitutional Convention has opened for business the suffrage headquarters at the Capitol are the scene of constant activity. Miss Anthony's labours with other Constitutional Conventions make her a general of experience, and under her direction the petitions from the different counties are being properly labelled and distributed among members of the Convention for presentation. Already 181,847 names have gone in representing twenty-six counties and others will rapidly follow. On Wednesday, the 23rd, Munroe County led off with its 30,973 names. Thursday (yesterday) thirteen other counties followed, and to-day fourteen more.

Each bunch of petitions is tied about with broad yellow ribbon, and the fourteen bunches scattered through the Convention this morning made a striking appearance.

The Convention opens at 10 o'clock. For half an hour before that time there is wild confusion in the petition room upstairs getting everything into final shape. Then the old coloured porter, who feels an exceeding friendliness to the ladies, carries armfuls of the yellow ribboned bundles downstairs to the Assembly Chamber, where Miss Anthony and Mrs. Greenleaf are waiting for them. By the way, women may enter the Assembly Chamber by the same door as the members and sit in the chairs outside the rail, or they may go inside and sit anywhere they choose, provided they do not encroach upon the area occupied by the members' seats.

Another lively scene follows the arrival of the petitions. Each one bears a card with the name of the gentleman who is to present it, and it must be carried to his seat. How to get it there is the question. Miss Anthony stands behind the rail with the different piles before her upon it, and searches the list of members, directs pages, and greets friends, all in the same breath. Some gentlemen come up and ask if their counties' names are ready and offer their services. In the meantime, Mr. Choate takes his place, calls the Convention to order, and all becomes quiet for a few moments while the Chaplain makes the prayer. The journal is then read; other business follows until the order is reached for the presentation of Memorials. A member rises in his seat, holding in his arms the package of petitions. He says: "I have the honour to present a memorial from — for example — Arria S. Huntington and 16,716 others, residents of Onondaga County, asking that the word 'male' be stricken from the Constitution." He then gives the number of men's names: the number of women's names and the total; the vote of 1893 and when we have been able to secure the data, the number of tax-paying women and the assessed valuation of their property. A page takes the package and runs with it up to the desk, where all the packages are placed as presented. The memorial is referred to the Committee on Suffrage, and immediately another member rises with another of our packages in his arms, goes through a similar presentation formula, and yields the floor to a third. They follow each other in quick succession until all that have been distributed are in. If all the women whose efforts are there represented could see the presentation they would go home resolved that lists which now number hundreds should number thousands before the time for receiving the suffrage petitions was past.

Yesterday, several thousands of " Anti " names were also presented, bound neatly and modestly in black cloth covers. Even the appearance of the book was conservative, and no doubt the ladies who planned it were pleased with the contrast it presented to our worn and heavy packages with their gorgeous ribbons. But they need not have felt so. Our colour is that of the sunshine, typical of liberty, generosity, and everything that is broad and free, and the wear has come from hands whose owners know the meaning of justice even though, when they held the book, their fingers were soiled with the day's toil.

Yesterday afternoon a hearing was given Miss Anthony and Mrs. Greenleaf in the Assembly Chamber by the Suffrage Committee. The day was the worst of the season, and no general notice had been given, but the great room was filled notwithstanding. The members sat in a stately row in front of the platform ; Mr. Goodell, of Syracuse, Chairman of the Committee, presiding. Miss Anthony and Mrs. Greenleaf occupied members' seats two or three rows from the front. Mrs. Greenleaf spoke first, presenting our cause in her forceful and dignified way, and recommending it by her stately and beautiful personality. Miss Anthony was greeted by the burst of applause which suffragists have come to expect whenever her name is mentioned in a public gathering. Never did our great leader speak more grandly. Never did she make the cause more clear. Toward the close of her address she asked for questions. After some hesitation several were put relating to certain of the objections which have special force just now among the " Antis." Miss Anthony had the brightest, most pointed answer ready on the instant. The hesitation was not upon her side.

The Women's Journal concisely says: "Woman suffrage petitions continue to pour in upon the New York Constitutional Convention. On May 29 ten more counties reported 30,059 signers, a total thus far of 211,906, with about half of the counties in the State still to be heard from. The 'antis' are buried out of sight. The claim that more women are opposed to woman suffrage than in favour of it ought to be laid to rest for ever, at least in New York State." The larger half of the signatures to the women's suffrage petitions were from women.

On May 31 Dr. Mary Putnam Jacobi, accompanied by members of the New York and Brooklyn Women's Suffrage Committee, appeared before the Suffrage Committee of the Constitutional Convention in the Assembly Chamber, Albany, New York, to urge that the word male should be stricken from the Constitution, and women allowed to vote.

Dr. Jacobi concluded a lengthened address with these words:— "Should in November a popular vote be taken, whether it prove favourable to our cause, as in Wyoming and Colorado, or adverse, as in Rhoda Island and Dakota, and prove adverse to the amendment, we shall bow, as is inevitable, to the popular will; we shall withdraw, and bide our time for another twenty years, when once more we, or our survivors, or our successors, will present themselves before a new constitutional convention to prefer — and then successfully — our claims."

ELECTIONS AND APPOINTMENTS.

DEPARTMENTAL COMMITTEE.

Miss Flora Stevenson has been nominated as a member of a Scotch Departmental Committee constituted to inquire into the treatment of habitual offenders and the best way of dealing with vagrants. Sir Charles Cameron is Chairman.

FACTORY INSPECTORS.

The ladies whose appointment as Factory Inspectors were announced in the April number, are:—Miss Lucy Deane—who had been recently appointed Sanitary Inspector by the Kensington Vestry; and Miss Adelaide Anderson, one of the ladies who have been acting as clerks to the Royal Commission on Labour.

UNDER THE LONDON COUNTY COUNCIL.

Miss Isabel Smith has been appointed Inspector by the London County Council under the Infant Life Protection and Shop Hours Acts. She was chosen from twenty-three applicants, and is the first woman appointed under the Acts.

Mrs. Kemp has been appointed Lecturer on Health for the London County Council.

Both these ladies, as also Miss Deane, received their training from the National Health Society.

SANITARY INSPECTOR.

The Kensington Vestry have appointed Miss Duncan, another pupil of the National Health Society, as Sanitary Inspector in place of Miss Deane.

SCHOOL BOARDS.

The following ladies have been elected on to School Boards in the past quarter.

Bedhampton (Hants), Mrs. Anderson (bye election).
Clovelly, Mrs. C. L. Hamlyn.
Croydon, Mrs. Grimwade.
Eastleigh (Hants), Miss M. Marriott.
Newton Montgomery (Derby), Miss A. S. Webb.

POOR LAW GUARDIAN.

Ormskirk (Southport), Miss Greenwood (bye election).

UNIVERSITY INTELLIGENCE.

CAMBRIDGE.

" The ladies have also scored several fresh successes this year, and several London papers have in consequence lectured us solemnly on our narrowness and bigotry in not allowing them to pay University fees and write B.A. after their names. This outbreak on the part of the press may now be regarded as an annual event." So says the *Cambridge Review*.

An annual event it will be likely to continue, so long as the papers can put " none " in the first class of the division, and then presently add a woman as filling the position declared vacant.

MATHEMATICAL TRIPOS, PART I., 1894.

In all cases of equality the names are marked thus (*).

WRANGLERS.

Cooke, E. H., Girton (equal to 28).

SENIOR OPTIMES.

Bartram, H., Girton (between 38 and 39); *Edwards, E. A. Newnham; *Gilford, B. M., Girton (equal to (*), 39 to 41); Ashbee, E., Girton (equal to (*), 42 to 45); Patterson, R., Newnham (equal to (*), 47 to 50); *Giles, K. A., Girton; *Home, E., Newnham; *Naish, G. V., Newnham; *Slater, E. E., Newnham (between 50 and 51); Muggeridge, E. H. A., Newnham (equal to (*), 51 to 52); Luker, E. J., Girton (between 53 and 54); Woodall, A. A., Newnham (between 56 and 57); Headridge, J., Newnham (below 59).

JUNIOR OPTIMES.

*Genge, E. M., Newnham; *Musson, H. E., Newnham; *Pierce, A. G., Newnham; *Todd, E., Newnham (equal to (*), 60 to 63); *Chambers, M. A., Girton; *Lovibond, E. A., Girton (between 63 and 64); Truman, R. C. M., Girton (between 67 and 68); Ratchinsky, M., Newnham (equal to (*), 69 to 71); Walford, A. H. B., Newnham (equal to (*), 87 to 90).

MATHEMATICAL TRIPOS, PART II., JUNE, 1894.

WOMEN.

Class I.—Division 1.—Johnson, A. M. J. E., Newnham.
Class II.—Division 2.—Stoney, E. A., Newnham.
N.B.—Miss Johnson's is the only name in First Division, First Class.

CLASSICAL TRIPOS, PART I.

WOMEN.

Class I.—Division 3.—Skeel, C. A. J., Girton; White, R. E. Newnham.
Class II.—Division 1.—Boyd, M., Girton.
Class II.—Division 3.—Millington, M. V., Girton.
Class III.—Division 1.—Dickson, I. A., Girton; Nicholson, M., Girton; Rouse, C. R., Girton; Stevenson, E., Girton.
Class III.—Division 2.—Wigglesworth, E., Newnham.
Class III.—Division 3.—Stuart, J. J., Newnham.

PART II.

Class I.—Pearson, E. R., Girton (Sec. II.); Purdie, E., Newnham (with distinction).

University Intelligence.

NATURAL SCIENCE TRIPOS. PART I.

Class I.—Castledine, H. M., Newnham; Philipps, E. G., Newnham; Skeat, E. G., Newnham.
Class II.—Bonnerjee, S. A., Newnham; Elles, G. L., Newnham; Wood, E. M. R., Newnham.
Class III.—Agar, W. Newnham; Ross, J. C., Girton. Attained to the standard of an Ordinary Degree.—Lawrence, A. L., Girton.

PART II.

Class I.—Baldwin, M., Girton (Botany).
Class II.—Booty, M. A., Newnham.
Class III.—Chesney, L. M., Girton; Wenham, N., Newnham.

HISTORICAL TRIPOS.

Class II.—Bake, C. H., Girton; Broadbent, J. B., Newnham; Nachbar, H., Girton; Shore Nightingale, M. T. B., Girton; Worthington, M., Newnham.
Class III.—Davies, E. G., Newnham; Henderson, M., Girton; Turner, M. A., Girton.

ÆGROTAT.

Jones, L. A., Newnham.

MORAL SCIENCES TRIPOS, PART I., 1894.

Class I —Division 3. —Fanner, G. L., Newnham; Fletcher, M., Girton; Meyer, B. E., Newnham.
Class II.—Division 1.—Hutchinson, W. M. L., Newnham. Division 3.—Stevenson, F. F., Girton.
Class III.—Division 1.—Waterhouse, E., Newnham. Division 2. —Evans, F. de G., Girton.

MEDIÆVAL AND MODERN LANGUAGES TRIPOS.

Class I.—Carmichael, G. W. (a, c),† Newnham; Cooke, L. M. (c)†, Newnham; Cunningham, E. M. (e)†‡, Girton; Roseveare, E. M. (a*, c*)†, Newnham; Sélincourt, A. de (c, e)†, Girton; Wright, E. L. P. (e)‡, Newnham.
Class II.—Bosanquet, E. T. F. †‡, Newnham; Fry, N. L., Newnham; Griffin, A. M.‡, Girton; Scott, A. M. M.‡, Girton; Sheepshanks, M. R.‡, Newnham; Smith, M. B., Girton; Stokes, M. G., Newnham.
Class III.—Grierson, A.†, Girton; Wilson, A. M., Newnham.
† indicates proficiency in the pronunciation of modern French.
‡ proficiency in the pronunciation of modern German.

OXFORD.

ASSOCIATION FOR THE EDUCATION OF WOMEN IN OXFORD.
The following Honours have been obtained :—

FINAL HONOUR SCHOOL OF NATURAL SCIENCE.
Class I. (Animal Morphology).—Lilian J. Gould, Somerville Hall.

PRELIMINARY EXAMINATION.
Chemistry.—Emily S. Curry, St. Kentigern's Hostel; A. Lucy Hodson, Lady Margaret Hall; Rachael S. H. Steel, Lady Margaret Hall.

Mechanics and Physics.—Emily S. Curry, St. Kentigern's Hostel; Rachael S. H. Steel, Lady Margaret Hall.

HONOUR MATHEMATICAL MODERATIONS.

Class III.—Winifred Ardagh, Somerville Hall.

FINAL EXAMINATION (HONOURS).
MODERN LANGUAGES.

Class I.—Bertha M. Forster, Lady Margaret Hall; Ethel C. Pemberton-Piggott, Oxford Home Student; Helen Redfern, Royal Holloway College, Egham.
Class II.—Edith L. M. King, Bedford College, London.
Class III.—Princess Catherine H. Duleep Sing, Somerville Hall.

ENGLISH LANGUAGE AND LITERATURE.

Class I.—Beatrice Boone, Lady Margaret Hall; Amy Kimpster, Somerville Hall.
Class II.—May Alexander, Somerville Hall.
Class III.—Amy Robb, Oxford Home Student; Crissy Shearson, Somerville Hall; Rosa T. Spackman, St. Hugh's Hall.
The following certificates have been obtained:—

RESPONSIONS.

Ida C. Olive, Oxford Home Student.

SECOND EXAMINATION FOR WOMEN (PASS).

Elizabeth M. C. Balfour-Browne, Lady Margaret Hall; Hannah M. Footman, Lady Margaret Hall; Mary Morshead, Lady Margaret Hall; Hilda M. E. A. R. Murray, Oxford Home Student; Frances Ward, St. Hugh's Hall; Mary Williams, Oxford Home Student. Of these Elizabeth M. C. Balfour-Browne gained distinction in French, German, and Modern History; Hilda Murray in French, German and Mathematics; Frances Ward in Mathematics, and Mary Williams in English Literature.

Lady Margaret Hall.—The Entrance Scholarships have been awarded as follows:—£50—Margaret Jourdain, Collegiate School for Girls, Corran, Watford (French and German). £40—Ellinor Lucy Broadbent, University College, Liverpool (Modern History). £35—A. Mary Wood (Mathematics). £30, the "Romanes' Scholarship"—Winifred Moberly, Sydenham High School (English Literature). £25, the "Old Students' Scholarship"—Lilian M. Pontifex, Croydon High School (French and German). Honourably mentioned—Margaret G. Dampier, Graham Street High School; Priscilla Bird, Miss Woods', The Laurels, Rugby.

St. Hugh's Hall.—The £25 Entrance Scholarship has been awarded to Evelyn M. Gunter, Kensington High School (Modern History). Honourably mentioned—Dora C. Abdy (English Literature).

The Mathematical Prize of £5 has been awarded to Melicent Wilson, of Somerville Hall.

OXFORD UNIVERSITY EXAMINATIONS FOR WOMEN.

(The following was issued too late for insertion in our April number.)

HONOUR SCHOOL OF NATURAL SCIENCE, DECEMBER, 1893.
PRELIMINARY EXAMINATION.
CHEMISTRY.
Mabel E. Cousins, Oxford Home Student.

ANIMAL MORPHOLOGY, MARCH, 1894.
Mary O'Brien, Somerville Hall: Rachel S. H. Steel, Lady Margaret Hall; Edith Serjeant, Oxford Home Student.

BOTANY.
Rachel S. H. Steel, Lady Margaret Hall: Edith Serjeant, Oxford Home Student.

HONOUR SCHOOL OF GREEK AND LATIN LITERATURE, MARCH, 1894.
Class I.—Lucy B. Bradley, Lady Margaret Hall; Elinor R. Price, Oxford Home Student.
Class II.—Evelyn A. Gardiner, Lady Margaret Hall; Nora Kirk, Somerville Hall; Jessie Watson, St. Hugh's Hall.
Class III.—Katherine Quelch, Somerville Hall: Gertrude V. Scriven, Lady Margaret Hall; Hannah M. Footman, Lady Margaret Hall, satisfied the Moderators.

The "Margaret Evans" Prize for English Constitutional History, has been divided between the two Candidates bracketed first in the Examination: Eleanor T. Joseph, Scholar of Somerville Hall; Ida B. O'Malley, Lady Margaret Hall.

Mary Croom Brown, Lady Margaret Hall; Agnes M. Wilson, St. Hugh's Hall; and Louisa Selby, St. Hilda's, distinguished themselves in the examination.

VICTORIA UNIVERSITY.

B.A.

Division 1—Dora L. Sandford, Univ. Coll., Liverpool; Lydia Taylor, Owens; Camilla D. Tennant, Owens. Division 2—Mary L. Beard, Owens; Evangeline Bramley-Moore, Owens; Ada Bryson, Owens; Gertrude L. Noble, Univ. Coll., Liverpool; Elizabeth G. Patterson, Univ. Coll., Liverpool; Janie A. Rowe and Lillie Rowe, Univ. Coll., Liverpool; Florence A. Wathew, Owens.

FACULTY OF MUSIC.—THIRD MUS. B. EXAM.
Division 1—Marian Millar, Owens. Division 2—Katherine Jones, Owens.

EXERCISE FOR THE DEGREE OF MUS. B.
Marian Millar, Owens.

CERTIFICATES OF PROFICIENCY FOR WOMEN.
Evangeline Bramley-Moore (Greek and Latin), Maria Davies (German), and Caroline E. Field (Latin), Univ.; Amy Fletcher (French and German), Owens; Mari J. Leather (Latin and French), Mabel M. Rich (Italian), Florence E. Roberts (French), and Dora L. Sandford (Latin, French, and German), Univ.; Thekla Wihl (French and German), Owens.

RECORD OF EVENTS.

WOMEN WORKERS AND THE FACTORY ACTS.
DEPUTATION TO THE HOME SECRETARY.

At the House of Commons on June 26, Mr. Asquith received, in Committee Room 15, a deputation from the Women's Employment Defence League, who represented the views of those working women who were opposed to the restrictions on women's labour proposed in the new Factory Bill. The Home Secretary was accompanied by Mr. G. W. E. Russell, M.P. (Under Secretary for the Home Office), Mr. Tennant, M.P. (private secretary), and Mr. R. E. Sprague Oram (chief inspector of factories), and the deputation was introduced by Mr. Gerald Balfour, M.P., and Mr. Charles McLaren, M.P. The deputation comprised among others Miss J. Boucherett (president of the league), Miss Ada Heather-Bigg (chairwoman), Miss Eleanor Whyte (hon. secretary, and secretary to the Society of Women Employed in Book-binding), Mrs. Houlton (Secretary, Shirt and Collar Makers), Mrs. Portbury (tie maker), Mrs. Briggs, Mrs. Boase, and Mrs. Addison (boot machinists), Mrs. Chappell and Mrs. Maloy (laundresses), Miss Letts (embroideress), Miss Stevens (dress-maker), Miss Hayes (shirt-maker), Mrs. Matthews (tailoress), Mrs. Bowden (umbrella maker), Mrs. S. Spring Rice, Mrs. Greenwood, Miss H. Blackburn, Mrs. Gerard Ford, Mr. F. D. Mocatta, Mrs. W. Burbury, Miss Jean Greive, Sister Mildred, Miss Ogle Moore, and Mr. Crofts.

Mr. GERALD BALFOUR, M.P., in introducing the deputation, said that the Women's Employment Defence League claimed to represent a large number of women engaged in various industries whose position would be injuriously affected by certain provisions in the new Factories and Workshops Bill. He enumerated the objections they felt towards the Bill, especially as regards restriction on overtime. He pointed out that in a considerable number of trades this restriction would be almost unworkable on account of the seasonal irregularities of the trade. The league looked upon it as striking a blow at home work. It was a very common practice for those who were employed in factories and workshops to take home work, not necessarily to be done by themselves, but to be done by, perhaps, their mother or sister, who although too weak to go to the factory, were still able to work for a certain number of hours during the day at work which was brought home from the factory. The league feared that this clause would discourage employers from giving out home work, lest they should be prosecuted for employing their hands overtime.

Several members of the deputation, including Miss Whyte (book-binders), Mrs. Houlton (shirt and collar makers), Mrs. Portbury (tie makers), Mrs. Briggs (boot machinist), and Mrs. Maloy (laundress) stated the effect which would be produced by the Bill on their industries.

The HOME SECRETARY, in reply, said that Miss Whyte had told them that this Bill was an attempt to treat women like children, and that there was some fear that the clause dealing with dangerous employments in the hands of male administrators and male inspectors might be construed so as to make any employment dangerous in which men competed successfully with women. He need not say that that was a most unfounded apprehension. He did not think that in the exercise of the power which Parliament conferred upon the Secretary of State in the Act of 1891 of declaring employments dangerous there were any serious criticisms from any quarter directed to show that employments had been so classified which were not really injurious to life or limb, and he could not doubt that, in whosesoever hands the administration of this Act might rest, the same principles of construction would be adopted. As to the general argument with reference to treating women like children, that had been employed from the earliest time against every piece of factory legislation. The whole of that legislation rested upon the assumption that public safety and public interest required that women should be treated in some matters, and among others in the hours of employment, on a different footing from men; and an

argument based upon the assumption that there was
no distinction between the two sexes and that they
ought to be treated alike was an argument fatal, not
only to the Bill now before Parliament, but to the whole
series of Factory Acts from the very beginning. They
could not expect him, therefore, to regard that objection as of much weight. There was a great deal of
misapprehension as to what the Bill really did. The
Bill did not limit the hours of labour to eight or anything of the kind. Except in the case of trades which
were certified to be dangerous and injurious to health,
and in the case of laundries (which for the first time
were brought under the Factory Acts), it did not deal
with hours of employment in a factory at all. Then,
as to Clause 7, the number of cases in which overtime
was really necessary upon five days in a certain week
was very small indeed. On the other hand, he was
satisfied there were a great number of cases where,
from perfectly avoidable mismanagement, the business
was rushed through in an unduly narrow space of
time, causing overtime recklessly, and to the injury of
the workpeople employed. The only object that the
Government had in proposing this legislation was to
protect the health of the workers. Then as to the
clause which dealt with taking work home. This was
one of the greatest abuses of their factory system. The
law which required that a child, a young person, and a
woman should be only employed a certain number of
hours during the day in a factory was perpetually and
habitually evaded by these persons, after they had
served the number of hours which the law allowed in
factories, having work given them to do at home, where
there was no power of inspection to see what the
sanitary conditions might be. He was perfectly satisfied that this was a very great abuse, and this was one
of the clauses to which he attached the greatest im-
importance and with which he would be most reluctant
to part. It was not aimed at the destruction of home
work pure and simple at all ; it was only aimed at preventing the evasion of the law. As to the dangerous
trades dealt with by the Bill, all that the Government
proposed was that that power of making special rules,

subject to appeal to arbitration, should be extended so as to permit the Secretary of State to prohibit the employment of persons or to limit their hours. He attached great importance to that because he had found himself constantly baulked by being unable to prohibit the employment of people who were obviously engaged in certain dangerous processes—the lead industry, for instance, and some branches of the chemical industry. It was in order that they might have the power of doing that, and also of seeing that, if people were employed in some of those dangerous trades, they should not be employed for dangerously long hours, that they had inserted this provision in the Bill. The last provision related to laundries—a thorny question on which he was not disposed to dogmatise. On the whole, however, he had come to the conclusion that there was not sufficient reason for exempting laundries from the general provisions which applied to other factories and workshops. Generally, he might say that the Bill was not dictated in any sense by any spirit of hostility to female labour. He was not wanting in sympathy with female workers, for he had appointed no fewer than four female inspectors, and he was well satisfied with the results, for they were finding out, by means of these lady inspectors, conditions of female labour which could never be disclosed to men inspectors. He was quite sure that the one desire of the Government was to limit such legislation as they proposed exclusively and entirely to those changes in the law which were necessary for the safeguarding of the health and lives of the female and infant children workers.

The following is a summary of the clauses in the new Factory and Workshops Bill which would specially affect Women.

§ 4. Forbids women to clean machinery in motion.
This seems a useful precaution in the case of heavy machinery, but otherwise unnecessary.

§ 7. Restricts overtime for any young person or woman to three instead of five days in any one week, in those trades where overtime is allowed. It does not however alter the total of 48 days overtime allowed in one year.

This adds a fresh point of friction between employer and employed.

§ 7. Line 6, page 3, omit the words "or woman."

§ 22. Extends the number of trades in which overtime is allowed—about 18 in all—by the insertion of the words "non-textile"—any non-textile factory.

§ 8. Forbids any young person or woman to take work to finish at home from the factory where she has worked in the day.

This opens a door to subterfuge and deals a blow at home work.

§ 8. Lines 15 and 17, page 3, omit in each line, the words "or woman."

11. Includes Steam Laundries under the Act as Factories—all other laundries as workshops—except (by sub-section 3) laundries where the work is done by servants, or members of the family dwelling on the premises.

By this section any woman who takes in washing and has not sufficient help in her own household, but has to bring in hired help from outside, will have to observe the daily limitations of hours prescribed for industries of a wholly different kind. This section will lead to evasion and subterfuge, or loss of work from resultant inconvenience.

§ 11. Page 4, omit entire Section.

§ 18. Enables the Secretary of State to forbid any person from working at any trade which is certified to be injurious.

This places freedom of contract for all persons, at the will of an individual.

§ 18. Page 7, omit entire Section.

LONDON COUNTY COUNCIL DOMESTIC ECONOMY SCHOLARSHIPS.

An excellent move for the encouragement of the study of domestic economy has been made, by the Technical Education Board of the London County Council, by the grant of seventy-six free domestic economy scholarships, for the children of parents whose pecuniary circumstances are such that they cannot reasonably be expected to allow their children to continue their education without such aid as the scholarships are intended to afford; 30 to be held at the Borough Polytechnic and 20 at the Regent Street Polytechnic.

These scholarships are to be awarded annually in January and July. The candidates must be either pupils about to leave school, being not less than 13 years of age and having passed the fifth standard, or ex-pupils who have left school for a period of not more than one year, having been 13 years of age at the time of their leaving, being not more than 15 years of age, and having also passed the fifth standard.

They must be provided with a medical certificate of health; and must undertake to attend the school of Domestic Economy on five days in the week, at such hours as shall be decided upon by the Governing Body, for a period of five months, during which they will be instructed in cookery, needlework and dressmaking, laundry work and housewifery.

All materials and books will be supplied by the Governing Body of the Polytechnic; and, in order to facilitate the attendance of children of the poorest parents, the scholars will be provided with dinner and tea on the days on which they attend the school, and will retain possession of the dress and other garments made by them during the needlework lessons.

The other six scholarships will be awarded at the Training School of Teachers of Domestic Economy, at the Battersea Polytechnic, the candidates for which must be not less than twenty nor more than thirty. The students will receive thorough training in the teaching of cookery, laundry, needlework, dressmaking and housewifery, also in hygiene and "first aid." Candidates for these also must be able to show that they are not in a position to afford their own training, and must be residents within the administration district of the London County Council.

All information can be obtained at the Technical Education Board, 13, Spring Gardens.

LADIES' COMMITTEE OF THE CHICAGO EXHIBITION.
CONCLUDING MEETING.

A Meeting of the Ladies' Committee was called at 53, Berners Street, on May 29, to receive the report of the committee and conclude the business for which it had been formed.

The Princess Christian, who as president has regularly attended the meetings the whole time the committee has been at work, opened the proceedings with an address of farewell. Her Royal Highness said:—" I do not desire to occupy your time with any unnecessary or lengthened speech, but I should be sorry if this, our last meeting, terminated without my expressing, as your president, a sense of my appreciation of the way in which the work of the ladies' committee has been performed by the ladies of the general committee, the members of the sub-committees, and their respective honorary secretaries. The idea of a section devoted specially to women's work was—at any rate, so far as international exhibitions are concerned—new, and I feel that in many respects you were called upon to arrange for, and make a selection of, exhibits as to which very little guidance could be derived from past experience. I believe, from the information which I have received, that the exhibits of women's work sent by Great Britain were highly creditable to the nation; and no doubt in any future exhibition, should a similar department or section be created, the experience which you have gained will be of great service to others. I feel that, in the way in which your work has been performed, you have shown great capacity for grasping the novel and by no means easy problems which had to be solved. It will, I think, be scarcely fitting that I, as your president, should propose, or that you should pass, any vote of thanks to yourselves; but I trust that this expression of my appreciation of, and gratitude for, the ready way in which you have responded to my invitation will not be unwelcome to you."

Sir Richard Webster (chairman of the Commission) moved a vote of thanks to the Queen for the exhibits contributed by Her Majesty. He afterwards made some comments on the general character of the work exhibited by the agency of the committee, which he considered did credit to their labours, especially seeing how novel and experimental the entire idea of the woman's department had been. The Princess Christian expressed her sense of the committee's obligations to the various gentlemen of the commission who had furthered theirs, as well as to their officers, Miss Lankester and Miss Stephenson. The report stated that the exhibits had returned, for the most part, in good condition.

NEW SOUTH WALES AND THE CHICAGO EXHIBITION.—The report from Lady Windeyer, as President of the Women's Work Committee, to the President of the New South Wales Commission, enumerates the nature of the exhibits sent by the women of that colony as follows :—" Thirty specimens of furs, a number of the most remarkable birds and animals, specimens in wood, various exhibits in photography and lace-making, knitting, illuminating, modelling, painting and printing. In the many branches of plain and fancy needlework the awards gained by our competitors testify that in New South Wales the skill in these arts, brought to this far-off land by our mothers and foremothers, has not degenerated. Especially Australian were the cabbage-tree hats and the gloves made from yarn spun from opossum fur."

BRITISH SILK ASSOCIATION.

The Silk Association of Great Britain and Ireland held its second exhibition from May 8th to 18th, at Stafford House, by the kind permission of the Duke of Sutherland. The first exhibition (a notice of which appeared in the REVIEW) was held four years ago at the house of Lord Egerton, of Tatton. It had, Mr. Wardle tells us in the valuable account of the British Silk Industry, appended to this year's catalogue, " a most successful issue, both industrially and pecuniarily ; no loss, but a small profit having been made." Unfortunately, he does not give data by which we can form a correct judgment of the actual work accomplished by the Silk Association during the past four years. We can compare 1828 or 1857 with the present year, but not 1890. If we are to judge by the number of exhibitors in the two exhibitions, the trade has retrograded rather than progressed, for there were 98 in 1890 to 60 in 1894. We miss the beautiful exhibits from Paisley, indeed Scotland is quite unrepresented, and we hear no more of the Cork Silk Culture Association. On the other hand the exhibits generally appear to be of a more important nature than those of four years ago; the quality has improved, and the Association can boast of British silks ordered by great ladies for drawing-rooms and state functions, and point with pride to the fact that H.R.H. the Duchess of York was married in English silk. "It was probably," says Mr. Wardle, "the first distinctly British silk marriage in this country, and I know the manufacturers of the country were intensely gratified and encouraged by this royal preference." "Already," he adds, "the looms of Spitalfields are increasing," but there is still work for the Society, when we realise that "the number of persons formerly interested in the silk trade of this country and its allied branches, directly and indirectly, was nearly a million. According to the last census returns, the number at present employed is 51,427 persons, *i.e.*, 18,750 men and 32,677 women." This is a sad diminution from 1828, when Spitalfields alone employed 62,000, and even from 1861 when the Coventry ribbon trade employed 40,000 people. The Government also have their part to do. "The silks for our British flags—banners of which we are so justly proud—are every year woven in Switzerland," and "until last year the contract for the spun-silk powder bags for our big guns, amounting to several thousand pounds per annum, was executed in Saxony," where the silk yarn of which the bags are made is still bought and made.

The exhibition was beautifully arranged. In the lobby at the entrance was a collection of silkworms and moths, living and dead. In the first room was a case of lovely silks and gauzes of marvellous shades of colouring, arranged with exquisite taste; near it was a stall of rich and heavy silks and brocades. There were specimens of cocoons and of the early stages of the raw silk, and Messrs. Debenham and Freebody showed a Jacquard loom, on which they were weaving a magnificent brocade for H.M. the Queen. Taffetas, silks, satins, velvets and brocades, tapestries and curtains were to be seen in profusion, and exquisite poplins from Ireland, displaying all the delicacy of colouring imaginable. Among these was a specimen of the dress brocaded with rose, thistle, and shamrock, worn by the Queen at her coronation.

In conclusion, we will point out that the revival of the silk industry means (in Lady Lathom's words) "reviving a means of support" to many of our countrymen and countrywomen, especially the latter, and that Englishwomen, as far as in them lies, ought to resolve, that neither in the Arts of Peace, nor in the benefits they bring, shall their country be behind the very chiefest of the nations.

HORTICULTURAL COLLEGE, SWANLEY.

The Woman's Branch of the Horticultural College, at Swanley, has just published its second annual report. The work done up to June, 1893, is recorded in the notice of the first annual meeting in our issue of July last. The report then read was forwarded to Chicago, where it excited considerable interest at the Horticultural Congress. At the Conference of Women Workers at Leeds in November last, Miss E. Sieveking (Hon. Treasurer) attended, and the result has been tokens of interest in the West Riding County Council and the local School Boards. In Kent the County Council has granted £300 towards the endowment of Scholarships for Women, and there is reason to hope that similar grants will shortly be made by other County Councils. The Scholarships at present offered to women are: Five Scholarships of £60 a year, each tenable by women, from 15 to 20 years of age, belonging to the Industrial Classes (*i.e.*, with an income under £400 a year); ten Scholarships of £30 a year, tenable by women of all classes. More appointments have been offered to women gardeners than the Committee have as yet been able to fill. Some specimens are quoted in the report, which points to the self-evident conclusion "that the fully-qualified woman gardener is not likely to lack congenial and remunerative occupation." The number of the Council and corresponding members has been considerably added to in the past year.

SOCIETY FOR THE EMPLOYMENT OF WOMEN.

The annual meeting of this Society was held at 22, Berners Street on June 1st, Viscount Grimston in the chair. Without presenting any new features the record of work of the preceding year was satisfactory. The most noteworthy incident of the meeting was a speech from Miss Orme, whose opinion, as senior assistant lady commissioner, naturally carries exceptional weight.

She deplored the tendency to restrict the action of grown-up women by law, and was sorry to see that women of intelligence and character were passing resolutions with regard to women's work which were most pernicious. She instanced the cry of "Equal pay for equal work," and said that not only would such a principle, if applied, rob vast numbers of women of employment, but it was possible to prove that the cry was raised with that very object. At the close of the proceedings a lady in the audience asked if it were a fact that 67,000 laundresses had been recently canvassed, and that 64,000 were in favour of limitation of their hours. The Hon. Secretary (Women's Industrial Defence Committee) replied that she had frequently heard it stated that such a canvass had been made, but knew nothing further. It was an undoubted fact though, that when a demonstration in favour of bringing laundresses under the Factory Acts had been recently held, not ten out of the 64,000 women alleged to desire the abolition of overtime had turned up to voice their wishes. She left her hearers to draw their own conclusions.

MEMORIAL TO JENNY LIND.

A medallion portrait of the famous singer—the last work of the late Mr. Birch—has been placed in Poets' Corner, Westminster Abbey, and was unveiled on April

20th by the Princess Christian. The memorial finds an appropriate site under the monument to Handel, of whose oratorios Mme. Lind Goldschmidt was for so long the greatest interpreter, and above the monument to the two children of the third Earl of Carlisle, with the bust of Thackeray on the right. Round the head are inscribed the words, "I know that my Redeemer liveth," and at the base on either side of a lyre wreathed with flowers the name and date of birth and death are given—"Jenny Lind Goldschmidt, born October 6th, 1820, died November 2, 1887." The proceedings began with the recital of a collect by the Dean of Westminster, and the Princess unveiled the memorial, after which the Dean said: "I have to announce that the medallion to Mme. Lind Goldschmidt is added to the monuments in the Abbey of Westminster."

REVIEWS.

British Freewomen, their Historical Privilege, by Charlotte Carmichael Stopes. Swan, Sonnenschien & Co., 1894.

THIS is the most complete study of the Women's Suffrage question, from the historical and constitutional point of view, that has yet appeared. Mrs. Stopes shows us the true position of the movement, not as an isolated fact of to-day, but as the necessary outcome of a long series of changes, which have imperceptibly modified our institutions; changes to which the women's vote has become a necessary counterbalance and completion.

The book opens with an introductory chapter on the remarkable degree of respect paid to women by the early Britons, and by the Anglo-Saxons, whose equal laws and customs in this respect advantageously influenced the Feudal System as developed in England.

The chapters which follow give the results of very
laborious and exhaustive researches into old records and
MSS. and historical documents, and show by a wealth
of instances that women were treated in all matters of
inherited property, privileges and duties, not as
creatures needing protection, but as human beings,
expected to fulfil the claims of their heritage.

We would gladly linger over these chapters and cull
some of these curious facts but for those engaged in
the actual work of the women's suffrage movement of
to-day the interest culminates in the chapter entitled
" The Long Ebb." " It is a patent fact," says Mrs.
Stopes, " that early in the seventeenth century men's
views regarding women became much altered, and the
liberties of women thereby curtailed. But there is
generally one voice that in expressing seems to lead
the opinion of an age. The accepted voice of this
period on this subject was not that of the ' learned
Seldon,' but of the ' legal Coke.' He first pronounced
an opinion on the disability of women, and as every
other *so-called authority* depends upon his, it is
necessary to examine the grounds of his opinion first,
as with him all his followers must stand or fall."

How that opinion fails to bear the test of such
historical examination as Mrs. Stopes here places before
us, we advise all readers to study for themselves; it
were too long to go minutely into the evidence here
collated, and we will only say that had the whole been
marshalled before the Court of Common Pleas, in the
famous case of Chorlton *v.* Lings, November, 1868,
as it stands marshalled in these pages, that famous
decision which took the last remnant of political franchises away from women in England had surely never
been pronounced.

After demolishing Sir Edward Coke's *dictum*, Mrs.
Stokes gives us a sketch of that eminent and admirable
lady, Anne Clifford, Countess of Dorset, Montgomery
and Pembroke, whose life was one long protest against
the encroachments of the time on those rights which she
should receive and hand down intact to her children.
After Anne Clifford, who thus protested against the
infringement of the Inheritance Laws, follows notice

of Mary Astell who, born a century later, protested against the withdrawal of educational advantages from women, and of Mary Wolstonecraft who, born in the eighteenth century, "protested against their social, civil and political degradation."

This chapter concludes with the decision of the Court of Common Pleas which left no Freewoman in Britain except the lady who sits upon the the throne; then we come to the "turn of the tide," and a spirited sketch follows of the progress women have made since 1868. Nor must we omit to mention a valuable paper which is given as an appendix, though originally we believe intended for a separate article, on "Women and the Universities." This paper succinctly records the various steps by which women have been admitted to educational advantages, with the dates and particulars of the charters of the Universities admitting women.

The book, originally printed in shorter form for the use of the Women's Suffrage Societies, has now appeared with numerous additions, as one of Messrs. Swan, Sonnenschein's Social Science Series. In her preface, Mrs. Stopes remarks that "Amongst the labour-saving appliances of the day may be classified collections of verified facts" and she hopes her book may reach the hands of those for whom it is written "brave women and fair men." We heartily trust so too, but only those who have essayed similar work will realise the saving of labour its pages will prove to students of "the woman question."

Letters of Harriet, Countess of Granville, 1810-1845, edited by her son, the Hon. F. Leveson Gower. In two volumes. Longmans & Co.

The period of history which borders most closely on our own times is frequently that of which we are most ignorant. It has scarcely taken its place in the history books of our schooldays, and it is not everyone who is blessed with older friends capable of instructing them in the doings of a bygone generation. Happy are they who have listened in their childhood to the old-world tales of a parent or grand-parent, and preserved the link which connects the past and the present. It is

this ignorance which makes the value, and this touch
of familiarity which makes the interest of letters and
memoirs of the early part of this century. We learn
from them history not to be learnt elsewhere, and we
meet in them personages whose names have been
household words in our youth. Those whom we have
seen as old men appear before us in the freshness of
their youth, and the vigour of their middle life. We
marvel at the unlikeness of men in those days to men
in these, and yet more at their likeness. The dinner
hour changes, the fashions alter, the mode of travelling
is transformed, but the human nature underlying them
remains, and the man and woman of 1810 is essentially the same as the man and woman of 1894. Essentially the same, yet, we feel inclined to ask after
perusing these charming letters of a charming woman,
is it only the effect of distance which makes them
seem so much more interesting than those now before
us ? Were the men really greater, the women more
beautiful and accomplished, the society more brilliant
in the first half of the century than, in spite of our
boasted culture, they are in the last ? Or is it, as in
the well-known mountain phenomenon, that we see
the grand silhouette cast upon the mist without the
petty details, which mar the grandeur of the form ?
Letter-writing, it has often been said, died out with
the advent of the penny post, but these letters of Lady
Granville are not the long, careful compositions which
one associates with the days before Rowland Hill.
They are many of them short and epigrammatic, and
for brevity might almost have been written yesterday.
But their style is so fresh, their fun so piquant that
they would still be delightful if instead of dealing with
kings, queens, great nobles and makers of history they
dealt with the Brown, Jones and Robinson of ordinary
middle class life. They are private letters, written by
Lady Granville, with no idea of publicity, to her nearest
relations and friends, and deal with private, rather
than public matters, though her husband's position
as Ambassador at the Hague and in Paris made public
characters her private friends, and public events
matters of private interest. She gives us in a few

strokes of the pen the most life-like sketches of her contemporaries. "Talleyrand crawled past me last night like a lizard along a wall," she says in one letter; and in another, "Did I tell you Talleyrand paid me a long visit on Wednesday morning? I never knew before the, as Mr. Foster says, power of his charms. First of all it is difficult and painful to believe that he is not the very best man in the world, so gentle, so kind, so simple, and so grand. One forgets the past life, the present look. I could have sat for hours listening to him."

Of Lord Lansdowne she writes: "He, who is not my beau ideal, is now revelling in his leisure. Beauty, music, small talk, a pains-taking *laissez-aller*, a most laborious frivolity." And on another occasion: "Lord Lansdowne is not quite the person, with all his great merits, to meet Madame de Lieven's piercing, unbounded understanding. I see her longing to box his placid ears." Madame de Lieven's receptions are constantly referred to. Here is one description: "Madame de Lieven in great beauty and high spirits. She has always an *entourage;* she can keep off bores, because she has the courage to *écraser* them. The sublimities sometimes clash, but that, for her taste, is a small evil. It would kill me to have Berryer and Molé *tête-à-trois*, looking daggers at each other, *mais elle sait nager* and gets out of every difficulty. The pleasantest women here, in my opinion, go constantly to her, Mesdames Appony, Schönbourg, Deirazzo, and Maire, who makes tea like a goddess. This scene *se répète* here, only with more assistance, merrier perhaps, but less genteel. Here fools rush in; there angels fear to tread. You will observe that there is a great deal of conceit in my humility." She describes the Queen, shortly after her accession, as "perfect in manner, dignity, and grace, with great youthfulness and joyousness." And we are able to compare this description with her picture of the king of the French. "Can you imagine the scene at Eu, Louis Philippe: how he will bow—roll over perhaps?" But the most perfect portrait is that she unconsciously paints of herself, one who in the midst of a life necessarily passed in the most brilliant society, found her truest happiness in the midst of her own family, who was the most popular of ambassadresses, the warmest of friends, an affectionate and admiring sister, a most devoted wife and mother, and an intellectual and accomplished woman.

We have found space to mention only a few of the procession of distinguished men and women who pass before us, in these pages. For the rest we must refer our readers to the volumes themselves, in which we can promise them abundance, both of entertainment and instruction.

A Plea for the Appointment of Police Matrons, by Florence Balgarnie. Published by the " White Ribbon " Co., Limited, for the National British Women's Temperance Association, 24, Memorial Hall, Farringdon Street, E.C.

A most important and necessary reform is strongly urged in this pamphlet and the benefits which have resulted both in Scotland and in the United States, from the appointment of police matrons, are clearly set forth. Difficulties there doubtless are, but they do not appear to be such as need or ought to stand in the way of a manifest improvement. The facts are well arranged and with a moderation which by no means detracts from the strength of the appeal.

The Relation of Women to Municipal Reform, by Herbert Welsh. Printed by the Civic Club of Philadelphia.

In this little pamphlet Mr. Welsh puts forward his ideas of the important part which women may play in Municipal Reform, and especially in staying the flood of corruption which stands in the way of improvement in American cities. He gives various instances of the capacity shown by women in organising and carrying out schemes for the public good. He credits them with " clearness of mental conception in planning, resource, skill . . subordination of all personal interests " to the public good, and urges them to " acquire the exact knowledge which will enable them to understand the situation clearly in detail, and the organisation which is requisite to effective application of their power." And he concludes by drawing a glowing picture of what Philadelphia will be when the influence of women—" none the less beneficent because of its inconspicuousness and its gentleness "—is felt in its municipal councils.

Le Grand Catechisme de la Femme. By **Louis Frank.** Bibliotheque Gillon, Paris and Verviers, 1894.

Mr. Louis Frank, the earnest friend to the women's movement in Belgium, has compressed a large amount of information on the legal and industrial position of women in various lands, into this catechism. The book, as the title shows, follows the style of question and answer, which, though wearisome to read and now fallen out of favour in England, nevertheless seems to give prominence to certain points. Two things are well forced on the attention of the reader by this interrogatory form, the exceeding narrowness of the Code Napoleon, and the persistent backwardness of Belgium, in all matters affecting women.

The following passage from the Ninth Lesson, on the savings of married women, will serve as a specimen of the style. The lesson opens with the inquiry whether wives in Belgium can dispose of their savings and elicits the reply in the course of further questions that leaving the savings of a wife at the disposal of her husband discourages saving.

"*Is it proved that Belgian women give up trying to save?*

"Yes, it is proved. I need only take one fact—Belgian wives who are under the authority of their husbands save thirteen times less than French wives who are freed from that authority.

"*Give an instance.*

"The French law of April 9, 1881, which recognised the right of a married woman to save and to dispose of her savings, has had most happy results in encouraging saving. In 1882, the savings of women were 13·52 per cent. less than those of men; this difference has diminished year by year and in 1889, fell to only 1·56 per cent. Whereas in that same year in Belgium the savings of women were 20·74 per cent. below those of men.

"*Is there not reason to fear that married women might*

embezzle to the detriment of their husbands when they can save?

"None!

"Prove this.

"In France in the space of eleven years from 1882 to 1893, the National Savings Bank has opened 517,513 accounts in the name of married women, 65,595 with the authority of their husbands, 451,918 without their help. That is to say, 87·32 per cent. have been direct accounts to set against them. There were but 32 cases of opposition in 1892 . . . . and of these but 10 were serious." The questioner then goes on to inquire into the case of other countries, and the various laws on the subject are enumerated.

The book is, we understand, about to appear in a Dutch and also in an Italian translation.

Woman and her Place in a Free Society, by Edward Carpenter. Manchester, The Labour Free Press Society, 59, Tib Street. Price 6d.

Why is this little book so difficult to read? was the mental query of the present writer. It has passages of eloquence; its writer has a lofty conception of what women ought to be and a generous longing to see all hindrances to the attainment of their highest freedom removed. Yet it has been a labour to read its forty short pages through!

Why? Surely because we have already had too much of this sort of dissection of the points of difference between man and woman; this anatomy of the functions which are dissimilar; and too little examination of the qualities, not of men or of women, but of human beings—too much of their separateness, too little of their oneness. Would that our reformers would write more of human beings, would do in letters what Sir Frederick Leighton has done in art, in his two glorious figures in this year's Academy. We gaze on the Spirit of the Summit with its upward yearning beyond the highest attainable on earth, and on Fatidica, with the eager vision into things beyond and think, not of the woman but of the human soul with its ever widening horizon of possibilities.

We wish we could have liked the little book better,

for despite a serious deficiency in his grasp of the full significance of family life, Mr. Carpenter has a generous conception of the relations between men and women, and to young men, at the age when they are forming their ideals, his upholding of the complete freedom of noble womanhood may teach nobler thoughts of the respect due to the human being.

PASSING NOTES.

TECHNICAL TEACHING FOR GIRLS AS IT IS IN IRELAND TO-DAY.

(A paper read by Mrs. Power Lalor, at a meeting held in Dublin in April, 1894.)

A slight retrospective view of female education in Ireland seems necessary to a proper understanding of the question. I have divided this into three parts: What has been done for practical education? What is doing now? and What is most necessary to undertake for the future?

There seem to have been no reliable statistics on female education in Ireland before the great census of 1841, and I find the startling fact recorded there by the Registrar-General that in 1841 58·7 per cent. of our female population, children and adults, were illiterates of the lowest type, as they could neither read nor write. The National system had then begun to replace the hedge schools of the country districts. I have always heard that good classical scholars were sometimes produced by these schools, but I fear girls occupied a very secondary and inferior place in their education. About thirty years ago I found one still existing in a very remote district. It was a small thatched building situated on a fork of land reaching out into a river, and the entrance to it was composed of stepping-stones through the water. A great hum of learning was heard outside, and on entering I found

a small room without a single vestige of educational
requisites save a rude desk, at which the master—a
picturesque old man—stood, and a *big stick*, which he
held in his hand. Some thirty scholars, girls and
boys, from 7 to 14, stood with their backs against the
wall, and read as fast as possible from the book each
held in his or her hand. It sounded most extraordinary nonsense, but it was some time before it
dawned on me that each child was provided with a
book totally different from that of his neighbour. One
had a National School reading book, another a prayer-
book, the next a song-book of a very secular nature,
and one—I suppose the future classical scholar—had
a copy of Pope. I have always regretted I did not
make a list of the varied literature. However, a year
later the hedge school was replaced by a National
School. Sir Alexander McDonald in his day, and
later Sir Patrick Keenan, with their able assistants,
have worked persistently at the primary education of
Ireland, and the proof of their successful exertions was
found in the census returns of 1891, when only nine-
teen instead of fifty-eight remained on the lists as
illiterate in the female population of Ireland. It is
evident, then, that the three R's—and Sir Patrick
Keenan's three R's carry most of the other letters of
the alphabet with them—have been fully developed.
The second question now arises at once. How stands
the practical training in practical matters by practical
teachers in Ireland for girls and women now?

The National Board recognised this need, and gave
a new industrial programme in 1890, which gives extra
fees for the teaching of Kindergarten, drawing, music,
book-keeping, dressmaking, sewing machine, lace,
cookery, laundry, dairy, poultry management, domestic
economy, type-writing, weaving, and shorthand, but,
as a rule, the high literary standard demanded of
female teachers has prevented their applying themselves to these subjects to any extent, and although in
about sixty schools extra teachers are paid for these
departments, this represents a small proportion out of
the National Schools.

Only 146,000 girls passed the needlework standard

in 1892, only 3,569 in machine sewing and cutting out, 948 in cookery, 229 in poultry management, so that we can hardly call the results from the National Schools satisfactory in practical teaching of these subjects, and as a fact comparatively few of the girls trained throughout the country can either cook or wash decently, nor can they sew well enough to make their own and children's clothes, and their knowledge of mending and darning is very poor.

The two dairy schools under the National Board are a brilliant success. 163 girls received instruction in Glasnovin and Munster dairy schools last year, and girls trained there are in great request, occupy good positions, and are in receipt of excellent salaries both here and in England.

The Kevin Street schools are doing a vast amount of good and deserve every encouragement, and the Pembroke schools, recently opened at Ringsend, promise most favourably for the future.

Cookery has been well taught at the Church of Ireland training school, and the travelling teachers employed by the ladies at the head of the Girls' Friendly Society for cookery, laundry and sewing, during the last 18 months seems to have done a vast amount of practical good in ten different counties.

Lace making is a flourishing industry and has developed enormously under proper teaching of drawing and design. Nursing also is very successful. Nurses are trained by the staffs of our large hospitals, and in private ones under eminent doctors, and in Ireland now Mrs. Gamp has been quite superseded by a bright and skilful Miss Harris. The Rotunda Hospital diploma carries a world-wide reputation; last week a lady trained there wrote me from Chicago: "My Rotunda diploma is a passport with every doctor." Thus three great industries are in a most flourishing state—nursing, dairying, and lacemaking. So far the great benefits of technical teaching for girls have been chiefly confined to the Convent Schools, to Societies like that of the Girls' Friendly, and to isolated places where ladies have taken up one or more subjects for their own particular industry or school.

We have arrived at our third and last, and most important point.

What is most necessary to develop in the future for the practical education of girls in Ireland? Our American cousins have coined a happy word in the education of girls—" home makers," and I think the chief aim of our meeting here to-day ought to be to consider how our girls can best be trained to be "home makers," in the best sense of the word; how we can bring a more widely diffused practical knowledge on practical subjects to the homes of our people; to teach our girls thoroughly the three R's, as it were, of technical education, on the three subjects necessary to the comfort and well being of every home, whether that of the poorest man or for the Palace of the Queen.

Cookery, needlework and laundry, adapted to the home for which it is needed.

In cookery, the training of country girls in simple invalid cookery is absolutely needed. How often have I seen a poor man trudge off four or five miles to the nearest butcher for the piece of beef for his ailing wife or child's beef tea ordered by the doctor, and then the scraggy, bony, stale piece that had been imposed upon him consigned to the depths of the large pot that had boiled the cabbage or potatoes for the dinner, and after a good boil up, the liquid offered to the poor invalid.

Washing, too, is of the roughest description, and it is impossible to get a man's shirt, or collar, or ladies' fine linen done locally. The fault of many of the classes for teaching these extra subjects lies in their being founded on too large a scale; laundry work is done by machinery instead of by hand, and consequently for the laundry work in small houses the teaching is comparatively useless.

This also applies to cookery. I remember a few years ago a teacher showing me with much pride a baking made by two girls for about 150 people; the bread was excellent, the kitchen and ovens spotless, and the girls knew to a nicety the number of stones of flour consumed, but when I asked one of them how much she would need to bake a single loaf, she was quite unable to answer.

Sewing for practical purposes needs development. A suggestion was made last week by the National Teachers' Conference in Dublin, that larger result fees should be paid to the female teachers for needlework, and that where there were 15 girls in mixed schools a workmistress should be provided. This would be very desirable in several mixed schools in Donegal, no needlework being hitherto taught, but I should like to see classes for darning, mending and patching. Sir Rowland Blennerhassett, our industrial inspector, says in his report (see page 33, record 1894) :—

"Ordinary household duties, the making of butter, caring of poultry, the method of rearing young cattle, knitting, making and mending articles of clothing, are what girls in industrial schools should be taught. If so trained they will be certain to obtain permanent employment immediately on leaving school, and be secured from temptations which wreck the lives of destitute girls unable to earn a respectable livelihood."

We therefore need practical teaching on those simple subjects for our homes, and as in large towns such teachers can be easily had, it is suggested we should have here a system of travelling teachers such as are referred to in report, page 33, November Record, 1891.

"The comfort of the working classes throughout the country may be largely promoted by instructing the wives and daughters in Cottage Cookery, the care of the house, and of children, sick nursing, laundry work and needlework.

"The system pursued is to supply a cook and nurse for two or three weeks (to a group of from five to ten villages). These travel round, giving one whole day a week to each place; they bring with them all necessary appliances, provide the food to be cooked, and distribute printed receipts and directions, by which their teaching may be remembered.

"All cooking is of the village or cottage description, is conducted on the rudest form of village stove, and is mainly directed towards teaching the right use of the simplest kinds of food, and the production of nourishing and palatable dishes from what is often wasted.

"The country might be covered by six of these cooks

and six nurses, taking three weeks' work each and teaching five days per week : thus sixty villages or more (according as a whole or a half day were given to each) might have demonstrations for a space of six weeks [Appendix 11 (b)].

"The salary of each teacher would be £6 per week, to include all travelling and other expenses incident to the teaching.

"Hence the total cost of twelve teachers working for six weeks would be £432.

"Laundry work and needlework might follow for another six weeks."

These could be chosen according to the needs of the different localities.

It is startling to read of what is actually doing in England, and to look at our incredible apathy on the subject.

I take at hazard the report of one English county's work—Cheshire—not a very large one. They voted for technical instruction £2,249; agriculture and dairy £2,000; sick nursing £250. Sanctioned instruction to be given in cookery, laundry, dressmaking, needlework, poultry and book-keeping, horticulture, commercial geography, commercial book-keeping and correspondence, shorthand, pattern-cutting, kindergarten, and also on five other subjects.

There can be no doubt the time has come to be up and doing if we wish to hold our own in the practical education going on in every country of Europe ; and I feel sure that the platform of useful education for our countrywomen is one in which those of every class, every creed, and of all shades of politics, can and will work together for the weal of their common country.

It is gratifying to note that since the delivery of above address, five ladies have obtained their diplomas from the National Union to which the training classes in laundry and cookery at 21, Kildare Street, are affiliated, and an influential movement is taking place to provide itinerant trained teachers in these subjects from this centre for the country parts of Ireland.

M. POWER LALOR.

REGISTRATION OF MIDWIVES.

A meeting of the Association for the Improvement and Compulsory Registration of Midwives was held on May 18, by the kind permission of Mrs. Ebden, at 29, Kensington Square. The chair was taken by Lady Mary Glyn, who, in earnest words expressed her sense of the urgent need that exists for better nursing among the very poor, and called on Miss Rosalind Paget, a trained nurse and certificated midwife, to read the first paper. In this excellent paper, which has since been published in pamphlet form,* Miss Paget pointed out how necessary it was to ensure proper care in all classes at confinements, but especially among the poor, among whom terrible cases of mismanagement were of daily occurrence, owing to their being left to the care of untrained and unlicensed attendants. England was the only country in which the licensing of midwives was unnecessary, and in which any ignorant woman could put a brass plate on her door and practise without hindrance, and could even be appointed to an official position. The consequence is, that awful risks are run by the poor, for evidence has been produced that seven out of ten births take place without a doctor in attendance. Miss Paget gave a slight sketch of the history of midwifery, and of the attempts of legislation on the subject in England from the sixteenth century, when midwives had to be licensed by the bishop—a point on which Bishop Bonner specially insisted. In the seventeenth and eighteenth centuries the subject was again ventilated, and in 1637 the first work on the subject was published, in Latin. Some years after, a certain Dr. Willoughby trained (among others) his own daughter. He insisted on a training of seven years. In our own century several attempts at legislation have been made.

In 1813 the Association of Apothecaries called attention to its necessity, but the House of Commons would not listen. In 1878 a Bill was introduced into the House of Lords, and in 1892, one into the House of Commons, but it was talked out by Mr. Bradlaugh.

---

* The need of Compulsory Registration and Better Training for Midwives. Liverpool: Gilbert G. Walmesley, 50, Low Street.

Another was stopped by the medical practitioners. Since then a select committee has been appointed to consider the compulsory registration of midwives, and evidence has been brought forward showing the large numbers of deaths and of permanent injury to mother and child caused by ignorant and unqualified practitioners. The question cannot be ignored, but it is not a party question, so may be thrust aside in favour of others which excite party feeling. It has been objected, first, that it will be disastrous to stand in the way of women helping one another. To this the reply is, that the interests of the village Gamp will be carefully safeguarded. Then, that there are not enough qualified midwives. But they will increase rapidly in number if they have a regular status. Then, that it will interfere with the medical practitioners. But this cry, which seems absurd in the face of the fact already mentioned, that seven out of ten births take place without the presence of a doctor, is raised only by some of the third- and fourth-rate men. The first-rate men see the necessity of legislation, and urge the profession to guide, not to oppose the movement. As long ago as 1646, a certain Peter Chamberlain urged on the Government to do something, saying that because things had been bad, it was no reason they should continue so.

Discussion followed in which Dr. ANNIE McCALL and Miss HUGHES, L.O.S., upheld the importance of registration.

CORRESPONDENCE.

PROGRESS OF WOMEN IN GERMANY.
TO THE EDITOR OF THE "ENGLISHWOMAN'S REVIEW."

DEAR EDITOR,—Many things have occurred since I was last able to send you a report. German women are astir and working in all parts of the country, and the aspect of our cause is improving more and more.

Shortly after I forwarded you my October letter, the political enfranchisement of women was for the first time discussed at the Imperial Diet. The most advanced party, the Social Democrats, numbering forty members of Parliament, pronounced themselves in favour of it; needless to say that the remaining 357 members were more or less disinclined to grant this right to woman, the question of Woman Suffrage being in Germany unattainable, because not alone sentiment opposes it, but it would involve an alteration in the German Imperial Constitution, a thing not easy in a sovereign Single-State, and all the more difficult in a Confederate State, such as the German Empire.

The Social Democrats show their political tact in trying to enlist, through this discussion, the sympathies of the women of Germany; but be this as it may, the fact remains, that the Woman Suffrage Question has been discussed at the German Imperial Diet, and, the beginning being made, will turn up again and again.

Another great step towards favourably influencing public opinion was the speech with which Prince Bismarck responded to a deputation of South German ladies, who waited on him upon his last birthday. After thanking them heartily for their great attention in travelling from the extreme south to the extreme north for the sole object of expressing their good wishes and admiration—a fact which the Prince designated as an honour which never before happened to a German statesman—he said that it was not only a personal joy for him to see the ladies in his house but also a great political satisfaction.

The Prince said that he considered the coming of the ladies as an acknowledgment of Imperial tendencies, and that this acknowledgment on the part of German women was the best guarantee for the future of the German Empire, that his confidence in the future was based upon the place which German women occupy, and that it was in his eyes a great achievement, that women are doing now what they would not have done before, that is, taking part in politics, and giving expression to their political sentiments. Prince Bismark thought that women did not change their convictions and their opinions so easily as men, and that there is much more reliance to be placed upon women than men in politics, and often in private life also.

Such an acknowledgment of the mental capacities of women, from the greatest but also the most Conservative German statesman, is the best proof of the progress of the woman question. Our women begin to be looked upon as grown-up persons, as individualities, and no longer as children, as before. Towards the end of March our metropolis was the *rendezvous* of the representatives of all German women's unions. After English and American models they constituted themselves into a Deutsche Frauenbund (United National Women Union), and intend to act in all great matters together. Let us hope that they will succeed in evoking amongst German women the much-wanted *esprit de corps*.

Yours truly, E. ROSEVALLE (Eliza Ichenhaeuser).

THE DECEASED WIFE'S SISTER.
TO THE EDITOR OF THE " ENGLISHWOMAN'S REVIEW."

MADAM,—The debate in the House of Lords on June 15, when the Deceased Wife's Sisters Bill was rejected by 129 to 120 reminds me of some queries which have long lain *perdu* in my drawer. Perchance you may care to give them to the readers of the ENGLISHWOMAN. Surely, whether they would respond to these queries by yea or by nay, many will agree that the Lords have acted fairly by women in delaying a measure which all must admit would directly affect (at least) two of the unrepresented for each one of the represented portion of the community, who would avail themselves of its provisions. Yours, &c., SOROSIS.

A SOCIAL SOLVENT.

Do you wish to loosen the bonds of intimacy between married women and their sisters? *Then vote for the Bill to Legalize Marriage with a Deceased Wife's Sister.*

Do you wish to make unmarried women eschew the society of their brothers-in-law? *Then vote for the Deceased Wife's Sisters Bill.*

Do you wish to separate orphaned children from the society of their aunts? *Then vote for the Deceased Wife's Sisters Bill.*

Do you wish to destroy pleasant intercourse between a widower and his sister-in-law? *Then vote for the Deceased Wife's Sisters Bill.* That Bill is a sure solvent. You need not be afraid that the poison will fail to act.

L'AVANT COURRIÈRE.

Madame Schmahl writes from Paris, just as we go to press, that the Bill promoted by the Avant Courrière to secure to married women the possession of their own earnings was introduced in the *Chambre des Deputés* on July 7, by M. Goiraud, *deputé des deux Sevres.*

"CHARACTERISTICS OF WOMEN'S PICTURES."

Notwithstanding the great attraction of the Guildhall exhibition, and of the unique collection of the portraits of fair women at the Grafton Gallery, the rooms of Burlington House and the New Gallery are daily crowded with visitors. Doubtless the average mind prefers the present to the past, and we all in a measure feel some responsibility for the work of our own day. The critics have decided that the Academy this year is even worse than usual; but from the women's point of view it is one of the best and most promising that has been noticed in this REVIEW. Women are more largely represented, and their canvasses better hung than hitherto, and many of their pictures have attracted well-merited attention.

"Psyche before the Throne of Venus," by Mrs. Normand, ranks first amongst the subject pictures and is the most ambitious and successful woman's work yet exhibited—one which could not have been executed a few years ago, when we had not the opportunity of studying from the life. The artist has chosen the scene when Psyche

> ". . . had wandered to the very home
> Of her most cruel and bitter enemy,"

and presents her prostrate before the throne of the Queen of Love, who is surrounded by beautiful attendants. The composition is good, and the colouring bright and harmonious. A soft hazy atmosphere pervades the whole picture, which is painted in Mrs. Normand's most delicate and refined manner, but more strength and less atmosphere around the throne, with light less evenly diffused, would have added importance to the chief group beneath the marble canopy, and differentiated the secondary group below the rose-strewn marble steps. The interest is too much distributed, and the eye wanders from Venus to her suppliant and attendants in the back-ground, instead of being arrested by the chief actors in the celestial drama. This picture goes to adorn the gallery of an Australian collector.

"Arrested" (311), by Miss Jessie Macgregor, is far in advance of any work she has hitherto accomplished. The figure of Fedora Alexandrowna is powerful in pose, expression, drawing and colour. The treatment is essentially dramatic throughout, and conspicuous for strength and vividity. Mrs. Stanhope Forbes, in "At the Edge of the Wood" (265), idealises an every-day subject by the simple means of harmonising her figures with the nature around them. A turkey-girl is shyly listening to a love tale under the orchard trees; her attitude is charmingly expressive as she stands, with dress tucked up and a stick in her hands. The two figures are well drawn, and in tone and feeling blend with their surroundings; the colour is true and pleasant, the painting throughout strong and firm. The white gate in the background is too white, hardly a fault in any other picture. "Two at a Stile" (24) belongs to the same class of work, but is inferior in conception and technique. Miss Noyes has done better in her little idyll (574) "The Hedonist," the landscape work of which is good and strong, but too green, and the background too close; the single figure is well drawn, but devoid of interest. "Flower o' the Elder" (384) is the best of Miss Erichsen's three exhibited pictures. Face and flowers are realistic, and fiercely painted, harsh and almost too strong in colour; but the faults are on the right side in this as in her other pictures, and there is none of that femininity so often noticeable in the manipulation of women's work. Miss F. Reid has two coarsely painted outdoor-subject pictures good in value; she has thoroughly studied French country town life, and represents it realistically, but quite unemotionally. Miss P. Clarke, in 526, contributes to this class a clever and ambitious but not well-balanced picture. Mrs. Lea Merritt treats whatever subject she chooses with originality and sympathy. "Watchers of the Strait Gate" (404) is no exception. Two angels guard the entrance, which so narrows that the spectator feels the impossibility of passing, and the Philistine demand that a picture should tell its story is satisfied. One angel holds the scales of justice, the other a wreath. The flesh colour of this picture is unpleasant, and mars the exceeding goodness of the whole; the backs of the watchers are coppery in colour and black in the shadow, a fault common amongst inferior mediæval painters of angels. In the same room "The Madonnina" (421), by Miss Amy Atkinson, a cleverly-studied child before a shrine. In "The First Audience" (392), by Miss M. Dicksee, the subject is well thought out and truthfully rendered. This artist's style tends to hardness, her figures become wooden from overworking; more breadth of treatment is needed to raise her pictures above the commonplace.

Amongst portrait painters, Miss Blanche Jenkins may be placed first. She has studied with much care the work of the Early English school, and endows her subjects with an indescribable old-world air, heightened by the artistic costume which carries no date, but is in accord with her style of painting. The two portraits (354, 668) are especially good in colour, well modelled, and very individual. Miss M. Porter has succeeded best with her picture of Lady Miles (288), also well hung in Gallery IV., near one of Luke Fildes' portraits; the careless drawing of the hands spoils otherwise good work. Mrs. Starr Canziani maintains her reputation by two good portraits: (930) a pleasant out-door picture of a little girl, and (853) a decorative drawing-room portrait. Miss Emily Way's large picture of the late Archbishop of Armagh, in ecclesiastical robes, is at once a good likeness and a dignified portrait; here, also, the hands are neither well drawn nor painted.

The general characteristic of the landscapes is less impressionist than of late, and, with a few exceptions, the work is rather amateurish. "Sand Dunes" (57), by Miss Anna Nordgren, cannot be fairly judged in its present position, but appears a disappointing specimen of this artist's work. Miss Hilda Montalba exhibits two skilfully painted Venetian subjects, but neither is clean in colour, nor satisfying in expression. Miss Elias—a new contributor, surely—has three delightful landscapes. "Pastures" (405) and "The Pathway" (728) are the best, and show technical knowledge, with appreciation of English scenery and colouring. The tone is low in both; there is no dramatic note, but the quality is good, and the feeling for the Northern grey day is truly expressed. So many landscape painters forget that the colour and sentiment of every country varies.

Miss F. Moodie remains the best painter of animal pictures, and her spirited drawings of puppies show her to be a real student of dog life and character. There are the usual number of flower studies; some have merit, but only one need be mentioned (575), "A Study in Blue and Green," by Miss Allport, very decorative and, at the same time, true to nature, is specially interesting as the work of a Tasmanian lady, and, we believe, the first that has gained entrance to the Academy. Miniature painting has again become a fashion, and several women exhibit cases in the water colour room. These are difficult to criticise, but the work of Miss M. J. Gibson possesses most of the qualities admired in this art of long ago.

The new gallery contains work by artists already mentioned, but Mrs. Swynnerton exhibits only in Regent Street. She has three portraits, of which No. 22 is the most striking, and an entire contrast to her usual style, as exemplified in No. 29. The former is a powerful study of a profile head, broadly and directly painted. Judged as a portrait it is unpleasant, as a study extremely clever, giving the idea of a swift impression. Mrs. Alma Tadema succeeds even better than usual in the style which she has adopted, and again, taking maternal love for her motif, treats it with delicacy of sentiment and execution. Miss Clare Montalba (51) has a beautiful picture of San Marco, and well as the subject is worn, her genius makes it new again. Miss Marianne Stokes' one picture (81) is disappointing; the landscape is good, but the fawn grotesque. Mrs. Stillman's four pictures have a charm of their own, though not belonging to modern art or times. "Afternoon in the Colonna Gardens" (262) belongs to the period, and speaks the language of the Italian sonnet.

In a short article it is impossible to do more than draw attention to the best work in the different classes of portrait, landscape and subject pictures. Women are to be congratulated on the large number of pictures that have been hung in all the galleries this year, and on the high average of merit attained. This success was inevitable when they began to regard painting not as a pastime, but a serious profession in which given equal opportunities they could compete on almost equal terms with their men rivals. The landscape work is least in importance and seriousness; yet Nature, with her countless moods, claims true and loving interpretation, and neither imitation, which is impossible, nor realism, which obscures sentiment, can satisfy her demands. It is a mistake to think that training is not necessary for landscape painting: knowledge and study are equally essential here as in subject work. Mrs. Normand and Miss MacGregor represent two distinct styles; the latter is strong in conception and execution; she paints with the force inculcated by the modern school, and probably her work is characteristic. The former plans and executes with delicacy and sentiment, investing her work with a charm essentially feminine. Composition, conception, colour, all are harmonious, and to the general public Mrs. Normand's pictures are most attractive, for they belong to the golden age, and offer a rest from the "storm and stress" of much modern work. In portraiture Mrs. Swynnerton and Miss Jenkins may be contrasted; in subject out-door work Mrs. Stanhope Forbes and Miss Reid. The picture lover must decide for herself on their comparative merits.

The one thing essential to the artist is to have an ideal. The form it assumes must depend on the character of the individual, and the period in which he or she lives; if absent from the consciousness, the best work will still lack something, whilst its presence will always redeem a failure.   H. H. R.

London School of Medicine for Women.

IN ASSOCIATION WITH
THE ROYAL FREE HOSPITAL.

THE Course of Study includes a complete preparation for the Medical Examinations of the University of London, the Royal University of Ireland, the Conjoint Examinations of the King and Queen's College of Physicians and the Royal College of Surgeons, Ireland, and the Conjoint Examinations for the Scottish Triple Qualification of the College of Physicians and College of Surgeons, Edinburgh, and the Faculty of Physicians and Surgeons, Glasgow. Also for the Diploma of the Society of Apothecaries, London, in Medicine, Surgery and Midwifery. For information respecting Scholarships, &c., apply to the Dean, Mrs. GARRETT ANDERSON, M.D., or to Mrs. THORNE, *Honorary Secretary*, 30, Handel Street, Brunswick Square, W.C.

EDINBURGH SCHOOL OF MEDICINE FOR WOMEN,
SPECIALLY RECOGNISED AS
Qualifying for the University of St. Andrews.

President:
H.R.H. The Duchess of Fife.

Vice-Presidents:
The Marchioness of Tweeddale. The Lady Helen Munro Ferguson. The Lady Reay.

This School forms an integral part of the Extra Mural School of Edinburgh. Its five years' curriculum is specially adapted to the requirements of the University of St. Andrews and of the Conjoint Scottish Colleges, but qualifies for all other examining Boards. Winter Courses, 100 Lectures each; Summer Courses, 50 to 60 Lectures each. Clinical instruction in the Royal Infirmary, with special cliniques in the Eye, Throat, and Ear, Skin, Gynæcological, and Lock Wards, with Clinical Lectures in Medicine and Surgery. School Fees, £75 in four instalments; or total Fees for qualifying course in School and Hospital, £95 in one payment. For information as to Scholarships, &c., apply to Dr. JEX BLAKE, *Dean;* or Miss BLACK, *Secretary*, Surgeon Square, Edinburgh.

THE UNITED SISTERS' FRIENDLY SOCIETY
(SUFFOLK UNITY).

"Work and Leisure" Court, No. 15.

The object of the Society is threefold; to afford
1. A weekly allowance in sickness.
2. An annuity commencing at the age of 65.
3. A sum of money (£6 or upwards) payable at death to the duly nominated representative of a Member.

All single women and widows of good health and character, between the ages of 16 and 45, are eligible for Membership in the "Work and Leisure" Court, subject to election by the Committee, and to a satisfactory Medical Certificate from a duly qualified Medical Practitioner. A further examination by one of the Physicians of the Court may be required by the Committee.

President: Miss L. M. HUBBARD, Editor of "Work and Leisure."
Secretary: Miss EDITH M. MASKELL, 7c, Lower Belgrave Street London, S.W.
(To whom all communications should be addressed.)

THE NEW HOSPITAL FOR WOMEN,
144, EUSTON ROAD, N.W.

THE PHYSICIANS ARE WOMEN.

Treasurer:—Mrs. WESTLAKE, The River House, 3, Chelsea Embankment, S.W.
Hon. Secretary:—Miss VINCENT, 6c, Hyde Park Mansions, N.W.
Physicians and Surgeons to the Patients:—Mrs. MARSHALL, M.D.;
Mrs. DE LA CHEROIS, M.D.; Miss COCK, M.D.;
Mrs. SCHARLIEB, M.D., B.S.Lond.
Physicians and Surgeons to Out Patients:—Miss WALKER, M.D.
Miss WEBB, M.B.; Mrs. STANLEY BOYD, M.D.
Ophthalmic Surgeon:—Miss ELLABY, M.D.
Assisted by a Consulting Staff of Physicians and Surgeons.

This Hospital is established to enable poor women to be attended by FULLY QUALIFIED WOMEN DOCTORS.

A Report and further information may be had on application to MISS MARGARET M. BAGSTER, *Secretary.*

Bankers:—BANK OF ENGLAND (Western Branch), Burlington Gardens, W.

WOMEN'S SUFFRAGE NEWS,
Edited by A. B. LOUIS.

Monthly.   **PRICE ONE HALFPENNY.**

Address—EDITOR, Women's Suffrage News,
Lyndhurst, Luton, Beds.

Society for Promoting the Employment of Women.
22, BERNERS STREET, OXFORD STREET, W.

Established 1859. *Incorporated* 1879.

This Society was established for the purpose of finding openings for girls to learn different kinds of trade and business. Also for aiding those already trained to procure employment. A register is kept for experienced and certificated Bookkeepers, Saleswomen, Matrons, Sick-nurses, Engravers, Law Writers, Printers, Gilders, and other assistants. Orders for copying MSS., circulars, &c., and for directing envelopes, are promptly executed.

Bookkeeping.

A class for training young women as Clerks and Bookkeepers is held on the evenings of Monday and Thursday.

PRICE ONE SHILLING.

New Series—Vol. XXV. No. IV.   Oct. 15th, 1894.

THE
ENGLISHWOMAN'S REVIEW

OF

Social and Industrial Questions.

EDITED BY HELEN BLACKBURN.

CONTENTS FOR OCTOBER, 1894.

ARTICLES.—Technical Training in the Counties, by Miss MACKENZIE. Proposed Imperial Exhibition of Women's Work, by Mrs. ROBERTS-AUSTEN. Changes introduced by the new Local Government Act.
WOMEN'S SUFFRAGE.—Notes of the Quarter. South Australia. New South Wales. Victoria. A New Zealand Experience. New York State. Incident at Leicester Election.
ELECTIONS AND APPOINTMENTS.
UNIVERSITY INTELLIGENCE. — London University. Royal University of Ireland. Glasgow University. Scotch University Scholarships.
RECORD OF EVENTS.—Institute of Journalists—Paper by Miss CATHERINE DREW. Barrack Life of Pauper Children. Post Office Telegraphists. Wesleyan Methodist Conference. Doctors at Swedish Institute, Clifton. Women and Order of Foresters. Lady Dufferin Fund. Labour Questions. Midwives' Registration Bill. British Association. Libraries Association. Japanese Ladies. Chelsea Hospital for Women.
OBITUARY.—Mrs. Augusta Webster. Miss Alice King. Mrs. Wm. Evans. Dr. Lange.
REVIEWS. — Our Exchanges. A German View of English Education.
COLONIAL AND FOREIGN NOTES.
PASSING NOTES.—Women as Stenographers. Medical Students at Geneva. British Silk Association.
PARAGRAPHS.

LONDON

PUBLISHED AT THE OFFICE OF THE "ENGLISHWOMAN'S REVIEW,"
22, BERNERS STREET, OXFORD STREET, W.

AND FOR THE PROPRIETOR BY
WILLIAMS & NORGATE, 14, Henrietta Street, Covent Garden, London
and 20, South Frederick Street, Edinburgh.

PUBLISHED QUARTERLY on the 15th January, April, July, and October.

WOMEN'S SUFFRAGE.

APPEAL

FROM WOMEN IN FAVOUR OF WOMEN'S SUFFRAGE

All enquiries and communications to be addressed to Miss Helen Blackburn, 10, Great College Street, Westminster, or Miss Gertrude Stewart, 29, Parliament Street, S.W., by whom books for signatures will be supplied on application.

Central Committee of the National Society for Women's Suffrage.

Hon. Sec.: Mrs. FAWCETT.   *Secretary*: Miss HELEN BLACKBURN.
Office: 10, GREAT COLLEGE STREET, WESTMINSTER.

MARRIAGE LAW DEFENCE UNION

An Appeal from the Women of England ...	1d.
The Woman's View of the Question ...	1d.
A Letter to English Wives. By Edith Mary Shaw ...	6d.
A Lady's Letter to a Friend, on behalf of those who do not wish to Marry their Brothers ...	½d.
What Miss Lydia Becker says ...	½d.
A Sister-in-Law's Plea for Mercy ...	½d.
A Woman's Opinion on the Wife's Sister Bill ...	½d.

MAY BE HAD AT
1, KING STREET, WESTMINSTER, S.W.

PERIODICAL PUBLICATIONS received during the Quarter :—
   AMERICA—*Woman's Journal; Woman's Exponent; The Woman's Tribune; Demorest's Monthly Magazine; The Cycle.*
   AUSTRALIA—*Dawn.*
   AUSTRIA—*Volkstimme.*
   BELGIUM—*Revendication du Droit des Femmes.*
   FRANCE—*Le Journal des Femmes.*
   SWEDEN—*Dagny.*
   NORWAY—*Nylaende.*
   DENMARK—*Kvinden og Samfundet.*
   SWITZERLAND (Zurich)—*Frauenrecht.*
   The Indian Magazine; Woman; Concord; The Lady of the House; Women's Union Journal; Review of Reviews; Threefold Cord; The Spinning Wheel; Nursing Notes.

A FAIR FIELD AND NO FAVOUR!

*Office for the Employment of Women as Compositors.
Girls trained and employed for the past twenty years.*

Ladies and Gentlemen are invited to place their orders for

PRINTING

WHERE THEY WILL BE EXECUTED BY

Women

IN A STYLE

EQUAL TO THE BEST.

NO SLIPSHOD WORK!
NO EXORBITANT PRICES!!

Estimates for Book and Magazine Work with Specimens.

JOHN BALE & SONS,

Steam Printers,

87-89, GREAT TITCHFIELD STREET,

OXFORD STREET, LONDON W.

Englishwoman's Review.

CONTENTS FOR JULY 16th, 1894.

ARTICLES :
>More Dangers to the British Workwoman. Report on the Employment of Women by the Lady Assistant Commissioners (*continued*), by Miss J. Boucherett. With all my Worldly Goods I thee Endow, by Mrs. Stopes.

WOMEN'S SUFFRAGE :
>Notes of the Quarter. Annual Meeting of the Central Committee. Report of the Appeal Committee. Results of the Election in New Zealand. Australian Women's Suffrage Society in Melbourne.

ELECTIONS AND APPOINTMENTS.

UNIVERSITY INTELLIGENCE.

RECORD OF EVENTS :
>Deputation to Home Secretary on Factory Bill. London County Council Domestic Economy Scholarships. Ladies Committee of Chicago Exhibition. British Silk Association. Swanley Horticultural College. Society for the Employment of Women. Memorial to Jenny Lind.

REVIEWS :
>British Freewomen. Letters of Harriet, Countess of Granville. A Plea for Appointment of Police Matrons. The Relation of Women to Municipal Reform. Le Grand Catechisme de la Femme. Woman and her place in a Free Society.

PASSING NOTES :
>Technical Teaching for Girls in Ireland. Registration of Midwives.

CORRESPONDENCE :
>Progress of Women in Germany. The Deceased Wife's Sister. L'avant Courrière.

CHARACTERISTICS OF WOMEN'S PICTURES.

THE
ENGLISHWOMAN'S REVIEW

(NEW SERIES.)

No. CCXXIII.—OCTOBER 15TH, 1894.

ART I.—TECHNICAL TRAINING IN THE COUNTIES.

"HE who does not teach his son a trade teaches him to be a thief," says the Jewish proverb, and the neglect of this axiom in our own country, if it has not taught dishonesty, has resulted in a terrible number of "unemployed," unskilled labourers who crowd the lower ranks of labour; and clerks in the middle ranks, whose chief qualification is writing a fair hand, and who are set aside for the better trained German with his commercial knowledge and acquaintance with modern languages. How many young men there are who have emigrated to the Colonies or the United States only to swell, for months, the army of the unemployed there, because they have not learned a handicraft. And how many complaints do we hear that the foreign workman, with his technical training, is causing permanent injury to English trades and handicrafts. The evil is no new one, and for many years praiseworthy efforts have been made to remedy it, by the establishment throughout the country of classes, schools, polytechnics, and colleges, for both men and women, by private individuals and local bodies of different descriptions. Many of these have done excellent work, and have resulted in permanent benefit to the localities in which they have been established; but many have been hampered by want of funds; by the low standard of knowledge among the artisans, who, leaving school early, often did not acquire the education requisite to profit by the classes opened for them; and by the want of capable teachers, who were not to be picked up on every hedge-side, for educated brains are often united with incapable hands; while men with capable hands were frequently unable to teach. In spite of disadvantages, however, splendid results were attained, and the way was prepared for a more extensive scheme. In 1890 it was decided in Parliament to adopt Mr. Acland's proposal, and to give to the County Councils the power to devote their respective shares of the duties under the Local Taxation Act to technical education. This action has resulted in an organised system of technical instruction which is spreading rapidly over the face of the whole country. We find everywhere: (1) Evening continuation classes to enable the less educated to profit by (2) Technical classes; (3) Special classes to prepare elementary teachers for giving instruction in technical subjects; (4) Technical schools for advanced instruction; and (5) A system of scholarships by which the most promising pupils can be passed into the technical classes, and again into schools and colleges. These scholarships or exhibitions, some of which are very valuable, can be held at the great technical colleges, such as the Yorkshire College, Leeds; or the Worleston Dairy Institute, Cheshire; or at endowed schools in certain counties, where special arrangements have been made for suitable instruction.

It is satisfactory to find that the claims of women and girls to technical education have not been overlooked. The articles which we published in 1890 (May, June, and July) showed that women had not been behindhand in helping themselves to obtain instruction; and in the movement now being made, their efforts are recognised and they are not left out in the cold. The table printed at the end of this article will give some idea of the openings offered to them. For the details we are indebted to the organising and education secretaries and clerks of the technical education committees of the County Councils, thirty-three of whom responded most kindly and courteously to our request for information. This will show that domestic subjects, *i.e.*, cookery, laundry-work, dressmaking and needlework, and nursing, including ambulance classes and lectures on health, are universally taught; dairy work, and especially butter making, are almost as common, and are attended almost entirely by women. In one of the counties it is recorded that one man attended, all the other pupils being women. In other agricultural subjects, bee-keeping, flower and fruit culture, and poultry-keeping, the classes are generally open to men and women on equal terms, though chiefly attended by men. Drawing, wood carving, and commercial subjects, such as shorthand, typewriting, book-keeping, languages, &c., are also open, and are largely attended by women. In some counties where there are special industries, women as well as men appear to be admitted to the classes.

In twenty-five counties there are scholarships open to girls; some of these are open alike to both sexes, some are founded specially for girls and women. There are fewer institutions open to girls than to boys, but, as a rule, a liberal spirit is shown, which appears to promise the opening of more if required.

We find, on studying the individual reports, that considerable differences exist in the working of the scheme in the different counties. These would be yet more marked if we were to take into account the county boroughs, but this paper deals only with the counties, and in consequence with technical training chiefly as it concerns agricultural districts. Where there is a special industry connected with any district this is always emphasized in the plan for that district. In Bedfordshire straw-plaiting and the machine sewing required in the making up of the straw into hats and bonnets attracts a large number of pupils. In Devonshire lace-making is taught; in Essex, Worcestershire, Somersetshire, Hampshire, and Cambridgeshire, basket-making. It is matter for regret, we may remark in passing, that this last subject is not more extensively taught. In our country's earliest days we are told, a Roman lady's room was not complete without a British basket. Now, Britons are content to get all their most elegant baskets from foreign countries. A proof that training in local industries militates for and not against general training, may be found in the work done in Cheshire and Lancashire. Here spinning, weaving and cotton printing attract pupils in the urban districts, while in the rural districts dairy work is taught with a thoroughness which, though it is a popular subject throughout the country, we scarcely find elsewhere, but these local subjects do not absorb the energies of the two counties; on the contrary, they seem to give point and thoroughness to the work which embraces at least as varied a curriculum as any other district in England. A total of over 20,000 individuals, of both sexes, have been affected by these technical classes, in Cheshire alone, and a very large number of these are women. We have not the details of boys and girls making up the whole number, but we have those of certain local classes which give males as 3,559, females as 3,421. In Lancashire the pupils of both sexes reach the enormous total of 45,709. Few of the reports give the details of attendances. In Devonshire we find it is about one female to three males, a very likely proportion for the whole country.

Ladies are to be found on several of the county committees, and on many local and sub-committees, where their work for their own sex is particularly valuable.

Let us now see something of the working of the scheme, taking Cheshire as our model county. "It is," says the organising secretary, "one of the few counties which has from the commencement devoted the whole of the money accruing to it from the Local Taxation (Customs and Excise) Act, for technical instruction purposes; and the committee charged with the administration of it has devoted to the subject an immense amount of careful attention, so as to have the work carried out in an economical, comprehensive, intelligent manner." Twenty-eight centres have been fixed upon as bases of operation, and the classes, which have now been carried on for three years show "a continuous and steady increase." Superior teachers have been obtained who are properly remunerated for their work. There is considerable development in the classes for commercial subjects, and an increase in numbers and an improvement in thoroughness in the instruction in domestic subjects. Lectures have been delivered at various centres on Dairy Farming, Horticulture, Poultry and Bee keeping, which have been well and regularly attended. "The Dairy Instruction" (says the Report) "at the western side of the county is placed under the Farm Management Committee, which arranges for demonstrations in butter-making and cheese-making at farm-houses in various parts of the district. . . . The time occupied at each demonstration in cheese-making is four days, and circulars are issued making known the centre at which each class is held, and inviting attendance, a small fee being charged, and the farmer allowed £2 for the use of his premises." In the Macclesfield district "Pupils are allowed to attend the classes free, and a butter-making competition is held at the end of the season when prizes and certificates are awarded." But the instruction does not end here. In the Worleston Dairy Institute, Cheshire possesses a fixed school which "influences to a considerable extent the whole character of the peripatetic classes in dairying. Such are intended to meet special difficulties in practice that have arisen, and to arouse interest and direct attention to the Institute. . . . The work at Worleston is intended to train up young people to a thorough knowledge of both kinds of dairy work, and fit them for undertaking the care of a dairy." The six summer months in the Institution are devoted to the instruction of females, the six winter months to that of males, and inducements are offered to encourage them to take a sufficiently long course to study the subject both theoretically and practically. "The County Council offered three sets of scholarships for females, ten in each case, tenable for eight weeks each. These have been eagerly competed for, and the candidates in each case have entered thoroughly into the work." Of thirty-five women candidates who presented themselves for an examination "of a searching character, embracing both practical work and theoretical knowledge," ten obtained first class certificates, "being considered sufficiently advanced to be entrusted with the management of a dairy," and thirteen obtained second class certificates. We cannot leave the subject of dairy farming which a pastoral county like Cheshire rightly feels is of paramount importance, without mentioning that the organising secretary has, by desire of the County Council, visited various centres in Switzerland, Germany and Denmark to obtain information as to the systems of instruction and methods of dairy work adopted in those countries. We must not leave it to be supposed that Cheshire women can hold only dairy scholarships. Four special scholarships for cookery, laundry work and dressmaking are tenable at the Birmingham and Midland School of Cookery; and two for sick nursing at the Royal Southern Hospital, Liverpool, besides scholarships at secondary schools and evening scholarships at technical institutions open to both sexes, and a few special day scholarships at higher seats of learning, which, however, seem to be chiefly intended for men.

The plan so completely carried out in Cheshire is followed, with varying details in other parts of the country. In the Northern counties opportunities are offered to women to carry their technical education to a higher point by the excellently planned Northern Counties' School of Cookery and Domestic Economy at Newcastle, open to all classes, by the Technical Colleges and Institutions in Yorkshire and Lancashire, and by the West Cumberland Dairy School, Aspatria. In the Midland counties are the Dairy Farm School, Halloughton, Whitacre; the British Dairy Farmers' School, Aylesbury, &c. In the South Western counties, the Bath and West and Southern Counties' Society, and the Gloucester School of Cookery and Domestic Economy, and in Sussex a technical school intended for the training of working-class girls in domestic subjects, are doing good work. Scholarships are to be obtained to all these institutions, and most of the counties have provided scholarships, tenable at certain grammar and endowed schools, which they have subsidized on condition of proper technical instruction being provided. These are already so popular that we hear complaints that all the clever children are going in for technical scholarships, and only the stupid ones devote themselves to Latin and Greek! Some of the County Councils give scholarships to the summer meetings at Oxford and Cambridge, which are highly appreciated by those who attend them. "I gained a scholarship," writes one lady, "which brought me here to the summer meeting, entitling me to *all* the lectures, also a special course on hygiene, and my board and lodging. Of course I came, and have worked hard and thoroughly enjoyed it. I have attended on an average five lectures a day, and in addition went on hygienic expeditions with our lecturer to sewage farm, waterworks, hospitals, workhouse schools, &c. . . . The meeting ended on Friday with a conversazione, but as I had to pay for the third week, having entered on it, I am staying till Wednesday morning. . . . I mean to try and get employment through the County Council later on. I have so enjoyed my time here. The lectures on history, literature and painting were splendid."

In some of the counties the training given is nearly, perhaps quite, as complete as that of which we have given a sketch in Cheshire. In almost all it proceeds on the same lines. Cookery is taught so universally that the hope dawns in our minds that the day is approaching when England will no longer deserve to be described in the words of the Frenchman, as "a nation where there are many religions and only one sauce." Dressmaking has been taken up with enthusiasm in many districts; nursing and ambulance lectures have been crowded. Even the laundry has had so many votaries that we may anticipate the day when an added brilliance will shine from masculine shirt fronts throughout the land, and our handkerchiefs will not emulate their stiffness. Almost as universal has been the teaching of dairying, and as we have given the general scheme of work in the earlier part of this paper, we will give here a description of a peripatetic dairy class in a Midland county, taken from the letter of one of the pupils :—

"I will certainly tell you what I can about the dairy classes, but am afraid it will not sound either very amusing or interesting, though in reality it was more or less both. We had the classes in a tent, the middle of which was boarded and covered with churns, workers, separators, &c. The ten pupils worked two at each churn, and spectators were allowed to fill up the tent and come as near as they liked, rather nearer in fact at times than *we* liked! It is such a bore to feel crowded when you are trying to work, and besides, the tent used sometimes to get frightfully hot. It is no joke, I can assure you, to have to make up your butter with the thermometer between 70° and 80°! In that case it really is not your fault if it comes out greasy and soft, but it is very annoying, as of course it is far more difficult to make up, and never looks nice, because the marks will not stay in, and look messy, instead of clear. We were frightfully awkward the first day, and the whole process took two hours and a half, and was very tiring, but we got quicker every day, and by the end of the time could get our butter finished, and our churns and workers scoured in an hour and three-quarters. People here seemed to like the new method very much, but they say it would not be much use to them, as none of them carry on dairying on a large enough scale to be able to buy the necessary appliances; or, as Mrs. F. puts it, 'It's very nice and clean, but you can't profit by it, without you 'ave h'all the h'applicants!' I don't think they can be got under £2; of course that only includes the actual things needed for the butter. A separator costs £12, I believe.

"The butter-workers are capital things, very easy to work, only they need a good deal of preparing, as they have first to be scalded, then well salted, the salt cleaned off, and finally they must be cooled.

"Really the preparing of the things takes far more

time than the actual butter-making. As we were all unaccustomed to the 'h'applicants,' rather comic scenes used to occur; people were continually forgetting to put the plugs in, and the consequence was that deluges, either of scalding or cold water, were continually occurring; and the instructress, who had rather a sharp and ready tongue, used to say she should have to take to wearing her skirt up to her knees. Once or twice people even forgot to put the plugs in their churns, and then, indeed, there was a scene. I saw two girls trying to hide their churn with their skirts, so that Miss H. should not discover the frightful mess of cream on the floor before they had shovelled it up. The thermometers, too, were a great puzzler at first; people used to put the wrong end into the cream, and hold it by the ball of quicksilver. There were two instructresses, and they had a page, in the shape of a rather uncouth but very willing boy, named Albert, who ran about with buckets of water. The tent usually resounded with cries of 'Olbert'; of course he was never on the spot when he was wanted. We used to make from fifteen to twenty pounds of butter a day. The cream came straight down from N―――― all ready to be churned. Some of the butter was sold on the spot, but most of it went to B―――― to market. We had four ordinary churns working by concussion; an old-fashioned barrel churn; a sort of eight-sided one, with a beater which had to be taken out before the butter could be removed; and two very nice little end-over-end churns. Then there was one of the new disc churns working by friction, which brought the butter in from five to ten minutes, and was most frightfully hard work, too hard for any woman, I think. We also learnt a little soft cheese making, that is, we were given the recipes and shown how to make them, and some of us used to help to put them in the presses. There were three kinds: milk cheeses, or Coulommier, as they called them, cream cheeses, and cream and milk cheeses, called Gervais. They were most excellent, and heaps of people bought them and liked them immensely; I think they were a novelty in this part of the world. The people who joined as pupils were chiefly daughters of small farmers; there were one or two people who joined, I suppose, out of curiosity, for it could hardly be much use to them—somebody's kitchenmaid and a little milliner person. No gentlefolk joined except myself, and the 'aristocracy' thought themselves too grand, I suppose. A good many farmers' and labourers' wives used to come and look on. . . . Early in November we begin cookery classes, which will also be very interesting, I think."

The complaint as to the "h'applicants" has been made and met elsewhere. The Lincolnshire (Kesteven) report says: " Although Lincolnshire is not considered a dairy county, a large quantity of butter is produced in most villages. The producers are in most cases owners of small dairies; two or three cows are usually kept, and rarely more than five or six. This being the case, simplicity and cheapness of methods taught become important points, and to these points due attention is paid. . . . Although it is usually thought best to use correct appliances and methods in the demonstrations, it is sometimes found possible and helpful to arrange for the exhibition of good methods adapted to 'old apparatus. This usually arouses much interest, and for many of our cottagers is perhaps the most useful form of demonstration." Devonshire has shown like common sense. "In the later courses," says the report, "instruction has been given in the Devonshire method of making butter from scald cream, as well as in the ordinary method, as it was felt that such a course would prove of the greatest value to the students." And the Devonshire instructress in cookery says: "I would here recommend that gas stoves should not be used; the pupils cannot have them in their own cottage homes, and I do not consider it fair to them to use anything but an ordinary coal stove, and even then it is necessary to explain how an open hearth fire can be made quite capable of cooking most dishes." Truly Fidele can have had nothing more when winning praise for

> "His neat cookery! He cut our roots in characters:
> And sauced our broths, as Juno had been sick
> And he her dieter."

Another complaint we must allude to before we close, and it is one which we have heard from several quarters. Why do so many of the County Councils insist on the lectures and classes being free? We know of one instance where the grant has to be supplemented by private subscriptions, because the local committee are not allowed to charge fees, which the people are perfectly able to afford, and would, we believe, be willing to pay. The teachers, and those who are best fitted to judge, concur in the opinion that free lectures are not as much appreciated or as regularly attended as those for which a fee is charged. If the pupils pay, they will take out the value of their fees by regular attendance. This error (as it appears to us) acts alike on the better and less well educated. We find from one of the reports that several courses of instruction for elementary teachers fell through, owing to the irregularity, "apparently from mere caprice," of the said teachers, who had themselves fixed the time of the classes.

Other dangers there are to which we cannot now allude; but mistakes and errors there must be in the beginning of a new scheme, and they will, we must hope, in time rectify themselves. We are much more struck by the care and thoroughness shown by the various committees. Want of space has prevented our mentioning by name more than a few counties, but there are many which would have served our purpose as examples as well as those we have chosen.

In conclusion we will quote once more the Report of the Organising Secretary for Cheshire:—" The work of technical education is yearly being better understood, and carried out more thoroughly and efficiently. More attention will, doubtless, be directed towards schemes for providing technical instruction of a higher character, and such as bear directly upon the manufactures and occupations of the various districts of the county. The seed time is but now passing, the time of ingathering or harvest can scarcely be looked for as yet, but that the work now being so carefully done will bear a rich store of fruit in the future is confidently anticipated."

A. M. MACKENZIE.

TABLE SHOWING THE WORK OF THIRTY-THREE COUNTIES FOR WOMEN AND GIRLS.

	Domestic Subjects.				Agriculture.													Remarks.
	Cooking.	Laundry.	Dress-making.	Nursing.	Butter.	Cheese.	Bee-keeping.	Flower and Fruit Culture.	Poultry Keeping.	Commercial Subjects.	Drawing.	Woodwork.	Science.	Straw Plaiting.	Lace.	Spinning and Weaving.	Basket Making.	
London	+	+	+	+	—	—	—	—	—	+	+	+	—	—	—	—	—	Ladies on the Board and on local committees. Excellent scholarships, open to both sexes, and special domestic economy scholarship for women.
Middlesex	+	+	+	+	—	—	—	—	—	+	—	—	—	—	—	—	—	Special scholarships for women tenable at "Maria Grey" Training College, &c. Scholarships open to women.
Kent	+	—	+	+	+	—	+	+	+	+	—	—	+	—	—	—	—	Ladies on local committee. Ten junior and two senior scholarships for women. Classes attended by 4,000 to 6,000 females.
Surrey	+	+	+	+	+	—	+	—	+	+	+	—	—	—	—	—	—	Scholarships open to both sexes. Those for girls tenable at Bonnell School, West Ham.
Essex	+	+	+	+	+	+	+	+	+	+	+	+	—	—	—	—	+	Four cheese scholarships tenable at Eastern Counties Dairy Institute. Classes attended by over 7,000 females.
Suffolk	+	—	+	+	+	+	+	—	+	+	+	+	—	—	—	—	—	This is the proposed scheme, but it is not yet working. Pioneer classes have been held.
Cambridgeshire	+	+	+	+	+	+	+	+	+	+	—	—	—	—	—	—	+	Junior scholarships open. Six dairy scholarships. Classes well attended.
Lincolnshire, Lindsey	+	+	+	+	+	—	+	+	+	+	+	+	—	—	—	—	—	Junior scholarships open. Four nursing scholarships tenable at Plaistow.
Lincolnshire, Kesteven	+	—	+	+	+	—	+	+	—	+	+	—	—	—	—	—	—	Many of the scholarships open. One special cookery scholarship.
Nottinghamshire	+	+	+	+	+	+	+	+	—	+	+	+	+	—	—	—	—	Ladies on local committees. Many open scholarships. Classes attended by over 7,000 women and girls.
Derbyshire	+	—	+	+	+	—	+	+	—	+	+	+	—	—	—	—	—	
Warwickshire	+	+	+	+	+	+	+	+	+	+	+	+	+	—	—	—	+	Four dairy scholarships. Dairy classes well organized and attended. Also wood carving classes.
Worcestershire	+	+	+	+	+	—	+	+	+	+	+	+	—	—	—	—	+	Ladies on local committees.
Oxfordshire	+	+	+	+	+	—	+	+	+	+	+	+	+	—	—	—	—	Ladies help in organizing classes. Scholarships and classes open to both sexes. 128 dairy students—

County																Notes
Northamptonshire	−	−	−	−	−	−	−	+	−	−	+	−	−	−	−	Many scholarships open. Also studentships at Aylesbury Dairy School. One county scholarship now held at Royal Holloway College.
Bedfordshire	+	+	−	−	−	−	−	+	−	−	−	−	−	−	−	Ladies' county committee. Nursing and cookery lectures numerously attended. 110 in dairy classes; 300 straw plaiting; 150 machining.
Buckinghamshire	+	+	+	+	+	−	−	+	+	+	−	+	−	−	−	Ladies on local committees. Minor scholarships open to both sexes.
Berkshire	+	+	+	+	+	−	−	+	+	+	−	+	−	−	−	Ladies on committees for domestic economy classes.
Sussex, East	+	+	+	−	−	−	−	−	+	+	−	+	−	−	−	Special ladies' committee. One scholarship at East Sussex Technical School, Uckfield, gained. Nursing the most popular subject.
Sussex, West	+	+	+	−	−	−	−	−	+	+	+	+	−	−	−	Special ladies committee. 1,442 women and girls attended classes.
Hampshire, Southampton	+	+	+	+	−	−	+	+	+	+	+	+	+	+	−	Attendance at cookery classes, 1,400 to 1,500.
Hampshire, Isle of Wight	+	+	+	+	−	−	−	+	+	+	+	+	+	+	+	Ladies on local committees. Scholarships at summer meetings at Oxford and Cambridge. Cheese scholarships. About 4,000 attendance.
Dorset	−	+	+	+	+	−	−	+	+	+	+	+	+	+	+	Ladies on local committees. Scholarships at Tiverton and Bideford. Studentships at summer meetings at Oxford and Cambridge. Attendance at classes about 17,000, in proportion of one female to three males.
Devon	−	+	+	+	+	−	+	+	+	+	+	+	+	+	−	Ladies on committee. Scholarships open.
Somerset	+	+	+	+	−	+	+	+	+	+	+	+	+	+	−	Ladies' committee. Dairy and nursing scholarships.
Salop	+	−	+	+	+	+	+	+	+	+	+	+	+	+	+	Many scholarships open. Special scholarships at Worleston Dairy School, &c.
Cheshire	+	+	+	+	+	+	+	+	+	+	+	+	+	+	+	All scholarships open. Most excellent organization. 45,709 pupils of both sexes.
Lancashire	−	+	+	+	+	−	+	+	+	+	+	+	+	+	+	Ladies on committee. Many scholarships open.
Yorkshire, West Riding	−	+	+	+	+	−	+	+	+	+	+	+	+	+	+	Scholarships open, and some specially for girls, tenable at High Schools, &c. 80 or 90 centres. Over 10,000 attendances by both sexes.
Durham	−	+	+	+	+	−	+	+	+	+	+	+	+	+	+	Ladies on sub-committees. Six cookery scholarships tenable at Northern Counties' School of Domestic Economy. Four dairy scholarships.
Northumberland	−	+	+	+	+	−	+	+	+	+	+	+	+	+	+	Scholarships open. Attendance at classes 6,000 of both sexes.
Cumberland	−	+	+	+	+	−	+	+	+	+	+	+	+	+	+	Ladies eligible for committees.
Westmoreland	−	+	+	+	+	−	+	+	+	+	+	+	+	+	+	

ART. II.—THE PROPOSED IMPERIAL EXHIBITION OF WOMEN'S WORK.

WHEN a young and rising nation wishes to take its place in the world of art and industry it is careful to secure adequate representation at an International Exhibition. Women are very much in the position of such a nation; they do not wish to enter into undue competition, or to range themselves as rivals with those who command the markets of this country, or of the world, but they do want recognition for their work on its merits, for they feel that the amount and excellence of the work done by women in England and her Colonies is absolutely unknown to the general public. An Imperial Exhibition of Women's Work would clearly be very useful.

Interest in the Exhibition is spreading so rapidly, that it may be well to place before our readers a brief statement of the aims of those in whose hands the preliminary suggestions for holding it are taking definite shape. The great object of the Exhibition is to afford such a complete illustration of the arts and industries in which women either do, or can, take a share, as will clearly show what are the respective fields in which men and women may work with the best effect and with the most satisfactory result to the nation as a whole.

There is at present great waste in the distribution of work, and the more those who have the true progress of the community at heart, investigate the relation between the industries of men and of women, the more it becomes evident that the possibilities of wiser regulations than those now in force are very great indeed. It is startling to find how great a share of modern industrial work devolves upon women, and we hope that an Exhibition such as is proposed, will be of great use not only to the women of England and her Colonies, but to the industrial interests of the nation.

On July 10 last, the first meeting to consider the question was held at the Society of Arts, the chair being taken by Lady Aberdeen, who was supported by such thoroughly representative women as Lady Kelvin, Lady Knightley, Mrs. Bedford Fenwick, Miss Maitland of Somerville Hall, Mrs. Kingdon Clifford, Madame Canziani, and Mrs. Lea Merritt, and many others. Among the men present may be mentioned: — Sir Richard Temple, Sir Donald Smith of Montreal, Sir Charles Fremantle, Mr. Wrightson, M.P., Mr. Liberty, and Major-General Webber. A very little discussion led the meeting to adopt as its main resolution :— " That it is desirable that an Exhibition, to be called the 'Imperial Exhibition of Women's Work,' should be held in 1897 or 1898 to celebrate the progress of women's work during the Victorian era," and the outcome of the various speeches which were delivered showed that the objects and scope of an Exhibition of Women's Work which should apply to all parts of Her Majesty's dominions were very wide; far more extended, perhaps, than might be supposed. One speaker said that the more they had investigated and subdivided the processes in most of the industries of modern times, the more they had found how large is the share of the work which devolves on women. As this growth has unconsciously been proceeding for many years, it was not surprising to find that the fact had been for several reasons much ignored. Hence many sceptics existed as to there being a field for such an exhibition.

There was even some evidence to show that trade organisations had done not a little in helping to conceal the large share women undertake of the manual processes of manufacture and production carried on indoors. Such an exhibition as was proposed would tend to throw light on the subject, and illuminate many corners which were now allowed to remain in the shade.

Speaking of the value of such an exhibition, General Webber said :—

Reports from many sources made it plain that employments which under existing conditions are injurious to health, may with proper precautions be kept open to women. Could there be any better objects for public exhibition, than the numerous apparatus and contrivances that have been invented with the object of enabling workers in industries essential to the community (for instance, lucifer match making), and which are suitable to the physique and constitution of women, to earn a good wage without losing their health, and with profit to the employer.

He claimed that the objects of this movement in no way need compete or come into collision with the legitimate and vast sphere of the work of men. *There was no question whatever in his mind of women versus men.*

They sought the help and support of both sexes, of any age, and of all ranks and classes. They hoped this meeting would come to a resolution that the time has arrived when the closing years of Her Majesty's glorious reign cannot be better inaugurated than by an exhibition of what her subjects of the same sex are doing and are able and willing to do.

It is satisfactory also to record that a paper on the proposed exhibition was read at the Meeting of the British Association, in Section F., by Miss Maitland, principal of Somerville Hall, Oxford, before a large and appreciative audience.

F. M. ROBERTS-AUSTEN.

ART. III.—CHANGES INTRODUCED BY THE NEW LOCAL GOVERNMENT ACT.

IT is impossible to estimate in advance the changes which will be wrought on rural life by the new Local Government Act, which replaces all the old authorities of Vestry, Churchwarden, Sanitary Authority, and revolutionises the Poor Law Guardian system by means of the new Parish Meetings, Parish Councils and District Councils. The following brief summary may at least serve to show what far-reaching changes—and it may be hoped, too, what far-reaching opportunities for reinvigorated life—are brought to the doors of the rural community by this Act.

It has undoubtedly brought to women enlarged opportunities for responsible action in the affairs of the community. Powers are placed now within reach of those women who may be elected by popular vote, which are the modern equivalent of those hereditary privileges possessed in former times by the Ladies as well as the Lords of the manor.

(1) *Parish Meetings.*

The Act provides in the first place that parish meetings must be held at least once a year in every parish, no matter what the population. (§ 1 and 2.) These meetings must not be held before 6 p.m. (§ 2, 3.) They are to be attended by the "Parochial Electors," that is, by all persons whose names are on the Parliamentary Register and the Local Government Register; and in addition, such married women as have a qualification separate from their husbands. (§ 3, 2.)

(2) *Parish Councils.*

Parish Councils are to be elected annually in every parish with over 300 inhabitants; to consist of from five to fifteen persons, elected by Parochial Electors. The first elections will be in November and December, 1894, after that annually in April. (§ 3.)

These Councils must not meet in public houses if any room suitable can be obtained free or at a reasonable cost. (§ 61.)

Persons eligible as Parish Councillors are Parochial Electors, or any persons who have been resident twelve months in the parish or within three miles of it. (§ 3.) The duties hitherto performed by vestries (with the exception of specially ecclesiastical duties) will fall on these Councils. They will also have the hiring of land for allotments (§ 10) and power to carry out what are known as Adoptive Acts, viz., the Lighting and Watching Act, 1833; the Baths and Washhouses Acts, 1846 and 1882; the Burials Acts, 1852 and 1885; Public Improvements Acts, 1860; the Public Libraries Act, 1892. (§ 7.)

(3) *District Councils.*

Any person is eligible as District Councillor who is a Parochial elector, or has resided twelve months in the district. (§ 23, 2.)

The District Councils will combine the duties of the Sanitary Authorities and Highway Boards (§ 25), and in rural districts the district councillors will also be the Poor Law Guardians (§ 24). In urban districts the Poor Law Guardians will still be a separately elected set of persons.

The District Councils will also perform sundry duties now performed by Justices of the Peace, viz., licensing pawnbrokers, gang-masters, dealers in game and persons having charge of infants under the Infant Life Protection Act. (§ 27.)

(4) *Special Changes as regards Poor Law Guardians.*

It will be noted that the system of Poor Law Guardian elections is completely changed by this Act.

The rate-paying qualification hitherto necessary for candidates for election is done away with. The method of increased votes for increased rates ceases. Every rate-payer, large or small, has one vote for each member, and no more. (§ 20, 4.)

All *ex-officio* and nominated guardians are abolished (§ 20, 1), but the Board itself has power to elect a chairman, vice-chairman, and two other persons, who in the first instance shall be taken from former *ex-officio* guardians. (§ 20, 7.)

The system of voting papers left at the house is done away with. All voting will be by ballot, at the polling booth.

The term of office will be for three years, one-third retiring each year.

(5) *Registration.*

The creation of these new bodies brings with it need for additional registration, so that at present returning officers have to distinguish voters as follows:—Electors who are on—

(1) *Parliamentary, County Council and Parochial register* = ownership voters who are men.
(2) *County Council and Parochial* = ownership voters who are women.
(3) *Parliamentary, Town or County Council, Parochial and School Board* = all male occupiers.

(4) *Town or County Council, Parochial and School Board* = unmarried women occupiers.
(5) *Parliamentary and Parochial* = men on service franchises and men on lodger lists.
(6) *Parochial only* = married women with separate qualifications.
(7) *Parliamentary only* = freemen, by ancient borough franchises.

(6) *Varieties in Voting.*

In School Board Elections the cumulative vote continues, *i.e.*, each elector has as many votes as there are members to be elected, and may give all to one, or otherwise distribute them as he pleases.

In Parochial and Poor Law Guardian Elections the voter may vote for as many persons as there are to be members elected, but he can only give one vote to each one; if he does not care to give one apiece to the full number, those votes are wasted.

A man may vote in several county districts if he has property there to place him on the Parliamentary Register. Women not being on the Parliamentary Register can only be qualified in the district where they reside.

But the point that perhaps claims most special attention of all, is the fact that these newly-created bodies should have added to the complications of the already so complicated system of registration. This fact adds fresh cogency to this claim of women to be included in the Parliamentary Register. Our politicians, in mere self-defence against the complications they have created, may come to welcome that further change which would abolish the need of a separate classification for women.

WOMEN'S SUFFRAGE.

NOTES OF THE QUARTER.

Nothing can at this moment so effectually strengthen the hands of those working for the extension of the Parliamentary Franchise to women, as a noble and wise use of the new opportunities which the Parish and District Councils' elections will afford to women.

Every parish in the land contains some women who will be entitled to vote, and few parishes there are which do not contain women who take a kindly and intelligent interest in the well-being of their fellow parishioners. To such women the new Act gives opportunity to change their hitherto indirect influence into direct and responsible influence, and many may there be who will avail themselves of the opportunity.

Particulars of the working of the Act are given above, suffice it here to urge that each and all will, in their own neighbourhoods, use all their efforts to spread understanding of the importance of the Act for the right ordering of the villages, and for drawing out the experience and influence of women for the public benefit.

The South Australian Women's Suffrage League have attained another step, in that the Legislative Council have read the Adult Suffrage Bill a third time. Whether the House of Assembly will confirm their vote we shall not know in time for this issue; but whatever be their decision, the struggle in the Legislative Council, of which a brief notice is given below, betokens a growth of power to the cause which calls for hearty congratulation to the indefatigable secretary, Mrs. Mary Lee, and her colleagues.

From New South Wales we receive an emphatic expression of his steadfast support from the veteran statesman, Sir Henry Parkes, and the expression of opinion quoted from Sir William Windeyer, Governor of the Colony.

In view of the presentation of the appeal from women in favour of Women's Suffrage next session, friends are reminded that all the secretaries of the various Women's Suffrage Committees will gladly hear of offers of help for increasing the mass of signatures. Sheets for three signatures, and books for twenty, can always be had, gratis, on application to the central offices, at 29, Parliament Street, and 10, Great College Street, Westminster.

COLONIAL.
SOUTH AUSTRALIA.

The Bill for Adult Suffrage passed the third reading in the Legislative Council of South Australia on August 13, after a slow and obstructed passage through committee.

As the Bill amends the constitution, an absolute majority of the whole House was required for the second and third readings. Its supporters were thirteen in a House of twenty-four, so that the loss of a single vote would have sacrificed the Bill. The opponents made every effort to bring about its defeat. They tried in committee to restrict the Suffrage to women with a proper qualification. Next they tried to make a higher age qualification for women than for men. When these attempts failed, it was proposed to grant women special rights of voting under the Absent Voters' Act, but the friends of the women's claims were not to be led into the perilous admission that there would be any danger or inconvenience to women in voting.

Finally, "In the last stages of committee (says the *Adelaide Advertiser*), amendments were proposed for a referendum on this subject, and for limiting the operation of the Act to a specified period—anything, in short, to delay the reform or to prejudice the Bill in the eyes of the other Chamber. It was all in vain. In one important respect, however, the measure has been amended. The clause prohibiting women from sitting in Parliament was struck out by a combination of the opponents of Women's Suffrage with a majority of its supporters. The votes of this curious alliance were no doubt cast with very different motives. Those of the voters who are favourable to the Bill favoured the excision of the clause because they desire the 'logical sequence' of Women's Suffrage. The remainder probably calculated that to extend to women the right to sit as well as to vote might have the effect of alarming the moderate supporters of female enfranchisement, and of changing votes in one House or the other. Possibly they were in hopes that, as a result of their action, 'something would turn up.' Something did turn up—a constitutional difficulty. The question was raised whether the Bill, with clause 4 omitted, is the same as that which was passed by an absolute majority on the second reading."

On this point the President gave his ruling that the Bill had not lost its identity because it had been amended in committee, and the third reading was passed, and the Bill now awaits the decision of the House of Assembly.

NEW SOUTH WALES.

The Sydney Morning Herald, of July 6, thus reports the words of Sir HENRY PARKES when addressing an election meeting :—" Since they had got the principle of the simple equality of voting power, he thought the time had come when they ought to think whether they could righteously stop at giving that power to the feeble-minded, the loose-lived and the drunkenly-disposed members of one half of the population, while giving no power whatever to the other half. In other words, was not the time come when the women of this country should have a vote?"

In a lecture on the "Tendencies of the Age," delivered at the University on July 29, Sir WILLIAM WINDEYER, Governor of New South Wales, enumerating the various steps by which the gulf between class and class are being gradually bridged over, referred to " the growing recognition that woman, in right of her womanhood and her subjection to the laws of her country, had a right to a voice in their making; that the ultimate perfection of the human race cannot be attained so long as the half with whom the responsibility of motherhood depends, was in any way prevented from developing its highest intellectual, social, and political capacity."

VICTORIA.

A Bill to extend the vote for election of members of the Legislative Assembly to women, was introduced on July 19 in the Melbourne Parliament by Mr. Malony. The debate seems to have come somewhat unexpectedly, and the friends of the movement were consequently not as much in force as they might have been. To judge by the reports of the Melbourne papers, the debate was not marked by any high degree of force or eloquence on either side; the most memorable saying being, perhaps, that of Mr. F. Madden, who said that the housewife who loves to do her duty to her children does not want the vote, and as to the platform women who advocated it, he would as soon give a vote to a cockatoo as one of them ; while the most important speech was that from the Premier, Sir James Paterson, who avowed himself in favour of the general principle, but he considered it would be better to leave the question to the Government, as there were many other matters connected with electoral law to be considered, and they should all be dealt with at one time. Though not altogether approving of the referendum, he thought it might be resorted to on the Women's Suffrage question.

The Bill was eventually talked out, or as it is expressed by the Colonial papers, "stonewalled," by Mr. P. M. Salmon.

A NEW ZEALAND EXPERIENCE.

The following is quoted from the *Leeds Mercury* of Sept. 15 :—" A gentleman in Napier, New Zealand, corresponding with a Leeds friend, writes as follows :—' So far as this question is concerned, the result has been quite up to expectation. The ladies seem to have caught an intelligent view of every question, which up till now has awaited decision. Of course they have voted strongly against the liquor traffic, as shown in their returning men of temperance views, with the result that in a number of districts in this colony a fair proportion of hotels for the selling of drink have been closed ; while in every other district the committees have responded to public opinion by placing such restrictions upon the traffic as will tend to reduce the evil very considerably, as, for instance, in compelling the hotels to close at 10 or 11 p.m., keeping them clean, and generally in enforcing better management. We, who are upon the spot, cannot but conclude that at no distant period drinking-bars will be closed altogether. This woman franchise has thus been an element for good to the entire community here. Here is something worth noting. Our girls are now being educated into taking an active interest in affairs political at the Girls' High School, where my girls attend. The reading lessons are not taken from the ordinary, old-fashioned reading-book, but from current English literature, English newspapers being generally used on these occasions. This is up to date, is it not? Over the tea-cups my girls and I talk upon questions of the hour, and thus they are led to form intelligent opinions upon the leading topics of the day. If at any time you hear female franchise disparaged, please champion the sex, and you are at liberty to draw upon my statements to back you up. Chatting this evening with my second daughter, aged 15, she informed me that, in addition to the reading lessons referred to, they are invited to write essays on the burning questions of the day, such as Home Rule, and, indeed, upon any question in which the future interests of the English-speaking nations are affected. With an electorate trained under such conditions as these, the result sooner or later would be seen in the substitution of right for might, leading to the enactment of justice and wiser laws all round.'"

NEW YORK.

The New York Constitutional Convention have rejected the petition of the 625,000 citizens of New York State praying that the word "male" be omitted from the constitution. Sixty voted in favour and ninety-seven against. But with sixty to vote in favour and with a petition signed by half as many as usually vote in the State elections, the women suffragists of New York feel that their demand has received a great momentum, and they are already making plans to collect additional signatures and press their claim on the State Convention. The Petition *against* contained 15,000 names.

INCIDENT AT LEICESTER ELECTION.

The recent bye-election at Leicester, when Mr. Broadhurst and Mr. Hazell were returned, has furnished a cogent argument for the upholders of women's claims to vote. A strong objection was raised against the latter gentleman by the Leicester Typographical Society, the principal objection urged being that Mr. Hazell employed girls as compositors in his printing works at Aylesbury. This led to a conference between Mr. Hazell and the secretaries of the provincial and of the Leicester Typographical Societies, in which it appeared that the latter were satisfied by understanding Mr. Hazell that as the women now employed left, their places would not be filled by women. Commenting on this Mrs. Beddoe wrote in a letter to the *Morning Post* of August 31, what most friends, and even some foes of Women's Suffrage will have shared with her in feeling, that the "condition that the candidate had had to make with regard to the employment, or rather non-employment of women compositors, furnishes one of the clearest proofs of the great injustice committed in withholding from women workers that strong political weapon which is now possessed by almost all those who compete with them in their industries, whether professional or industrial. When the new Member for Leicester considers the case of the thousands and tens of thousands of women who have, by sad necessity if you like, to support themselves, he ought to be, as we hope he will be, one of the strongest supporters in the House of the Women's Suffrage Movement, and thus the hardships to the few may, as is so often the case, lead to the benefit of the many." It is gratifying to add that Mrs. Beddoe's hope is fully justified by the following letter received by Miss Gittins, hon. sec. of the Leicester Women's Suffrage Society :—

"DEAR MADAM,—I have long been of opinion that women who are qualified, except as to sex, should have the power of voting, and I hope that this alteration in the law would tend to raise the moral tone of political life. It might not be a gain to the Liberals and Radicals, but it seems to me a just measure, and that is quite enough for me.
"Yours faithfully,
(Signed) " WALTER HAZELL.
" Miss Edith Gittens."

ELECTIONS AND APPOINTMENTS.

THE LOCAL GOVERNMENT BOARD have nominated Mrs. S. A. Barnett as one of the Commission appointed to enquire into the condition of pauper schools.

THE SECRETARY OF STATE FOR INDIA has appointed Miss Annette Benson, B.Sc., M.D. (Lond.) as first physician to the Kama Hospital, Bombay, in succession to Mrs. Edith Pechey Phipson, M.D., resigned.

MRS. BAIRD of Cambusdoon has just been presented with the freedom of the Royal and ancient burgh of Dunbar, in recognition (as her burgess ticket recites) of "the benefit conferred upon the burgh by her magnificent gift of an esplanade for the use and enjoyment of the inhabitants of the town and neighbourhood."

WELSH COUNTY SCHOOLS.—The Carmarthen County Council have elected Miss Schaw Protheroe on the Board of Governors of Intermediate Schools of the County, and also as one of the managers of the Whitland Board for the Intermediate School.

IN Flintshire several ladies have been nominated governors of the county schools.

MISS HELEN GLADSTONE has been nominated governor of the Hawarden School by the Hawarden Board of Guardians.

SCHOOL BOARDS.—*Apsley Heath* (Beds), Mrs. Anne Stuart; *Salford*, Mrs. M. Jordan (by election).

POOR LAW.—The Strand Board of Guardians have elected Mrs. Evans as a Representative Trustee of the Parish Estate Charities of St. Mary-le-Strand.

MRS. PERCY FLEMING, M.D. (Lond.) and Miss Piercy, M.B. (Lond.), have been elected members of the Anatomical Society.

MISS ELEANOR FLEURY, M.B. (R.U.I.), has been elected a fellow of the Medico-Psychological Society.

MRS. J. R. GREEN has been elected on to the Committee of the London Library.

MISS C. E. WHITE has succeeded Miss Johnson as head of the Alexandra Hall of Residence, Dublin.

THE *London Diocesan Magazine* says that a new departure is being taken by the committee of the Missions to Seamen, in the employment of a lady worker, Miss Alice Barton, for the port of London.

UNIVERSITY INTELLIGENCE.

UNIVERSITY OF LONDON.
MATRICULATION EXAMINATION, JUNE, 1894
HONOURS DIVISION.

Hicks, Amy Maud (Prize of £5), North London Collegiate School for Girls.
Rickword, Beatrice, Ipswich High School.
Atcherley, Lily, University Tutorial College.
First Division.—179 girls.
Second Division.—100 girls.

ROYAL UNIVERSITY OF IRELAND.

The Summer Examinations of the Royal University of Ireland give the following results as regards the women students:—

MATRICULATION EXAMINATIONS.

Thirty-eight girls passed in various subjects, making in all 61 passes. Of these—Katherine S. H. McCutcheon, Methodist College, Belfast, obtained an Exhibition of £24 ; and the following obtained Exhibitions of £12—Annie Wilson, Strand House School, Londonderry ; Florence B. Adamson, Victoria College, Belfast; Dorothea C. Harden, Alexandra College, Dublin; Elizabeth W. Leebody, private study and Ladies' Collegiate School, Londonderry.

FIRST UNIVERSITY EXAMINATION.

Thirty-three girls passed in various subjects, making a total of 45 passes. Of these—Edna Hudson, Victoria College, Belfast ; Elizabeth M. A. Baxter, Victoria College, Belfast ; Mary Murphy, Ursuline High School, St. Angela's, Cork, and Agnes Hanna, Victoria College, Belfast, each obtained an Exhibition of £15.

SECOND UNIVERSITY EXAMINATION.

Fifteen girls passed in various subjects, making a total of 38 passes. Of these—Annie McElderry, Victoria College, Belfast, obtained an Exhibition of £36. Margaret S. Brittain and Isabella Dewar, both of Victoria College, Belfast ; Catherine E. Duffy, St. Mary's University College, Dublin ; Cecilia A. L. Hitchcock, Alexandra College, Dublin ; Elizabeth G. Kennedy, Loretto High School, Dublin, obtained Exhibitions of £18.

Eva M. McGuire, Victoria College, Belfast, also obtained an Exhibition of £18, and the Stewart Scholarship in Arts, £90, as a reward of her successes in two consecutive years.

FIRST EXAMINATION IN LAW.

Mary E. Clements, private study.

FIRST EXAMINATION IN MEDICINE.

Isabella A. Tate, Queen's College, Belfast.

THE FIRST LADY GRADUATES OF GLASGOW UNIVERSITY.

The candidates for the final examinations for degrees in medicine and surgery in Glasgow University numbered 135, of whom 69 passed in all subjects, and 30 in all but one. Of the 30, 21 were referred for three months in surgery. There were 8 withdrawals and 28 rejections. Of the candidates 4 were ladies, of whom 2 passed in all subjects, and 2 in all but surgery. The graduation took place on July 19, among the graduands being the two ladies mentioned. These ladies have the unique distinction of being the first lady graduates of this more than three centuries old University, and their names ought to be recorded. They are Miss Marion Gilchrist, of Bothwell, and Miss Alice L. L. Cumming, daughter of Dr. Cumming, of Blythswood Square. Both are students of Queen Margaret College, Glasgow, where each took a preliminary training in

Arts before entering on her medical studies. Miss Gilchrist is an LL.A. of St. Andrew's, and has the additional honour of graduating with high commendation. Queen Margaret College has reason to be proud of her first University candidates.—*British Medical Journal.*

THE SCOTTISH UNIVERSITIES AND SCHOLARSHIPS FOR WOMEN.

Acting under the Scottish Universities Act of 1889, the Scottish Universities Commissioners, in August, published an Ordinance with regard to regulations for admitting women to Bursaries, Scholarships and Fellowships which will give the Universities ample powers to admit women to share in the advantages they have to offer.

The Commissioners ordain as follows:—

I. (1) It shall be in the power of the University Court in each University, after consultation with the Senatus Academicus, to make regulations from time to time for the purpose of appropriating for competition without restriction as to sex, or for competition among women students only who are proceeding to a degree in any Faculty, such number, if any, of open bursaries, which have taken effect prior to August 30, 1864, as the University Court may think fit: provided always (a) that the Court and the Senatus in each University shall, in making such regulations, have regard to the number of bursaries in that University specially appropriated to women by the terms of the deeds of foundation; (b) that no bursary shall be appropriated to students in any other Faculty than that to which it is at present attached, except under Section III. of Ordinance [General No. 19.—Regulations as to Bursaries, Scholarships, and Fellowships].

(2) It shall be in the power of the University Court of each University, in like manner, to open to competition, without restriction as to sex, such number, if any, of Scholarships or Fellowships tenable by graduates, which have taken effect prior to August 30, 1864, as the said Court may think fit.

II. Save as hereinbefore provided, women shall not be allowed to compete for or hold any Bursary, Scholarship, or Fellowship, which is not expressly open to competition by women by the terms of the deed of foundation.

III. Women competing for Bursaries, Scholarships, or Fellowships under the provisions of this Ordinance shall be subject to all the provisions prescribed by Ordinance [General No. 19.—Regulations as to Bursaries, Scholarships, and Fellowships].

IV. This Ordinance shall come into force from and after January 1, 1895, or as soon thereafter as it shall be approved by Her Majesty in Council; provided that nothing herein contained shall extend to, or affect the interests of, any person holding a bursary, scholarship, or fellowship at the date of its coming into force.

RECORD OF EVENTS.

THE INSTITUTE OF JOURNALISTS.

The first International Conference of the Press which took place at Antwerp in July (the reports of which came just too late for mention in the last Review), and the Sixth Annual Conference of the Institute of Journalists, held this year at Norwich in August, both furnish proof of the equal position which our English journalists are ready to accord to the women members of their profession. Women journalists attended the Conference in Antwerp from France, Russia, and America, as well as from England, but it was the English Institute of Journalists who sent the only two women who attended as delegates. Miss Catherine Drew and Miss Grace Benedicta Stuart were both elected as representative members of the London district of the Journalists' Institute, and Miss Stuart was invited to contribute a paper on the position of English women in journalism, which was received with every mark of attention and approval. Moreover Mr. Clayden, in his address in his capacity as President of the Institute of Journalists, took occasion to remark that the institute made no distinction between man journalists and women journalists.

Similarly at Norwich, the London district renewed its expression of confidence by electing Miss Drew as one of its delegates, and by asking her to contribute a paper. The President (Mr. Clayden) acknowledging the welcome of the Mayor and Corporation, said he might "point out that Norwich was the birthplace of the most illustrious of lady journalists, Miss Harriet Martineau, whom he had had the honour to succeed in the position which he had now occupied for many years."

In the paper which closed the proceedings of the Conference, Prof. Jebb, M.P., concluded by saying: "It was a pleasure to observe that among the members of the Institute there were many ladies. Those who appreciated the present position of journalism, and who wished well to its highest interests, would agree that able and cultured women could contribute elements of a quite unique value to its educational influence."

The paper read by Miss Drew on the second day of the Conference was received with special interest, and touched on points of so much moment for women journalists as to invite the production of as large a portion as space permits.

PAPER BY MISS CATHERINE DREW, "WOMEN AS JOURNALISTS."—After a few preliminary remarks Miss Drew said :—

The indulgence asked for the subject chosen is not for women as women, but for women as journalists, workers in the same field with the men who have made the Press in England a power, morally, politically, economically, and socially.

There is yet a graver reason for choosing my fellow-workers on the Press as my theme to-day. It is the first time in England that a woman journalist has been allowed the privilege of holding a brief, and stating a case for her own sex. If special pleading obtrudes itself, the novelty of the situation must plead my apology.

The admirable paper read at Antwerp by our late President, Mr. Clayden, is now, in printed form, in the hands of all our members. Listening to it, seated in front of the daïs from which it was delivered, its spirit came home with a force and impressiveness that merely scanning its pages scarcely conveys.

On page 6 you will find this passage:—" There is no more democratic body in the world than the Institute of Journalists of the United Kingdom. It rests on universal suffrage as its basis, it knows no distinction between man journalists and woman journalists."

This is the only allusion to difference of sex in journalism that Mr. Clayden makes, but that one is enough to make every woman member think seriously of the situation, how far that section to which she herself belongs is likely to realise the ideal set before her, and live up to such a lofty conception of a journalist's aims and work.

The admission of women to membership was a great

experiment. Some people called it a rash measure, and others went farther, denouncing it as dangerous. Even the Laodicean critics considered the innovation uncalled for, as the women would certainly prove themselves to be nuisances.

For good or ill, women have been taken into the Institute. In the future they will justify one or other of these censorships. Either they will raise the Institute by accepting the intentions of the founders, striving daily to live up to its highest aims, or they will ignore every consideration but individual interests, dragging down the organisation, and making it a byeword and a disgrace to the great profession to which we must all be proud to belong.

Very little seems to be known, even in the ranks of our own profession, of the work done by women journalists; of the incessant toil; the untiring endeavour to keep pace with public tastes and the requirements of advancing civilisation; the ever-recurring disappointments and discouragements borne with heroic endurance, suffering, intensified by privations that womanly as well as professional pride tries to keep out of sight.

Enlarged ideas on women's education first originated about a quarter of a century ago, slowly taking practical shape. It is only within the last ten years that the results of the movement have been evidenced in the number of women taking part in the everyday work of the world.

In 1841 but 15 women were professionally engaged as authors, editors, and journalists. In 1861 the numbers had risen to 185. The next ten years added but 70 more to the ranks, making 255. When the next census was taken the wider advantages of education had begun to bear fruit, for authors, editors, and journalists rose to 452. In this (1881) census the reporter and shorthand writer for the first time makes a separate and very modest appearance, represented by 15 ladies. The last census gives but 660 authors, editors, and journalists; but the shorthand writers had added 127 to their ranks. There were, besides, a number of women engaged in scientific pursuits, who, without being classified as journalists, were regular contributors

on special subjects to newspapers and magazines. In
those early days when the professional writer was so
small a factor in production, probably the writers were
quite sufficiently numerous for the readers. The ordinary journalist woman gave her time to fashion
magazines. The exceptional woman, of which there
were three brilliant examples, contributed to the best
leading journals of the day able reviews of scientific,
philosophical, and literary books, with essays on what
is now known as sociology. Two of these, the Hon.
Mrs. Norton and Miss Harriet Martineau, have laid
away their pens for ever ; but the third, Miss Frances
Power Cobbe, still lives, and we claim her as one of
our honorary and most honoured members.

So recently as in 1882, when there were 2,137 newspapers in the United Kingdom, 50 of which were
denominational, the organs of different religious bodies,
and 92 for young people, there were but 42 for ladies,
exclusive of trade journals. Six of these were high
class, treating of many topics interesting to, and beneficial for, women, only making fashion an incidental
feature ; while of the 36 remaining, modes and domestic
management were the great themes, and fiction and
miscellaneous topics only introduced as padding.

The difficulties under which an editress carried on
her paper before women were trained to be accurate
and punctual can scarcely be imagined in these advanced
days. Specialists now abound who make themselves
responsible for their departments, and relieve the woman
at the helm of much anxiety. Dress illustrations in
those days were literally " made in Germany." They
came over in electro-type form by way of Paris, having
first done a little duty in French papers. From Germany came also work patterns, with illustrations
and descriptions, emanating from the admirable Victoria
Institute, presided over by the Crown Princess, now
the Empress Frederick of Germany. The translations
were usually done by young ladies who had brought a
little knowledge from boarding schools, but very little
sense of responsibility, and with Lady Morgan's fine
contempt for figures as a woman's concern. The
editress had to test every proof herself—this is a study

from the life—so that her crotchet needle lay in the inkstand, her knitting needles in the table drawer, and her evenings after office hours were spent in trying the cookery receipts, to be quite sure whether an ounce or a pound of flour was suggested as the correct quantity for a pudding.

The exceptional woman, like Mrs. Crawford, of Paris, and Miss Shaw, of the *Times*, must be separated in classification from the bulk of women journalists, for they cannot be ranged.

After these ladies come those who are contributors on literary, artistic, and scientific subjects, who work chiefly at home, sending out their contributions on well-digested subjects in cleverly constructed articles, some signed, others anonymous, that take their place as leaders, or descriptive articles in the daily papers.

A large number of women are found doing office work, who are neither original thinkers, nor brilliant writers; but they are accurate and painstaking, and are not the less journalists because they have to arrange, condense, and often re-write, the work of others.

Nor can the sketcher be overlooked in these days of illustrated journalism. She is an indispensable member of the staff, but, unfortunately, she is as yet the worst taught, and the most unmanageable quantity in the world of journalism.

The fiction writer contributes her share to journalism, but as she is, more or less, of the associate type, she scarcely takes rank with the actual worker on newspapers.

The great majority of women journalists are what in the medical profession would be known as "general practitioners." Of these an all-round knowledge is expected of people and things, great and small, with a faculty for presenting topics in an attractive manner to readers. The general practitioner must be quick to observe, keen to appreciate, cautious to accept statements, with a well-balanced sense of proportion, and a ready adaptation to circumstances. Her knowledge, theoretical and practical, must range up and down a gamut of subjects not included in any curriculum. She must live on a kind of watch tower, looking over a world with domestic as well as social interests ; nor may her vigilance relax where political changes are concerned, those forces that control and alter all conditions of life. To-day she may have to soar to an organ stop, and to-morrow drop down to a new frying-pan. Pinafores may be weighing down her spirits while she is being called upon to consider improved mechanism for a piano. A new embroidery silk may have to await her needle until she has tested a patented potato peeler. Attendance at social functions requires tact and delicacy. She must also possess that faculty ascribed to an illustrious personage, of remembering faces and fitting the right names to them. To confound one Duchess with another, or ascribe the charitable work of a Marchioness to a Countess, would be one of those blunders which amounts to a crime.

No woman need attend a loan exhibition of art treasures without having trained her eye to discriminate the work of one period from that of another. Family traditions, as imparted by their owners, are avalanches that have rolled down the centuries, gathering size and importance by the way ; and lace, jewels, pictures, and many other treasures are not always what they seem.

These papers have become of really great national importance as mediums of communication between producers and consumers of an infinite number of home industries. A whole army of women is engaged in this service of viewing, testing, and reporting on the novelties produced. On the verdict of the women journalists often depends the success, or the failure, of a venture on which a large sum of money has been expended. The manufacturer, at least, recognises the importance to the trade of the country of the woman journalist.

Were those cynical objectors to women in the ranks of the profession allowed to wipe out the women that to-day I represent, and also their readers, it would be nothing short of a national calamity. The Commissioners of Bankruptcy might sit day and night, relieving one another, and at the end of a year find the undischarged insolvents of the commercial world still blocking up the doorway. Ladies' papers, and the interests they serve, have become a great social and economic power. In no country of the world is this so fully understood as in England.

For the woman journalist the fact ought to be placed on record that English manufacturers and proprietors of journals are building up large fortunes by her labours, yet she has no share of the profits. Co-operation is confined to the labour itself, not to its results. No women own these great ventures, neither newspapers nor factories, but to the former their work is so valuable, and their services are so indispensable, that without their help doors might be closed. The woman's wage is often far removed from being a living wage; rarely has she a margin that allows for preparation for old age. Many women have aged and invalid relatives dependent on them, and some are widows bravely doing their best for their little children. For the woman journalist the eight hours day has yet to dawn, for her work is never done. It may come in the future, it is not in the present, and it never was in the past.

In the labour world there is no sentimental element. Women are not employed out of generosity or benevolence, but because they know their work and do it well, and they themselves recognise and accept these conditions.

In a society, one of the few in existence that offers a woman equality, it is rather a humiliating confession to make that she is the weaker sister. To her professional life is new, and, in its uncertainty, depressing. In her path lies every temptation to live to a low rather than a high standard, regarding illegitimate means of adding to her income as fair and incidental to her calling. It is difficult to persuade one who is underpaid and over anxious, that the honour of the profession calls upon her to work with clean hands.

Gentlemen of the Institute—It depends upon you what the woman journalist becomes in the future. It rests with you, her employers and fellow-workers, to treat her professionally consistently with the same spirit in which you welcomed her within your ranks. She is in your hands, either to do honour to her membership or to cast a shadow over the whole profession.

Truth, and a high sense of honour are to be expected of her, but fair and generous dealing must meet her, at least, half-way. Her path is a difficult one, and no hindrances to her keeping a straight course need be put in her way.

This plea is not one for the present hour, but for all time through which such an organisation as ours shall last. We of to-day are moulding the journalists—men and women—who will take our places when we have passed away. The responsibility is not a light one, but it must be shared equally—by men and women alike.

You have set us a standard, and the women I represent are prepared to accept it, and with all their powers to try and live up to it. When the terrible innovation, dangerous and revolutionary, that you have made becomes an old story, you will, I doubt not, have learned fully to appreciate and to respect women as journalists.

THE BARRACK LIFE OF PAUPER CHILDREN.
DEPUTATION TO THE PRESIDENT OF THE LOCAL GOVERNMENT BOARD.

A very large and influential deputation waited on the Right Hon. G. J. Shaw Lefevre, President of the Local Government Board, at the Local Government Board Office, on July 23rd, to lay before him the evils of the present system of massing pauper children in huge schools, and to urge upon him the desirability of appointing a Royal Commission or some other mode of public inquiry to investigate the conditions under which pauper children are educated in barrack or associated schools. The deputation included some 200 representative persons, and was one of the largest and most important ever received at the Board. Among those present were the following ladies:—Mrs. S. A. Barnett, Miss F. Davenport Hill, Miss Emma Cons, Mrs. Ernest Hart, Miss Brodie-Hall, Mrs. Eva Maclaren, Miss Donkin, Mrs. A. Hicks, Miss Townsend, Mrs. Shaen, Miss Spence, Mrs. Hall, Miss A. L. Browne, Mrs. F. Raikes.

Sir JOHN GORST, M.P., who introduced the deputation, explained its object, which was not to make an attack upon the management of the great district schools, but to go a great deal further, and urge that the time had now come when a public inquiry ought to be made into the whole system of the treatment of the children, and in the light of modern experience to consider, not only whether the schools were ill or well managed, but whether the system of herding children together in large numbers must not necessarily produce evil results, detrimental to the State and the children themselves.

Mr. ERNEST HART made a general statement on behalf of the deputation, and was followed by several speakers, including Mrs. S. A. BARNETT, who said: I venture to speak to you to-day because I have had some experience in this matter. For sixteen years I have been a manager of the Forest Gate District School. For nearly twenty years I have been a working member of the Metropolitan Association for Befriending Young Servants, the Society which was founded by Mrs. Nassau Senior, and which exists mainly to look after girls trained in the pauper schools. For nearly fifteen years I have taken girls from the schools straight into our own home, and have thus had 135 under my personal observation. I began my work as a manager, believing that the system of associated schools could be made to serve the purpose of educating and up-bringing these children in a right and suitable way; but slowly and reluctantly I have arrived at the opposite opinion. There may be defects in boards of management or superior officers, but when both are enlightened and benevolent, the *system* of educating large numbers of children together makes their efforts ineffective. The requirements of administration oblige them to keep to rule. They cannot give rein to their affections, or time and tenderness to small mites who need special care. As one of the school officials said to me : " I often have to tell a child that she is shamming when I would like to cosset her a bit; but what should we come to if we petted up every child when there are so many?" The requirements of administration also compel the large majority of those engaged

in the up-bringing of these children to be unmarried.
The schools, which are the only home of hundreds of
children, are to the officers and servants merely their
workshop. Themselves homeless, they cannot (even
should they wish to do so) share with their charges
their fireside pleasures or their family interests. My
own experience, as well as that of a number of other
ladies, enables me to say that many of the girls brought
up in these barrack schools have faults peculiarly their
own. They are : (1) Self-indifferent—indifferent to vice
as well as to virtue, to vanity as well as to affection, to
scolding as well as to ambition. (2) They are of a
temper that combines sulkiness and rage, spite and
stubbornness, and it is this "pauper temper" which
frequently causes them to lose their situations. (3)
They are ignorant of the commonest dangers of the
world, frequently as powerless to keep themselves
clean as to avoid temptation, and were it not for the
devotion of the 1,050 ladies who, as members of the
M.A.B.Y.S., unflaggingly watch, guide, and protect
these girls, the results, I fear, would not be far other
than they were when Mrs. Nassau Senior's inquiries
elicited the fact that fifty-three per cent. of girls
brought up in pauper schools had to be classed as "unsatisfactory and bad." (4) They know nothing of
domestic affairs. The mistakes they make would be
comic if their consequences were not apt to be tragic.
They have been trained too much by machinery, too
little by "mothering"— turned out according to
pattern, they miss the individuality which might make
life a pleasure to themselves and a help to others. I
promised you, sir, to be brief, so I will say no more;
only allow me, on behalf of the many girls who are
under State care, to join my voice to those who ask for
an inquiry that will lead to reform. I know that
boarding out can only provide for a small proportion of
rate-supported children, but an inquiry may bring to
light, not only the evils under which the children now
suffer, but also other methods by which they can be
wisely educated—methods which will allow the more
permanent children to be divided from the "ins and
outs," namely, the children of the degraded from those

of the decent widow; methods which will permit each child to be brought up as an individual with its own character and tastes, an individual who needs to be loved as well as to be drilled, to be developed as well as to be disciplined.

A commission of inquiry was subsequently appointed, and the name of Mrs. Barnett is announced as one of the commissioners.

POST OFFICE TELEGRAPHISTS.

A parliamentary return—moved for by Mr. Provand, and ordered by the House of Commons to be printed in July—has now been published, showing the number of telegraphists employed by the Post Office, their wages and conditions of employment in 1872 and 1894, from which the following figures are taken—

	Number.		Percentage of Whole Number.		Average Mean Salary.	
	Men.	Women.	Men.	Women.	Men.	Women.
LONDON:						
1872.						
Supervisors	87	66	12·7	6·4	£173	£99
First Class Telegraphists	115	132	16·7	12·7	115	72
General Body	486	840	70·6	80·9	61	43
	688	1,038				
1894.						
Supervisors	342	105	13·9	8	218	131
First Class Telegraphists	698	342	28·2	26	135	89
General Body	1,428	869	57·9	66	76	57
	2,468	1,316				
PROVINCES:						
1872.						
Supervisors	183	—	5·2	—	154	—
First Class Telegraphists	222	—	6·4	—	104	—
General Body	3,102	—	88·4	—	58	—
	3,507					
1894.						
Supervisors	535	43	12·5	2·8	190	115
First Class Telegraphists	1,037	353	24·2	23·6	122	81
General Body	2,708	1,101	63·3	73·6	68	50
	4,280	1,497				

THE WESLEYAN METHODIST CONFERENCE.

WOMEN DELEGATES.

The representative session of the Wesleyan Methodist Conference, which met in Birmingham on July 23, was met this year by the perplexed question, whether a lady could attend as a representative?

A number of ladies for the first time, we believe, attended as visitors; but in addition to these, Miss Dawson attended as the elected representative of the Third London Synod.

Immediately on the commencement of business, the Rev. OWEN WATKINS drew attention to this circumstance. He submitted that the constitution of the Conference provided for 242 ministers and 240 "laymen," and that such an innovation could not come about in that way. He contended that it was not respectful to the Conference, and it was not respectful to the Methodist Church. He moved:—

"That the lady elected to the Conference by the Third London District be allowed to take her place, and that such admission be without prejudice to the case; and that a committee be appointed to consider the whole question and report; and that no further election of ladies take place until the Conference has decided the whole question of the admission of ladies as representatives to the Conference." Whatever their views might be, they could not settle this question offhand. It was a grave departure from Methodist usage.

Rev. PRICE HUGHES did not think there was any good in debating it at length. There was nothing so very awful in the admission of a lady.

After an animated discussion, the following amendment, moved by the ex-President (the Rev. H. J. POPE), and seconded by Mr. QUIBELL (Newark), was carried by a large majority:—

"That the attention of the Conference having been called to the presence of a lady representative, elected by the Third London District, resolves, in view of all the special circumstances of the case, and without deciding the validity of this election, to proceed to the order of the day, but directs that in future no chairman of Synod shall receive the nomination of a lady representative until the Conference shall have determined by legislative action to admit ladies as representatives, and until such new legislation has been submitted for approval to the District Synods."

The announcement of the acceptance of this amendment as a substantive motion was the signal for loud cheers, in which the visitors and other strangers in the gallery heartily joined. During the discussion there was great excitement at times, and the President had difficulty in maintaining order. The result is that Miss Dawson retains her seat for this Conference, but that in so doing the matter of women representatives is without prejudice for the future.

Commenting on this discussion in the *Review of the Churches* for August 15, Mr. Percy Bunting writes:—"Women are admissible to office unquestionably as leaders, and no doubt in other offices, and as such are members of the quarterly meeting of this circuit. In that capacity they have votes for election to the District Synod. It is doubtful whether they are eligible as members of the District Synod. In the rules of such elections the word 'layman' is used, but also the word 'gentleman.' At the same time circuit stewards are members of Synods, and it would require to be shown that a woman cannot constitutionally be elected circuit steward. Women have, in fact, been so elected. If this point is settled in favour of women, then it would follow that the word layman, in rules relating to the Synod, includes a woman, and it might well be held that the same construction applies to the Conference itself.

"With regard to Connexional Committees, women are habitually appointed, and the list printed in the 'Minutes of Conference' includes their names. The list is headed 'Lay Members.' It is inserted by express resolution of the Conference, which also directs that in the provisional list of such committees, printed in the 'Conference Agenda,' the postal address of each 'layman' shall be given.

"The language of all these rules is somewhat loose, and perhaps no clear conclusion can be arrived at from it. The most important argument is that the eligibility of a woman as circuit steward has never been challenged; that women are members of quarterly meetings, and presumably, in the absence of express prohibitors, eligible for the Synod; that either *ex-officio* or by election, they may therefore be members of Synod; that the Synods elect representatives to Conference; and that the choice of the Synod is expressly fettered only by the qualification that a representative must either be a member of the church of five years' standing, a trustee, a member of a quarterly meeting, or a member of Synod, every one of which qualifications may be filled by a woman. The question, so far as it turns upon the present law, therefore, seems to be whether the somewhat ambiguous use of the word 'layman' can over-ride this presumable eligibility." *

DOCTORS AT THE SWEDISH INSTITUTE, CLIFTON.

During the visit of the British Medical Association to Bristol in the last week of July, Miss Theodora Johnson and Fröken Dahl gave a demonstration of Dr. Ling's system of physical training, at their Swedish Institute, 20, Vyvyan Terrace, Clifton, which was attended by several members of the Medical Association. Dr. W. H. Harsant, F.R.C.S., presided.

Miss JOHNSON prefaced the practical demonstration by a short address, in which she pointed out that in Ling's system physical training was based on scientific principles, each movement having a definite physiological aim, and producing a definite physiological result. She gave a short account of the system, the college for which was established in 1815 in Stockholm. The Hampstead Training College, at which Miss Johnson had had the honour of being the first student—was established in 1885.

With the assistance of a class of some twelve young girls, Miss Johnson showed the nature and purpose of the Swedish gymnastics, pointing out the effect of the various movements on different muscles. The visitors were especially interested in the use of the ladders and

---

* Conf. news from the Wesleyan Church of Australasia, page 274.

bars, which form a feature of the system, the pupils
going through the manœuvres with grace and zest.

After this Miss DAHL gave a demonstration of massage and medical movements, Miss Johnson entering an emphatic protest against the degradation of the term massage, which resulted from its employment by rough and untrained persons. With regard to medical movements, an interesting object lesson was afforded by two former patients, who were both quite cured of spinal curvature, and who proffered their help. Miss Johnson closed by urging the need of well-regulated systematic training in every school, and especially pointing out its value to the blind, and to the deaf and dumb.

At the close, Dr. HARSANT expressed the thanks of the doctors and himself for what had, he said, proved a most interesting and instructive afternoon.

WOMEN AND THE ORDER OF FORESTERS.

The inaugural address of the High Chief Ranger at the Foresters' High Court held in Cambridge on August 6, gives some interesting facts as regards the position of women in the large Friendly Society, which it will be remembered they were admitted to from courts of their own in 1892. The High Chief Ranger (Brother W. P. Littlechild) remarked that he had an exceedingly pleasant privilege in being the first High Chief Ranger to welcome female delegates to a High Court. It would be one of the most pleasing recollections of a happy year of office that the ladies began in his year to take a part in their work, and to show their male brethren they had not a monopoly of sympathy or of the zeal which tireth not in the service of humanity. At the end of December, 1893, the Order had a grand total of 876,493 members of all kinds ranged under its banner. This large total included 3,657 adult women benefit members, and 16,839 widows contributing for funeral allowance. There were in all 59 female courts. Altogether the Cambridge Executive looked back upon the issuing of so great a number of dispensations for female courts with justifiable pride. Might the earnestness and zeal which had set in be continued, and the membership in the male courts receive a great impetus and encouragement from the success of the female branches.

THE LADY DUFFERIN FUND.

The Editor regrets that pressure of space prevented the following passage from the article in the Times of April 16, appearing in the last issue:—

The annual meeting of the Lady Dufferin Fund in Calcutta shows how a good work once started on right lines continues to give good results. The five years during which Lady Lansdowne has ably directed the movement, have been years of continuous progress, and Lady Elgin now takes over an organization which has grown out of an effort of private philanthropy into a great national institution. It is not too much to say that the Marchioness of Dufferin and Ava has created a system of medical aid for the women of India which, twenty years ago, would have been regarded as an impossible dream. Her aim was to bring relief within the reach of thousands of Indian females and young children who suffer needlessly, and who die for want of knowledge. That aim, after nine years of unremitted effort, is now being realized to an extent that perhaps even Lady Dufferin herself would not have dared to anticipate. Before she left India she had created a system of relief which, in 1888, afforded hospital treatment to 2,500 in-patients, and about 100,000 out-patients. In 1893 the numbers had risen, under Lady Lansdowne's care, to 12,500 in-patients and 600,000 out-patients during the twelve months. The local committees had also been able to extend gratuitous treatment to patients, whose caste precluded them from coming to the hospitals, but whose poverty rendered them unable to pay fees. If any proof were required of the capacity of British ladies to initiate and direct great movements, this magnificent organization for bringing medical relief to the women of India, planned by Lady Dufferin and developed by Lady Lansdowne, would conclusively furnish it.

There is probably no scheme of philanthropy now before the public which yields so large a result from such small resources. The Indian chiefs and communities liberally contribute their share. But money is wanted in England for scholarships to enable Eurasian and Indian female students or practitioners, who have proved their capacity in India, to complete their studies in this country. The English managers of the fund decline to spend money on untried pupils whose aptitude for the medical profession is uncertain. But they are anxious to be enabled to help young women who have studied or practised in India, and who are recommended by the Indian committees for a further training in England. It is from this class that any large or permanent system of medical aid to the women and children of India must be recruited. Lady Dufferin and Lady Lansdowne have laid the foundations of a female medical profession for India on indigenous institutions and on native Indian agency under skilled British control. It is to be hoped that philanthropic men and women in Great Britain will help in this beneficent work.

LABOUR QUESTIONS.

WOMEN'S EMPLOYMENT IN SHOPS.—The National Federal Council of Scotland for Women's Trades has just issued a report of an inquiry conducted on its behalf into women's employment in shops by Miss Irwin. The report is, as Miss Irwin herself warns the reader, a "Grievance Report." She has dealt very briefly with the " large class of shops where the arrangements as to hours and general conditions of employment are excellent," and has dealt mainly with those where bad conditions prevail. She concludes with suggestions that not only the weekly but the daily limit of hours be fixed by law, and legislation should be directed to all shops where assistants are employed, including adult workers of both sexes. She also recommends compulsory provision of seats, and a " sufficient number of shop inspectors of both sexes."

We begin to suspect that this continual cry for legislation as a remedy for every evil is altogether a lazy way of doing things. It is such an easy thing to say, "Here is something wrong, let's have a law." We own

to a profound mistrust of any report which deals, as this
one avowedly does, with the bad side only, and then
flies to an Act of Parliament, without consideration of
how the better conditions on the other hand have been
brought about. Law is a two-edged sword, and often
cuts where it is not expected, ay, and sometimes more
than where it is expected.*

THE TRUCK ACTS.—A pamphlet has been issued by
the Women's Trade Union Association entitled, "The
Truck Acts: what they do and what they ought to do."
It has been compiled by Mr. Stephen N. Fox and
Miss Clementina Black, and is a careful enquiry into
the abuses of the Truck Act. Any work undertaken
by two such earnest and indefatigable workers as Mr.
Fox and Miss Black is worthy of careful study, but to
this writer it seems the remarks above applied to Miss
Irwin's report apply here also—it has too much of the
"Grievance Report" about it. However perfect the
law, its effectiveness must depend on the human beings
who come under it; the greedy and the grasping will
abuse any and every law, nor should it be forgotten
that if the good workman needs rights against the bad
employer, equally the good employer should have rights
against the bad workman.

MIDWIVES' REGISTRATION BILL.

The Midwives' Registration Association has, after
twenty-three meetings, drawn up recommendations for a
Bill for the compulsory registration of midwives, which
will, no doubt, be the basis of any legislation proposed
next year, and will have important bearings on the future
of the profession. The Association consists entirely of
medical men, but it has shown a certain spirit of fair-
ness in that it proposes that the Midwives' Institute,
being the only corporate body representing the midwives' interests, should have representation on the
Central Board to which the Bill proposes to give powers
of a very far-reaching kind over midwives. It is proposed that this Board frame the rules for instruction,
examination and registration of midwives. An ex-

---

* Compare the American experience recorded on p. 282 of this Review.

planatory note gives the Midwives' Registration Association's definition of a midwife :—

"For the purposes of the Act a midwife is a woman who undertakes to attend cases of natural labour without the direct supervision of a medical practitioner. (Nothing in the Act should be construed to prohibit a person not registered as a midwife from rendering gratuitous assistance in case of emergency.)

"The interpretation of the term 'natural labour' should be included in the regulations laid down by the Central Board under the direction of the General Medical Council.

"The certificate granted to the midwife should contain a clause to the following effect :—' This certificate does not entitle the holder to treat any complication or abnormal condition in mother or infant, to treat or prescribe for any case of illness, or to perform any obstetric or other operation.' In such cases the services of a registered medical practitioner should be obtained."

BRITISH ASSOCIATION.

Of the papers contributed by women to the meeting of the British Association at Oxford, those bearing most directly on the interests of this Review were Miss Maitland's in the Economic Section, on the proposed Exhibition of Women's Work; and another by Miss Kennard on the Life of Factory Girls. This, we understand, has been published in pamphlet form.

In the Botanic Section, Miss Layard explained her system of preserving botanical specimens, and exhibited a number of casts in wax of the models of flowers intended to be used for study when natural specimens could not be procured. The various botanists present pointed out how useful these would be, and hoped Miss Layard would persevere in her endeavour to preserve flowers in their natural condition.

In the Anthropological Section, Mrs. Stopes was down to read a paper on Neolithic Implements. By the time her turn came, the hour fixed for adjourning for lunch had been considerably over-passed, and a little conversation passed between the chairman and Mrs. Stopes, who was sitting near by, as to the advisability of reading the paper then—when, as Mrs. Stopes said, she was tired and hungry, and so were the audience—or deferring it to next day; and it was deferred. A most commonplace incident in itself; but a reporter sitting near caught at the one word "hungry," and announced to the wide world that the lady had broken the ruling of the chair, and refused to read her paper because she was hungry!

Miss Weld and Miss A. W. Buckland, who also had papers in the Section, fared indifferently, for Miss Weld's was taken as read, and Miss Buckland was requested to shorten hers down into five, instead of the twenty minutes allotted for papers. But luckily for them no reporter was present, hungry for sensational "copy."

THE LIBRARIES ASSOCIATION.

In a paper entitled "Our Readers and what they Read," which was contributed to the annual meeting of the Libraries Association (held in Belfast in September) by Mr. Elliott, chief librarian of the Belfast Free Library, it was stated that on Saturdays the demand for books was larger than on any other days. Some of the borrowers wish for what they call nice books for Sunday, and the favourite writers of such books are—Mrs. Worboise, Mrs. Wood, Mrs. Craik, Grace Aguilar, Charlotte Yonge, Miss Carey, E. P. Roe, S. and A. Warner, Mrs. Charles, Edna Lyall, Annie Swan, and Mrs. Whitby.

Papers were read at the conference by Miss Petherbridge, on "The American Library School;" and by Miss M. S. R. James, late librarian of the People's Palace, on "Boston Home Libraries."

JAPANESE LADIES AND THE WAR.

The terrible war now raging in the East, with all its possibilities of far-reaching changes in the destinies of Asia, stands outside the province of this Review. But one thing is to be noted with gratification, and that is, that in this wonderful combination of the ancient fast-rooted civilisations of the East with the modern appliances of the West, the Japanese women have shown themselves imbued with the same spirit of improvement which characterises the men. The *Times* correspondent at Tokio (September 20) states that "The Empress of Japan, as chief patroness of the Japanese Red Cross Society, has personally set the example of preparing lint and bandages for the wounded.

In this humane work her Majesty is actively supported by all the ladies of the Court, whose handiwork is to be distributed between the wounded Japanese and Chinese soldiers without distinction."

CHELSEA HOSPITAL FOR WOMEN.

The following members of the Ladies' Committee of the Chelsea Hospital for Women have tendered their resignations to the Board of Management, namely: Mrs. R. P. Ebden, Vice-President; the Hon. Flora Macdonald, Mrs. Brend Batten, Miss Dudin Brown, Mrs. Edis, Mrs. Furley, Mrs. Hussey Walsh, Mrs. Newton, Mrs. Reeves, Mrs. Alexander Ross, Mrs. F. F. Schackh, Mrs. Travers, and Mrs. Webb Peploe.

OBITUARY.

MRS. AUGUSTA WEBSTER, *Jan.* 30, 1837—*Sept.* 5, 1894.

We have the sorrow to record the death of Mrs. Augusta Webster, which took place at Kew on Sept. 5. Daughter of Admiral Davies, for many years chief constable of Cambridge and Huntingdon, and wife of Mr. Thomas Webster, Fellow of Trinity College, Cambridge, Mrs. Webster has earned for herself a double right to a tribute of grateful remembrance in these pages, in that she was the writer of poems whose force and power give them high place in English literature, and that she was also one of the most ardent sympathisers and for many years an active worker for the advancement of women.

When the Central Committee of the National Society for Women's Suffrage was formed in 1872, Mrs. Webster was one of its most hard-working members, and rendered much service in the drafting of letters and papers for the Committee, which in the early days of its existence was located at 9, Berners Street; she occasionally also took part in meetings. In 1879 she was elected a member of the London School Board for Chelsea, coming in 4000 votes ahead of the next candidate. She now applied herself indefatigably to the work of the Board. Her attention was specially devoted to the books used by the schools; she was indeed practically the school books' committee. She also took great interest in the women teachers, being always accessible to them, ready to see them at any time; she fought many battles on their behalf, but they were battles fought with that conciliatory spirit which arouses not antagonism but friendship. It was hard work, and after the first three years Mrs. Webster retired. She was, however, again elected in 1885.

Her translations of the "Prometheus Bound" of Æschylus and the "Medea" of Euripides, published in 1868, were the books which first drew attention to the new poet, though she had published earlier under a *nom de plume*. These translations were followed by numerous works, many of them dramas, and all partaking of the dramatic instinct, which adds force to her terse expression and clear delineation of character. "The Auspicious Day" (1872), "Disguises" (1879), "In a Day" (1882), are her principal dramas, but there are none of her writings in which dramatic power stands forth more clearly than in "Portraits" (1870), the work on which, more than any other, probably, her fame as a poet rests. But "Lu Pe Ya's Lute" stands not far behind, a poem in which Chinese life and character are described with a vividness and accuracy which have astonished readers well acquainted with China. "A Book of Rhyme" (1881) contains many sweet songs, and from one of them a few lines seem to come at this moment with sad appropriateness.

> "Not by her grave; it is too still, too cold,
> And save my loss is nothing with me there.
> What memories have I there of her of old?
> They came not there, the dear lost days that were.
> Not *she* lies there, but only my despair;
> Not *she*, but death, and all my loneliness.
>
> . . . . . .
>
> Not by her grave; some day will I return,
> When sorrow keeps its wont unvexed by place,
> And, sitting on the turf beside, will learn
> To call before me there her waking face.

> Not that white face that slept and took no trace
> Of change because I kissed, nor for tears.
> Some day; for now I should forget her so,
> Lose the fair woman, and not know
> The coldness and the silence when she died,
> Lose her all so."

Mrs. Webster contributed frequently to the *Examiner* for about two years before that paper ceased, and her essays collected thence were published under the title of a "Housewife's Opinions." She also wrote frequently for the *Athenæum* up to a very short time before her death.

MISS ALICE KING.—The death is recorded some weeks ago of Miss Alice King, the blind novelist. She was the daughter of the Rev. J. M. King, a scholar of some note, and was born at Cutcombe Vicarage, Somerset, in 1839. Her eyesight was defective from her birth, and at seven years old she became totally blind. In spite of this misfortune her education was carefully attended to by her mother, and she acquired seven languages. Her first book, "Forest Keep," was published in 1862, the proceeds being devoted to a stained glass window in Cutcombe Church. This was followed by numerous other novels, among them "Queen of Herself," "Hearts or Coronets" and "A Strange Tangle." She was also a frequent contributor to the *Quiver*, *The Argosy* and other Magazines, and her writings are distinguished by an excellent tone.

MRS. WILLIAM EVANS, OF LEICESTER.—The death of Mrs. William Evans, which took place on May 20 at Leicester, has removed one of the early subscribers to this Review, and a pioneer worker in her native town. Mrs. Evans inherited from her father, the late Rev. Joseph Dare, a great enthusiasm for education, and while strongly in sympathy with all other forms of philanthropic endeavour, her own energies were mainly directed in that channel. She took a warm interest in the work of the School Board from the time of its formation; in 1879 she was elected a member, and again in 1888, in the interval retaining her connection with several of the schools as manager. In 1878, Mrs. Evans became one of the managers of the Wyggeston High Schools for Girls, a position which she occupied until shortly before her death. She took an active interest in the formation and working of the Leicester (now the North Midland) School of Cookery, joining the Committee of Management in 1886; and was also the first lady to give a course of Health Lectures in Leicester, where she was for several years connected with the District Nursing Committee. "All Mrs. Evans' work, whether in public or in private," writes a Leicester correspondent, "was characterized by 'sweetness and light,' and she received a touching tribute from the Board School teachers testifying their appreciation of her sympathy, her insight, and her clear understanding of the aims and ends of education."

DOCTOR LANGE (Fröken Emmy Kramp).—We deeply regret to record the loss sustained by the Medical Faculty of Denmark in the death of Dr. Lange, which took place a few weeks ago. Fröken Emmy Kramp had the distinction of being one of the early pioneers who faced the disapproval with which any woman was regarded who studied or sought to enter a profession twenty years ago—disapproval alike from her family circle, and from the world beyond it. She was the fourth woman to enter the medical profession in Denmark.

After taking her degree Fröken Kramp worked at the Almindelig and "Frederick's" hospitals in Copenhagen, winning the respect and love of the staff and of her patients. The charm of her personality was very great, she seemed to bring a gleam of sunshine and beauty wherever she went, with the brightness of the dark, clever, kindly eyes, regular, clear-cut features and fresh complexion in a setting of beautiful grey hair—prematurely grey at twenty years of age.

Shortly after entering upon her career Fröken Kramp married Dr. Christen Lange, and it would be impossible to picture a more ideal marriage, where love and sympathy found the strong additional bond of professional companionship. Their home in Copenhagen was the *rendezvous* of the keenest intellect and most advanced thought in the whole country, for her vivacious temperament turned with large-minded sympathy to all subjects which tended to advance the welfare of mankind. Yet first and foremost Doctor Lange was wife and mother, queen of her home, and she lost her life in giving life. She died two days after the birth of twin sons, at the comparatively early age of 43. She belonged to no particular church or creed, but spent her life in the service of humanity. Besides the home left desolate, many a sick bed will be more lonely and many a bitter tear will be shed by her patients in the hospitals when they hear that their "little lady" can visit them no more.

REVIEWS.

OUR EXCHANGES.

OF the many Exchanges which reach this Review from far and near, and especially those from far, it is often a regret that so little mention can be made. Nevertheless, if not often yielding occasion for special reference, they all come most gratefully acceptable as bringing each its portion of witness to that general activity amongst women everywhere, which it is the aim of these pages to record as fully as may be practicable.

Of none can this be more truly said than of the *New Cycle*, the official organ of the General Federation of Women's Clubs in the United States (edited monthly by Mrs Croly, 222, West Twenty-third Street, New York). The pages of the *New Cycle* present an astonishing record of the growth and energetic life of the women's clubs that are springing up throughout the States, and forming centres of intellectual and social intercourse, which must have a far-reaching influence on the lives of its citizens. Its pages also contain interesting literary articles. The September number contains, for instance, a paper on " Three Chinese Women," which reveals the higher standing of women in China in the olden time, before its habits and laws had become crystallised. " In the good old times of Chan," runs the preface of a Chinese book of memoirs of distinguished ladies, written 125 B.C., "the honourable women set such an excellent example, that they influenced the customs of the empire, an influence which descended even to the times of the Ching and Wei states."—But it were too long to treat further of this article now.

Demorest's Family Magazine (published monthly at 15, East Fourteenth Street, New York) surpasses all other family magazines that we know, in its varied matter and wealth of illustrations. At the present time it is issuing month by month a series of portraits of distinguished men and women of all countries. The October number, just arrived, contains portraits of Ralph Waldo Emerson, Sebastian Bach, the two Alexandre Dumas—father and son—Alice Cary and Phœbe Cary (American author and poet), Alexander III. and Thomas A. Edison.

To the *Women's Journal* (founded by Mrs. Lucy Stone, and published at 3, Park Street, Boston, Mass.), and the *Women's Tribune* (edited by Clara Bewick Colby, and published at 1325, Tenth Street, N.W. Washington, D.C.), these pages are oftenest indebted for direct quotation, for these are the two journals which gather up, week by week, notice of all that pertains to the many-sided interests of women.

The *Woman's Exponent,* from Salt Lake City, comes

to remind us that women there are taking their active share in the advancing movement.

In Australia *The Dawn*, a journal for Australian women (edited monthly by Louisa Lawson, 402, George Street, Sydney), continues, we believe, to be the only periodical which relates specially to women's interests in Australia. We think we see indications of more strength of material finding its way in amongst the domestic interests with which its pages chiefly deal, indications, we trust, of a brightening dawn. May the little journal grow and prosper.

The *Journal des Femmes* (edited by Madame Martin, 107, Rue Mont Cenis, Paris), together with the occasional publications of the *Avant Courrière* (12, Rue Gazan, Paris), are the papers to which we turn for news of all that affects the public interests of women in France.

In Belgium, *La Revendication des Droits Feminins* (edited by Claire La Nauze, 71, Rue Berckman, Brussels), is performing valuable educational work, and has just entered on its third year.

Frauenrecht, under the able editorship of Frau Dr. jur Emilie Kempin, comes monthly from Zurich, full of valuable matter for those who are working to spread the leaven of women's advancement. At the present time an abstract of the laws of the Swiss Cantons relating to women is appearing in *Frauenrecht*.

The sheet entitled *Das Recht der Frau*, which forms part of *Volkstimme*, the organ of the Democratic party in Vienna, has articles on various questions concerning women. The legal position of married women has been lately treated therein.

Our Scandinavian contemporaries continue their steady work of recording the progress of women at home and abroad. As the news from abroad often preponderates over that from home, they do not always afford news for this Review, but they always show themselves fulfilling their important function for their respective countries, viz., *Dagny* (published by the Frederika-Bremer Union) in Stockholm, *Nylænde* (edited by Gina Krog), in Christiania, and now in its eighth year; *Qvinden og Samfundet* (published by the Danish Women's Union) in Copenhagen, and now in its tenth year.

To turn to home Exchanges, the *Indian Magazine* (Constable & Co., 14, Parliament Street) lays this Review under constant obligation for valuable information regarding India.

Concord (the Journal of the International Peace and Arbitration Association), *Nursing Notes*, *Women's Union Journal*, are welcome for their respective circles of information. *Woman*, and the *Review of Reviews*, are too well known to call for more than a grateful acknowledgment.

The *Three-fold Cord*, we regret to learn, is to be suspended.

The *Spinning Wheel* (published weekly at 199a, Strand), which has gradually risen in interest, has now, we trust, a firm foot-hold, and we wish it heartily good speed. The same may be said of our Exchange from Ireland, the *Lady of the House* (published on the 15th of the month by Messrs. Wilson & Hartnell, Commercial Buildings, Dublin). A series of papers on Women's Colleges began in the August issue, with one on Swanley College, by Miss F. W. Currey, and was continued in September by one on Newnham, by Miss L. S. P. Wright.

A GERMAN VIEW OF ENGLISH EDUCATION.

There is no doubt Germany is making strides in the woman's question, and whatever reproaches (not in every case unfounded) there may be against its leaders, such results as the "Mädchengymnasien" and the partial admission to the Universities are proofs of good work on the one side, and an awakening necessity for higher female education on the other. A further sign of advancement in the right direction is the rapidly increasing literature on the subject. To-day it is not only one or the other of the struggling women themselves who write, but men of science and repute are seriously beginning to take up their cause.

The book I wish to give an account of is dedicated to Professor Kussmaul of Heidelberg, one of the most celebrated physicians of our time. Its title clearly tells its subject: "Die höhere Frauenbildung in Grossbritanien, von den ältesten Zeiten bis zur Gegenwart," von Karl Heinrich Schaible, Karlsruhe, 1894. Its author, Doctor of Medicine and Philosophy, formerly Professor at the Royal Military Academy at Woolwich, Examiner at the University of London and the College of Perceptors, and member of various other educational societies, devoted the best years of life to the educational questions of this country, and brings to his task, besides his wide personal experience, the unbiassed judgment of another nationality, united to the sympathetic understanding of an Englishman.

Professor Schaible's book is mainly historical, but historical in the right sense, showing female education in its *progressive development* instead of using history (after the manner of some writers) as an argument for the greater or lesser stability of things, in order to show that because women did not attain to a higher level three or four hundred years ago, they can and must not do so now. Yet even the "dark ages" were not by any means so dark as we like to think. Ladies at the time of St. Boniface composed Latin verses and wrote Latin letters of high refinement of feeling and expression. In the sixteenth century Sir Thomas More already spoke ardently in favour of knowledge and even learning in women, as a means of making them more fit companions for their husbands, better mothers and more intelligent educators for their sons; and at the end of the last and the beginning of this century women like Mary Astell, our first apostle, Hannah More, Mary Wolstoncraft and a grand array of others, stood up courageously for women's rights. In 1836 James Simpson published his "Philosophy of Education," in which he advocates the same intellectual training for both sexes, on the plea that, as it ennobles a man's moral character, it must do the same to woman's—declaring all arguments against this as invalid and unsubstantial. At about that time a considerable number of books on this subject were published by women. About 1851 Mary Carpenter began her life of noble work, proving by her own example the capacities of women. John Stuart Mill, by taking up the cause of women, marked a turning point in the history of mankind, and Miss Emily Davies in 1869 inaugurated, by founding Girton College, a new era in women's education.

Coming to our own time, Professor Schaible gives a most clear, and in its leading features complete, picture of the different pedagogical institutions and societies for women's higher culture and scientific training. He shows a wealth of information based on his own extensive experience, corroborated by such authorities as Dr. Garrett Anderson, Dr. Fitch, Dr. William Hodgson and many others. By frequent quotations from the excellent book "Women and Work," by the late Emily Pfeiffer, he does justice to a noble-minded writer, all too soon forgotten by her countrywomen. Two chapters are devoted to the subject of women's capacity; the results of his own observations being as interesting as they are gratifying. He was filling the post of Examiner at the London University when, in 1867, the first female candidates were admitted to an examination, and in 1878 to all degrees, prizes and distinctions on equal terms with men.

As a physiologist and doctor of medicine the author also treats at some length the physical capacity of women for serious studies, and refutes convincingly the standing stock-in-trade of objections, amongst them that of the smallness of our brain; and he winds up with the famous story of the celebrated Professor Bischoff, whose brain after death was found to be lighter than the average woman's brain, after he had during his lifetime maintained the superiority in weight of the male one. Dr. Fitch says (quoted by the author as motto on the title page), "the true measure of woman's right to knowledge is her capacity for receiving it, and not any theories of ours as to what she is fit for or what use she is likely to make of it." I agree with Professor Schaible that inability will find its own limit in itself, and that the supposed danger of a diminution in the number of wives and mothers will be warded off by nature herself, who always takes care of her own laws; and I believe with Dr. Fitch in the undeniable truth which the history of educational development in

England during the last thirty years has made evident, that at the present state of our knowledge and experience all attempts at differentiating the intellectual vocations of men and women are premature, for education is essentially an inductive science. But I should like to go still further. The point in question is not the establishment of a theory as to our capabilities for an education equal to that of men, or the way in which we should utilise it, but the simple granting of it as a simple human right, to find out for ourselves and take upon us, whatever may be the consequences; this purely ideal character of our claim to education is well expressed by the author. In the nineteenth century only did a higher sense of duty awake towards girls. One gradually became conscious that human beings, whether male or female, are put into this world, not for the purpose of earning a livelihood, but for that of living, that their life depends mainly on what they know and for what they interest themselves, on the extent of their intellectual sympathies, on their love of truth, on their power to influence and inspire other minds ; and that for these reasons the culture of the mind stands in as close a relation to the requirements of the life of a woman as to those of a man ; all this is seen in a clearer light to-day than in former times. This is certainly a distinct sign of advancement towards a state of higher culture, and, therefore, a proof that the movement must be a good and a sound one.

The women of England have attained much already; but what is better still, they have never lost an inch of ground once gained. In reading the chapters devoted to their achievements from the University Colleges, training hospitals for doctors and nurses, down to the secondary schools, we may feel thankfully proud, but also very hopeful that social and political rights must follow for a certainty the educational ones.

Woman is the keeper of her nation's moral standard. Should she not be better capable for it by an increase of her intellectual forces? In Germany there are still some amongst its best thinkers who seem to doubt it. Prof. Schaible's book, with its calm scientific expositions, its simple statements of wide personal experience, will do more to dispel old prejudice than hot-headed and aggressive arguments. To ourselves it will prove scarcely less valuable, dealing, as it does, with one of the most vital of our aims. To English readers, who are still arrayed on the side of our opponents, it cannot fail to carry some conviction.

I shall close with the author's second motto, "Je ne sais pas un père de l'Eglise ni un moraliste, qui jusqu' à présent ait prétendu que la parabole des talents ne regardait pas les femmes aussi bien que les hommes."
—Dupanloup, Evêque d'Orléans.

CAROLA BLACKER.

COLONIAL AND FOREIGN NOTES.

(For Women's Suffrage Intelligence see pages 237-239).

AUSTRALIA.

The erection of the Woman's College, in connection with the University of Sydney, was completed in May last, and the building has been duly opened. The building stands on a portion of the University Reserve, and has been granted *in perpetuo* by the Government. Parliament voted the sum of five thousand pounds, and an equal sum has been subscribed. The Government also makes a small annual grant toward the stipend of the lady principal. The college is open to all women undergraduates of the University of Sydney who are in the process of graduation, and is absolutely neutral on all matters of religion, being on the question of religion exactly on the same basis as the Sydney University itself.

The Triennial Conference of the Wesleyan Church of Australasia and New Zealand, was held in Adelaide in May. In these countries the Wesleyans are very numerous and influential. John Wesley, in his rules, forbad the recognition of women preachers, excepting under very special circumstances ; but the feeling of the equality of the sexes has powerfully taken hold of the Wesleyans of the Southern World, and at the above Conference they abolished John Wesley's rule, so that now there is no bar to the recognition of women preachers among the Wesleyans under the Southern Cross. The Wesleyan clergy everywhere in these parts, labour for Woman's Suffrage.

SOUTH AFRICA.

In the Transvaal Volksraad, on August 13, a memorial was presented from 1,300 women of Johannesburg, and two memorials from Pretoria, praying for the abolition of barmaids and more stringent supervision as regards the adulteration of liquor.
Messrs. Celliers and M. J. Joubert sympathised with the memorialists, but saw no chance of giving any effect to the prayers; Mr. Celliers pointing out that if any legislation were to be enacted with regard to the abolition of barmaids the possibility existed that morality would be endangered. The country had not sufficient industries to provide for women out of employment.

A proposal by Mr. Celliers, seconded by Mr. Jooste, to this effect, was tabled.

INDIA.

A most interesting paper by Mrs. Steel, on "Pupils and Teachers in the Punjaub," is reported in the July number of the *Indian Magazine and Review*. She draws attention to the variety of races and religions, and consequently manners and customs in India, the ignorance of which causes people in England to make so many mistakes in generalising on the social condition of the people of India. "In no point is this ignorance more remarkable than in the all-embracing commiseration bestowed so indiscriminately on Indian women." In the peasant class, not only are the women not secluded, but "the recognition of woman, as above all things the hearth-mother, the bringer of children, places her on a far higher pedestal than we Western nations are inclined to admit." Even in towns, the purdah has no hold, or only a very partial one, on a large number of women. The number of women, "under the most liberal allowance," is one quarter of the total. She corrects, also, the impression that most men in India are polygamists. "Considerably under 1 per cent. of the men in the Punjaub are polygamists." In a paper in the same review, by Syed A. M. Shah, on "The Status of Muslim Women," these facts and figures are confirmed; he asserts that "according to the Indian census, Muslim polygamists are only 1 per cent.," and quotes that, according to Islam: "At the feet of the mother lieth paradise," and states that "the lower classes go about openly in public, and the custom [of seclusion] is relaxed in the case of ruling princesses." Mrs. Steel does not minimise the evils caused by seclusion—on which she evidently feels strongly—nor those entailed by child marriage. On the question of enforced widowhood she points out that this applies only to the Hindus, and that Mahommedan widows are expected to marry again, that in many cases "widowhood entails few disabilities save the loss of right to form a new connexion," a right of which many would not wish to avail themselves, while in the too numerous cases of "harshness, cruelty and wicked suffering heaped into a widow's life," the evil deeds of those who ill treat them are "utterly unwarranted" by their religion.

Misses Bonnerjee and Rukhmabai gained certificates at the distribution of prizes on June 26, to the Students of the London School of Medicine for Women.

Miss Jaganadham, L.R.C.P., late House-Surgeon to the Cama

Hospital, Bombay, daughter of the Rev. P. Jaganadham, London Mission, Vizagapatam, died on July 27, aged 30.

The Secretary of State for India has appointed Miss Annette Benson, M.D. London, First Physician to the Cama Hospital, Bombay, in succession to Mrs. Pechey Phipson, M.D., resigned.

Miss Hemlati Sen has received the award of the Viceroy's cholarship, and another Scholarship at the Campbell Medical School.

Miss Cornelia Sorabjee gave an interesting lecture at Wilson College, on July 7, on "The Legal Status of Women in India," in which she pointed out that custom, rather than law, stood in the way of Indian women claiming their proprietary and personal rights. Custom prevents an Indian woman, deprived of her natural protector, from applying to a male lawyer in any legal difficulty. Women lawyers would supply a want which is much felt, and would supplement—not supplant—men's work.

A Course of Eight Lectures in Tamil, to Hindu ladies, has been delivered in Madras. The idea originated with some Hindu gentlemen, and the lectures were arranged by Mrs. Brander, the Inspectress of Schools, and delivered by some of the mistresses in girls' schools. Only women were allowed to attend. The number of Hindu ladies attending, omitting visitors and children, was 20. The highest number attending on any occasion was 40. The lectures were considered fairly successful, and the promoters hope to continue them on a more organised footing.

FRANCE.

The latest publication of the *Avant Courrière* (Rue Gazan, Paris), is the Bill introduced in the Chambre des Députés by M. Goirand, for enabling married women to dispose of their own earnings—preceded by the explanatory preamble (*exposé de motif*) usual in French Parliamentary Bills.

This preamble indicates how the present condition of hardship to so many wives in France is an incidental result of the arrangement as regards property between husband and wife, known as *communauté de bien*, which is much the most prevalent of the arrangements recognised by law.

The Bill briefly provides that—

"Whatever be the *régime* adopted by the married couples, the wife shall have the right to receive the sums proceeding from her own personal work, without the concurrence of her husband, and to dispose of them as she will.

"The powers thus conferred on the wife are not to be a check to the rights of third persons on the property held in community."

The friends of women in France are to be congratulated on having obtained the services of a deputy of such high legal standing as M. Goirand, solicitor to the Civil Tribunal of the Department of the Seine, and President of the *Conseil Géneral* of Deux-Sevres.

HOLLAND.

The total number of students in the four universities of Holland is 2,972, of whom 19 are women.

SWITZERLAND.

UNIVERSITIES OF SWITZERLAND.—The number of students in the various Universities of Switzerland during the present summer semester is officially given as follows :—Basle, 155 men, 3 women ; Berne, 162 men, 42 women ; Geneva, 173 men, 43 women ; Lausanne, 84 men, 19 women ; Zurich, 235 men, 80 women.

UNITED STATES.

MICHIGAN.—The *Woman's Journal* of July 28, says :—" One of the most important advances in favour of women that has been made recently is the unanimous adoption of the following resolution by the Board of Regents of the State University of Michigan :—

" ' *Resolved*, That henceforth in the selection of professors, instructors and other assistants for the University, no distinction be made between men and women, but that the applicant best fitted for the position receive the appointment.'"

PASSING NOTES.

WOMEN AS STENOGRAPHERS.

Abridged from the report of an address given by Mr. Svend Hogsbro (advocate at the Supreme Court of Denmark) before the Gabelsberger-Stenographic Association in Christiania, August 13 to 15, 1894.

After expressing his own conviction that shorthand is an eminently suitable occupation for women, Mr. Hogsbro went on to say that in his own country, Denmark, a woman had fourteen years ago come out at the head of the examination necessary for an appointment as assistant parliamentary stenographer. She was highly complimented, but did not receive the appointment. Four years ago another woman passed the same examination, and had received the appointment. The year after another followed, and the year after that two others passed the examination, but one of the male competitors was preferred, though they had come out higher. The other parliamentary stenographers protested against this injustice, and last year these two women again passed the examination, again came out at the head, and were now both appointed. There are thus now four women in the parliamentary service as assistant shorthand writers in Denmark. Whether they will be allowed to rise to the higher rank is still an open question. Outside Parliament women have not as yet found much opening in the profession in Denmark.

Mr. Hogsbro then passed on to give particulars he had gathered from various other countries. In the United States he was informed that women's work in connection with shorthand and typewriting was chiefly writing from dictation, whether as clerks in business firms or as having offices of their own. They are also engaged in public offices, usually passing the requisite examination more successfully than men. At the World's Congress in Chicago last year a calculation had been made that women in the United States had earned 28,000,000 dollars in one year by shorthand and typewriting.

From England his information had been supplied through the medium of this Review, and would not present anything novel to our readers. In Holland and Belgium no great effort seems to have been made to bring women forward in this line. In Hungary he was informed that the Minister of Public Instruction had established commercial schools for girls in which shorthand was an obligatory subject.

As regards Germany and Austria, the Secretary of the Royal Academy of Stenographers in Dresden had told him that there were thirty-seven associations where women were taught shorthand in Germany, and several thousands of women had there received instruction, generally with better results than the men, which was probably to be attributed partly to their having more time to devote to the study, partly to their generally belonging to the upper classes ; but " God be praised," added the Secretary of the ac ademy, none were engaged in parliamentary work. They found work chiefly in reporting lectures, sermons, &c., and in writing from dictation for authors and in business firms, also in taking down conversations through the telephone for the press, but very rarely as reporters at public meetings.

In Finland the Secretary of the Stenographic Association to whom the parliamentary reporting is entrusted, informed him that two women were engaged in the parliamentary service. In Sweden many women practise shorthand, especially in Stockholm, where one lady, Miss Bäskow, had a very extensive practice. In Norway, as in Denmark, women were engaged on the parliamentary work, but very little elsewhere.

From all the details thus gathered together the lecturer was of opinion that women had amply proved their capacity to take down from dictation; their efficiency as reporters was as yet hardly sufficiently tested, but he urged they should have full opportunity to try their powers. Finally, he wished to impress on the women who entered the profession the great importance of an all-round acquaintance with the public matters of the day, and that if they would succeed as shorthand writers they should give more attention than was their wont to the political parts of the newspapers. He concluded by moving a resolution "That this meeting express its opinion that women ought to have the same liberty as men to cultivate and use their powers in the service of stenography." After some discussion this was unanimously carried.

BRITISH SILK ASSOCIATION.

In our notice last month of the Exhibition of this Association we mentioned that the number of exhibits in 1894 was smaller than that in 1890. We hear from the President the cause of this diminution : "All the silk branches were excluded, except the two most important ones for dress and furniture, for a two-fold reason. First, there was not room to display every kind of British silk goods. Secondly, the Duchess of Teck, the President of the Ladies' National Silk Association, wished to show the ladies of England what British looms could do in these two respects, in order that if successful, the British ladies could demand from their drapers and dressmakers to be supplied with British silks." "We are paying at this time," Mr. Wardle says, in the same letter, "more than one million sterling per month for silks manufactured on the Continent, and as our silk people are in some places starving, it is quite time that the sympathy of the ladies should be enlisted." The Ladies' National Silk Association already numbers among its members many important names, a number which Mr. Wardle is naturally anxious to increase, and he hopes in the course of time to have a thorough county organisation. Ladies interested in the prosperity of this national industry are requested to send their names and addresses for enrolment as members of the Association, to Mr. Thomas Wardle, Honorary Working Secretary, Leek, Staffordshire. Members undertake to encourage and promote English, Scotch and Irish silk manufactures by all means in their power, inquiring for them when buying, and giving preference, when possible, to silks of home manufacture.

A RESIDENTIAL SCHOOL for the Training of ladies in Household and Domestic matters has recently been opened at Camp End, Malvern, under the direction of Mrs. Buck, Hon. Sec. of the North Midland School of Cookery, and Miss Brander, a Diplomée of the same school, and for some years Poor Law Guardian and Member of the School Board in Surrey. Here instruction is given in all kinds of domestic work and in elementary hygiene, and the mental education gained in high schools and colleges is supplemented by thorough instruction in all that the mistress of a house ought to know. Ladies can take a longer or a shorter term of instruction according to the time they have at their disposal, the terms for board, lodging and teaching being 30s. a week. Reference is permitted to Mrs. Garrett Anderson, M.D., Mrs. Sidgwick, Newnham College, Cambridge, and many other well-known ladies; and particulars can be obtained from Mrs. Buck, Birstall Holt, Leicester.

WOMEN MEDICAL STUDENTS AT GENEVA.

A paragraph recently went the rounds of the foreign press, stating that of the 175 women who have studied medicine in Geneva during the past seventeen years, 115 had been lost sight of, and a very small fraction had pursued their studies with any degree of success.

As the paragraph was given publicity in England

by the *Lancet*, it seems desirable to quote the comments of the late Dr. W. Lowenthal, Professor at the Academy of Lausanne, who wrote in *Der Frau* for June :—" I can only say that those accounts, even if they are perfectly correct, have no value whatever for those who desire to pronounce on the subject of women's studies; they merely prove, once again, on what frivolous grounds statistics may be compiled. As a matter of fact, these statistics only show that out of 175 female students, 14 completed their studies in Geneva, and that 161 left Geneva before finishing their studies. That is all! What in the world justifies us in assuming that these 161 came to grief? May not many of them have carried on and concluded their studies elsewhere—in Switzerland, in Paris, in Russia, or in England? I happen to have personal acquaintance with various women students at Geneva, who afterwards studied in Paris: and I have heard of a number of Russian women students, who, seven or eight years ago, were obliged to leave Geneva and return to Russian Universities, because the Russian Government did all it could to prevent Russian students from remaining at Swiss Universities, especially at Geneva (probably on account of the large number of Nihilists who were then staying there). By far the larger number of ladies studying in Geneva were, as it happens, Russians. Finally, it is to be observed that for some years Paris has had a great attraction for students who speak French, because access to the Paris hospitals, previously denied to women students, has been conceded them, and thus Geneva is again affected. In a word, instead of superficially asserting that they have made shipwreck of their lives, it may be taken for granted, without more ado, that the greater part of the 161 Geneva students have simply pursued their studies elsewhere."

In this connection it may be appropriate to notice a pamphlet lately published by Clara Schubert-Feder (Dr. of Phil.) on the "Life of Women Students in Zurich." The author writes from personal experience, and is able to give interesting details of the student life. Touching evidence is given (pp. 24, 25) of the affectionate esteem and actual enthusiasm with which the women doctors are regarded by the poor, who have had experience of their sympathetic tenderness in the hospitals. The pamphlet, which has reached a third edition, is published by R. Boll, in Berlin.

PARAGRAPHS.

CHILD LABOUR.

THE following experience in New York, which we quote from the *New Cycle* for May, is well worthy the consideration of the philanthropists who repair to legislation as the cure for every evil they combat :—

"The repressive laws in regard to labour for the children of the poor have assumed mischievous proportions, and are sustained by unwholesome sentiment rather than judgment based on knowledge and experience. A recent enactment has thrown boys and girls upon the street at fourteen and fifteen years of age, who in many cases were not only earning money which was sorely needed, but at the same time acquiring knowledge of an art by which they could earn a livelihood. The very poor usually have large families, they cannot afford to keep their children at home till they are sixteen, nor clothe them so as to be presentable at school, even if the schools could find space, which they cannot. The boys and girls are therefore thrown on the street at an age when they are most liable to suffer from vicious association and companionship. Idleness goes hand in hand with mischief, and together breed crime ; and these local enactments which are supposed to be in the interest of education and opportunity are creating communities of criminals and paupers.

"Work that is not too hard is good in itself, far better than idleness and the street. A boy under fifteen, but the oldest of seven children and the only help of a widowed mother, wept bitterly, recently, at being ordered to leave his shop because he was under age. 'Come home with me,' he pleaded, 'and see the children. They have not enough to eat, and I am all the help mother has got.' The boy had to turn a little wheel that cut the leaves of artificial flowers, work that had never before cost the manufacturer more than three dollars a week. But the faithfulness of the boy and his anxiety to earn money for his mother, induced the employer to raise him to four. The sum added to the mother's washing and charing was all the family had to subsist upon, yet he was compelled to give up the employment."

London School of Medicine for Women,
IN ASSOCIATION WITH
THE ROYAL FREE HOSPITAL.

THE Course of Study includes a complete preparation for the Medical Examinations of the University of London, the Royal University of Ireland, the Conjoint Examinations of the King and Queen's College of Physicians and the Royal College of Surgeons, Ireland, and the Conjoint Examinations for the Scottish Triple Qualification of the College of Physicians and College of Surgeons, Edinburgh, and the Faculty of Physicians and Surgeons, Glasgow. Also for the Diploma of the Society of Apothecaries, London, in Medicine, Surgery and Midwifery. For information respecting Scholarships, &c., apply to the Dean, Mrs. GARRETT ANDERSON, M.D., or to Mrs. THORNE, *Honorary Secretary*, 30, Handel Street, Brunswick Square, W.C.

EDINBURGH SCHOOL OF MEDICINE FOR WOMEN
SPECIALLY RECOGNISED AS
Qualifying for the University of St. Andrews.

President:
H.R.H. The Duchess of Fife.

Vice-Presidents:
The Marchioness of Tweeddale. The Lady Helen Munro Ferguson. The Lady Reay.

This School forms an integral part of the Extra Mural School of Edinburgh. Its five years' curriculum is specially adapted to the requirements of the University of St. Andrews and of the Conjoint Scottish Colleges, but qualifies for all other examining Boards. Winter Courses, 100 Lectures each; Summer Courses, 50 to 60 Lectures each. Clinical instruction in the Royal Infirmary, with special cliniques in the Eye, Throat, and Ear, Skin. Gynæcological, and Lock Wards, with Clinical Lectures in Medicine and Surgery. School Fees, £75 in four instalments; or total Fees for qualifying course in School and Hospital, £95 in one payment. For information as to Scholarships, &c., apply to Dr. JEX BLAKE, *Dean;* or Miss BLACK, *Secretary,* Surgeon Square, Edinburgh.

THE UNITED SISTERS' FRIENDLY SOCIETY
(SUFFOLK UNITY).

"Work and Leisure" Court, No. 15.

The object of the Society is threefold; to afford
1. A weekly allowance in sickness.
2. An annuity commencing at the age of 65.
3. A sum of money (£6 or upwards) payable at death to the duly nominated representative of a Member.

All single women and widows of good health and character, between the ages of 16 and 45, are eligible for Membership in the "Work and Leisure" Court, subject to election by the Committee, and to a satisfactory Medical Certificate from a duly qualified Medical Practitioner. A further examination by one of the Physicians of the Court may be required by the Committee.

President: Miss L. M. HUBBARD, Editor of "Work and Leisure."
Secretary: Miss EDITH M. MASKELL, 7c, Lower Belgrave Street London, S.W.
(To whom all communications should be addressed.)

[ENGLISHWOMAN'S REVIEW.]   *Advertisements.*   [OCT. 15th, 1894.

THE NEW HOSPITAL FOR WOMEN,
144, EUSTON ROAD, N.W.

THE PHYSICIANS ARE WOMEN.

Treasurer:—Mrs. WESTLAKE, The River House, 3, Chelsea Embankment, S.W.
Hon. Secretary:—Miss VINCENT, 6c, Hyde Park Mansions, N.W.
Physicians and Surgeons to the Patients:—Mrs. MARSHALL, M.D.;
Mrs. DE LA CHEROIS, M.D.; Miss COCK, M.D.;
Mrs. SCHARLIEB, M.D., B.S.Lond.
Physicians and Surgeons to Out Patients:—Miss WALKER, M.D.
Miss WEBB, M.B.; Mrs. STANLEY BOYD, M.D.
Ophthalmic Surgeon:—Miss ELLABY, M.D.
Assisted by a Consulting Staff of Physicians and Surgeons.

This Hospital is established to enable poor women to be attended by FULLY QUALIFIED WOMEN DOCTORS:

A *Report and further information* may be had on application to MISS MARGARET M. BAGSTER, *Secretary.*

Bankers:—BANK OF ENGLAND (Western Branch), Burlington Gardens, W.

The Nursing Record
Edited by Mrs. BEDFORD FENWICK.
PUBLISHED EVERY SATURDAY, PRICE ONE PENNY.

Contains all the Nursing News of the week; Articles by well-known Medical Men and Nurses; Notes on Science, Art, Literature and the Drama; Hospital News; Discussions by Matrons in Council; Full Official Reports of the Royal British Nurses' Association and the National Health Society, &c., &c.

Order from Local Bookseller, or from the Office—
11, ADAM STREET, STRAND.

Prices—At Home, 12 Months, 6/6; 6 Months, 3/6; Abroad, 12 Months, 9/-.

Society for Promoting the Employment of Women.
22, BERNERS STREET, OXFORD STREET, W.

Established 1859.   *Incorporated* 1879.

This Society was established for the purpose of finding openings for girls to learn different kinds of trade and business. Also for aiding those already trained to procure employment. A register is kept for experienced and certificated Bookkeepers, Saleswomen, Matrons, Sick-nurses, Engravers, Law Writers, Printers, Gilders, and other assistants. Orders for copying MSS., circulars, &c., and for directing envelopes, are promptly executed.

Bookkeeping.

A class for training young women as Clerks and Bookkeepers is held on the evenings of Monday and Thursday.

For Product Safety Concerns and Information please contact our EU representative GPSR@taylorandfrancis.com
Taylor & Francis Verlag GmbH, Kaufingerstraße 24, 80331 München, Germany

www.ingramcontent.com/pod-product-compliance
Lightning Source LLC
Chambersburg PA
CBHW070232230426
43664CB00014B/2271